# CORNEILLE

## HIS HEROES AND THEIR WORLDS

# CORNEILLE

## His Heroes and Their Worlds

*by*

## Robert J. Nelson

## University of Pennsylvania Press
### Philadelphia

SBN: 8122-7384-2

Printed in the United States of America

# Acknowledgments

This book has been made possible by the generosity and encouragement of a great many people and the institutions they represent. I am grateful to the trustees and faculty of Yale University, who granted me a year's leave of absence (1957-58) from academic duties under the terms of a Morse Fellowship to begin intensive study of Corneille both here and in France; the officers of The American Council of Learned Societies who awarded me a "Grant-in-Aid" to continue this study in the summer of 1960; the Faculty Research Committee of the University of Pennsylvania which provided funds for research and for the preparation of the manuscript in the academic years 1959-60, 1960-61, and 1961-62; Professor Henri Peyre of Yale University, who supported my requests for aid from the institutions cited, thereby continuing in this project the professional support he has graciously given over many years; Professors Nathan Edelman of The Johns Hopkins University and Georges May of Yale University, who supported my requests for aid from the institutions cited; Professor William Roach, who also supported my requests for aid from various institutions and who, as my Chairman, has provided an atmosphere in which scholarship has been a real possibility as well as a responsibility.

There are, of course, many others who have helped less directly, but as mightily to bring this book to the point of publication: my wife and children, who have suffered that their home serve so often as an "office"; Miss Joan Manson, Miss Deborah Goldberg, Mrs. Nancy Williams, and Mrs. Josette Egli, who rendered invaluable secretarial services; countless colleagues on whom I have all too often imposed my throes of composition. Finally, there are those whose influence has been more remote, but nonetheless significant—family, former teachers, and friends of many years' standing who have shaped me as a man and as a scholar. It is to the memory of one of these that this book is dedicated. May he rest in the assurance that he, like all those cited here, has helped to shape only what is worthy of his high standards in the pages that follow.

With slight variations, portions of this book have already appeared in the following: "Pierre Corneille's *L'Illusion comique*: The Play as Magic," *PMLA, LXXI* (1956), 1127-1140; *Play within a Play: The Dramatist's Conception of His Art—Shakespeare to Anouilh.* New Haven, Yale University Press. 1958; "The Dénouement of *Le Cid*," *French Studies, XIV* (1960, 141-148); "The Unreconstructed Heroes of Molière," *Tulane Drama Review, IV* (March 1960), 14-37.

I wish to thank the editors of these publications for permission to use this material in this book.

# A Note on Texts and Procedures

Except where critical editions have been used, I have based my study of the plays on the original versions (by recourse to variants when necessary) as given in *Oeuvres de P. Corneille,* ed. Ch. Marty-Laveaux. Paris, Hachette, 1862-1868. 12 vol. (called M-L here). The critical editions in question are of: *Melite, Clitandre, La Veuve, L'Illusion comique, Le Cid* and *Rodogune.* In citing them I have preserved seventeenth-century spellings both for quotations and references to names of characters throughout this book: for example, Melite from the play of that name; Chimene and Diegue from *Le Cid;* Cleopatre and Timagéne from *Rodogune.*

There are two kinds of notes: expository and referential. Expository notes, indicated by an asterisk or a dagger, are found at the bottom of the page which they elaborate. Referential notes, indicated by a number, are grouped at the end of the book (pp. 298-301). Footnote numbers begin anew with each chapter.

I have also provided an Appendix of plot résumés of the plays discussed at length.

To the Memory of

Pierre Clamens

*Que tout ici soit aussi juste que lui*

# CONTENTS

# Introduction*

Until quite recently Corneille's reputation in English has been pretty much taken on faith from the French. Synthetic studies, in particular, have derived from a school of French critics, best represented by Gustave Lanson (*Corneille*, 1898), for whom Cornelian drama is essentially a moralistic struggle between love and duty in which the stern virtue triumphs. In a less prevalent conception, Cornelian drama has also been viewed as both an autobiography of its creator and a gallery of post-medieval noblemen and noblewomen rhetorically clinging to a declining feudal ideal (see, for example, Lee Davis Lodge's largely biographical *A Study in Corneille*, 1891). Again, his reputation having been established, Corneille, the dramatist, has been relegated to second place in a mass of "sources-and-influences studies." Leon Vincent's *Corneille* (1901) for example, amounts to little more than a cursory sketch of theater conditions of the period of Corneille. Dorothea Frances Canfield's *Corneille and Racine in England* (1904) recites for nearly three hundred pages successive translations of the French dramatists from their own time to the early nineteenth century, but contains almost no literary criticism of the dramatists themselves.

Miss Canfield's title points to what might be described

---

* For works cited in the Introduction complete information may be found in the Bibliography.

as Corneille's unhappy fate at the hands of nearly three centuries of critics, French and English: the misleading comparison with Racine. An inability to consider Corneille on his own terms seems to beset nearly every critic who studies him. I am not speaking of the fact that the critic must take a stand, although one can hope that the stand be based on more understanding than is the case in Martin Turnell's summary interpretations of Corneille and Racine in *The Classical Moment* (1948). Rather, I am speaking of the long-standing teleological view of French dramatic literature in which Corneille is a precursor—albeit a refractory one—of the high point of French classical tragedy, Jean Racine.* A greater readiness to assess Corneille on his own terms (quite literally) informs E. B. O. Borgerhoff's study of Corneille in *The Freedom of French Classicism* (1950) , but even this critic's views of Corneille as a skillful craftsman and magician, close as they come to the essentials of Cornelian dramaturgy, tend to reduce Corneille's stature.

Borgerhoff's essay apart, studies of Corneille in English during the last quarter century have failed to keep pace with their French counterparts in either depth or range. In the very heyday of the Lansonian approach, Péguy was laying the groundwork for a more dynamic interpretation (*Victor-Marie, comte Hugo,* 1910; *Note conjointe sur M. Descartes,* 1914). The circumstantial orientation of Lanson and earlier academic critics has persisted in French criticism, to be sure, but recent academicians have been more probing and more sophisticated, less univocal in their preoccupations and preconceptions. Louis Rivaille (*Les Débuts de P. Corneille,* 1936) and Georges Couton (*La Vieillesse de Corneille,* 1949) have explored in depth sepa-

---

* The view is summarized in Lanson's observation: "Quinault et Corneille, si inégaux de génie, sont les deux points de départ de Racine." *Esquisse d'une histoire de la tragédie française,* p. 81.

rate phases of the dramatist's creation, but they have understood the continuity of the canon in more flexible terms. And if Couton, in particular, has nevertheless tended to follow an earlier criticism in imposing Corneille's "time" *upon* the work, Robert Brasillach (*Corneille,* 1938) has tended to seek the time as he believes it to be found *in* the work. An even more textual, if still moralistic, approach has yielded Louis Herland's illuminating study of "La Notion de tragique chez Corneille" (1946), an article whose theses are developed in depth in his *Horace, ou la naissance de l'homme* (1952). Again, in some ways continuing an outlook found in Péguy's many writings on Corneille, Octave Nadal's *Le Sentiment de l'amour dans l'oeuvre de Pierre Corneille* (1948) has shown that if criticism of Corneille must be psychological and historical, it can at least strike out beyond the mechanistic premises of earlier criticism. Nadal has also shown that the literary influences upon Corneille are far more diverse than is suggested in J. B. Segall's *Corneille and the Spanish Drama* (1902) or Martinenche's more general study of the same influences, *La Comedia espagnole en France de Hardy à Racine* (1900). Similarly, Paul Bénichou shows in *Morales du grand siècle* (1948) that Cornelian "heroism" cannot be reduced to the *sententiae* of classroom recitations and that a true history of Corneille's heroes will place them neither in the schoolbook history of Rome nor in the unfinished history of the critic's time, but in the emergent history of Corneille's time with its clash of feudal and centralist political values.

In an entirely different vein, standing in sharp contrast to the circumstantial orientation which has culminated in Couton's recent *Corneille* (1958), French criticism of the past quarter century has also produced an impressive body of "intrinsic" or "esthetic" criticism. A number of scholars have provided us with critical editions based on the original editions of certain of the plays: *Melite* and *La Veuve* (by Mario Roques and M. Lièvre, 1950 and 1954, respectively), *Clitandre* (by R. Wagner, 1949) *L'Illusion comique* (by Robert Garapon, 1957), *Le Cid* (by Maurice Cauchie, 1946) *Rodogune* (by Jacques Schérer, 1946) *Sertorius* (by J. Streicher, 1959). These editions cannot, of course, seriously affect the utility of Marty-Laveaux's monumental *Oeuvres de P. Corneille* (1862, in 12 volumes)—where the variants can be found—but the convenience of the critical edition and the new perspectives of many of the individual editors have done much to remind us of the variety and flexibility of Corneille's canon.* A more conscientious attention to the canon itself has yielded Georges May's fruitful comparison, *Tragédie cornélienne, tragédie racinienne* (1948) while still another critic, Roger Caillois, has protested the tendency of his fellow countrymen to deny Corneille his richness and grandeur in a demeaning comparison with the presumably thin and narrow Racine ("Un Roman cornélien," 1938). Again, Jean Schlumberger's *Plaisir à Corneille* (1936) suggests a Corneille very different from the imposing, sententious figure inherited from Lanson and his school by generations of French *lycéens* and English critics. Still another French critic has sought to correct—and has perhaps overcorrected—the psychological orientation of academic criticism by suggesting that if we must be concerned with psychology, the psychology of the spectator is far more important for an understanding of Corneille's *art* than the psychology of the dramatic character (Jean Boorsch, "Remarques sur la technique dramatique de Corneille," 1941). Léon Lemonnier's *Corneille*

---

* Streicher's edition of *Sertorius* seems to me an exception, offering little advantage in its text over M-L. I have used the latter here.

(1945) has also pointed to the dramatic versatility of Corneille, but insisted more on the inapplicability of voluntaristic categories to many of the "heroes." All in all, the Corneille who has emerged in these and other French works is a dynamic, flexible, and many-faceted writer little known to the cultivated English-speaking world.

In this book I attempt to bring many of these recent perspectives to bear on the particular subject of the "Cornelian hero." I shall also rely on the partial studies of recent English critics—L. Harvey, J. Hubert, *et al.* For the most part, however, I shall rely on independent reading of the plays themselves. Lest it seem that I insist upon my independence, let me hasten to add that I am well aware that no critic is utterly independent—he is the sum of all the forces of biology and culture which have brought him to the moment of writing. Indeed, the forces which have influenced me in particular features of my interpretation will be evident to adepts of Corneille even in those instances where I have not indicated a specific source as a point of departure or difference. Yet, I am sure most readers will agree that perhaps more than any other major French writer, Corneille must be rescued from the mass of documentation which has accumulated about him in nearly three centuries of criticism and that, for the most part, a work attempting to study the entire canon must, in the name of clarity and coherence, forsake to a considerable degree the criticism of criticism which so much commentary turns out to be. Furthermore, the history of Corneille criticism to date inevitably leaves many of my studies of individual plays "independent," since that criticism, though fruitful, has cut through the tissues of separate plays, thereby tending to ignore and on occasion to belie the organic character of each play: themes (Nadal, Bénichou, Bernard Dort's *Pierre*

*Corneille: Dramaturge,* 1957); periods (Rivaille, Couton); techniques (May, Boorsch, and Jacques Schérer's *La Dramaturgie classique,* 1950) ; language (Crétin and Merian-Genast on Corneille's metaphors). These studies have regarded a theme or a technique as a constant of the canon rather than as a variable in the context of a particular work. Other studies have treated separate plays as units, but not always as organic units. Voltaire's famous *Commentaires sur Corneille* (as prefaces to his editions of the dramatist in 1764 and 1774 and in a separate format in 1764) does not live up to the promise of the *Préface du commentateur* (of the *Remarques sur "Médée,"* 1764 edition, and repeated in the *"Avertissement"* of the 1774 edition) to study all the plays. It ignores the early comedies, and, in its own way, disregards context, concentrating chiefly on *"les beautés"* and *"les défauts"* of Corneille. A less arbitrary approach characterizes H. C. Lancaster's truly comprehensive study of the plays in his multivolume *A History of French Dramatic Literature in the Seventeenth Century* (1929-42), but the plays are treated in a scattered fashion due to Professor Lancaster's chronological approach to all of the dramatic literature of the century. The result is a loss of focus and of coherence in the treatment of the canon. Again, Lacy Lockert has provided us with studies of individual plays in his prefaces to his translations of Corneille (*The Chief Plays of Corneille,* 1952, and *Moot Plays of Corneille,* 1959) but this comes to only fourteen of Corneille's thirty-three plays (including *Psyché*) and the studies, which Mr. Lockert has included, with slight alterations, in his *Studies in French Classical Tragedy* (1958), are less studies of the individual plays than records of critical evaluations of them. The most interesting attempt to consider individual plays as organic works has been A. Donald Sellstrom's "The Structure of Corneille's Masterpieces" (1958), a study of the political tetralogy (*Le Cid, Horace, Cinna, Polyeucte*). I have been less concerned with technique as such, concentrating more on themes. However, I have, like Mr. Sellstrom, tried to follow an organic principle in treating themes. I trust that the results will be as interesting.

I concentrate in particular on the themes of the hero and his world. I am especially concerned with what Lucien Goldmann has called, in another context, "les lois constitutives de l'univers de la pièce"* and with the way in which a given hero behaves with respect to those laws. *Le généreux* is the central concept, of course, one far more important for an understanding of Corneille than the overdebated "unities." It conveys far more than its English cognate "generous" or the parallel usage of the term in modern French: "kind," "bounteous," "charitable." In its seventeenth-century usage, *généreux* is closer to its etymological meaning: "Latin *gens, gentis,* f. [root Gen, *gigno,* that which belongs by birth or descent], a race or clan embracing several families united together by a common name and by certain religious rites. Orig. only patrician, but, after the granting of the connubium between patricians and plebeians, also plebeian." [1] It is strictly its patrician sense that obtains in Corneille: "Le choix," Bénichou observes, "de personnages princiers ou royaux n'est pas seulement chez lui un procédé d'amplifi-

---

* "Nous appellerons 'tragédie' *toute pièce dans laquelle les conflits sont nécessairement insolubles,* et 'drame' *toute pièce dans laquelle les conflits sont ou résolus* (tout au moins sur le plan moral) *ou insolubles par suite de l'intervention accidentelle d'un facteur qui—selon les lois constitutives de l'univers de la pièce—aurait pu ne pas intervenir." Jean Racine: dramaturge,* p. 13 (italics in text).

cation ou une convention théâtrale: c'est une condition du drame, sans laquelle tout s'effondrerait, les démarches et le langage de la gloire perdant tout leur sens chez des personnages du commun."* Whether kings or less than kings, Corneille's heroes owe their sense of self to the *maison* of which they are born (or, in the case of certain problematic heroes, to their sense of how those so born should behave). Rodrigue's celebrated torment derives precisely from the fact that he is the son of the noble Diegue; neither young nor old Horace can forget his loyalty to his house. Indeed, in most of the plays of the canon, this derived sense of self exists with a purity perhaps unknown in historical annals. This is to be expected: the framework is poetic, not historic or sociological or anthropological. The sources of power and position are not traced by the dramatist to some conjectured primitive state in which Horace's forebears would have "existentially" won their power through might and main. Power and position are presumed in the Cornelian universe. In spite of the poetic framework, it has been assumed by some critics that the political conventions of the Cornelian universe literally reflect the politics of Corneille's own time. (Couton, in particular, reads the plays as historical documents). Such readings are a distortion of and a distraction from the internal dynamics of the Cornelian universe. Whatever the historical fate

---

*Morales du grand siècle*, p. 22. Also, Nadal notes in his study of the term *générosité* that "Le généreux, la généreuse sont de souche noble" (*Le Sentiment de l'amour dans l'oeuvre de Pierre Corneille*, pp. 298-299). Cotgrave's *A Dictionarie of the French and English Tongues* (1611) also gives this meaning as primary. The dramatic use of the concept does, of course, predate Corneille:

> On ne pense jamais qu'un homme généreux
> Soit engendré de sang imbécile et poureux.

Antoine de Montchrestien, *Hector*, V. First published in 1604.

of the concept of "the divine rights of kings," the affirmations and betrayals of the concept within a given play must first command our critical attention. In the greater number of plays, by far, the Cornelian *généreux* is noble and virtuous (Latin: *virtus,* manly as well as morally pure) in birth and in station and *thus* noble and virtuous in deed. His duty may, as Nadal and others have stressed, be to himself, but his sense of self is derived, not forged. Though it is often not apparent till the end of the play, the ethos is "essentialist" rather than "existentialist."

The *généreux* is a convention of the Cornelian theater, even as it is of the theater of his contemporary dramatists. The heroism of the hero in those plays of the canon which Corneille and his contemporaries called "tragedies" or the purity of the hero in those plays he called "comedies"— these were assumptions within which Corneille constructed his plays and within and against which his spectators found themselves being thrilled, shocked, surprised, edified, horrified, and reassured by Corneille's heroes. Perhaps the two most frequent traits for which the self-critic of the "Examens" praises himself are *"nouveauté"* and *"invention."* This is ironical when one considers Corneille's fortune at the hands of critics other than himself. Most of the treatments I have just reviewed have tended to force heroes as diverse as Tirsis, Rodrigue, Cleopatre, Sertorius, Pertharite, and Suréna into the single mold of the "Cornelian hero." It has been recognized that there are differences, of course, but these are usually explained in such terms as anticipation, apprenticeship, decline, etc. Such explanations falsify the realities of the worlds in which these differing heroes live. They have led to a misleading neglect of the other figures of those worlds and have thereby led to a too rigorous unity in the conception of the "Cornelian hero." There is a unity, to be sure: the values of all the plays, including the comedies to a certain extent, are those of the "political tetralogy" (*Le Cid, Horace, Cinna, Polyeucte*) ; *générosité, estime, gloire, mérite, devoir*. But these values are not postulated in the same way in every play.

This does not mean that each of the thirty-three plays of Corneille (including *Psyché*) is as unique within the canon as its creator's emphasis on originality would lead one to think. That emphasis has fruitfully led many of the critics I have cited to seek the differences between Corneille and his historical or literary sources. However, the dramatist's emphasis on his originality can also lead to fruitful internal comparisons. In making such comparisons, the political tetralogy, because it is so well-known rather than because it is assumed to represent the basic "direction" of the canon, can serve as a kind of "magnetic north." An exploration of the canon along these lines leads me to believe that there are five significant "compass points" or four reorientations within it:

1. *Melite* to *L'Illusion comique:* the hero as *damoiseau*.
2. *Le Cid* to *Pompée:* the hero as *généreux*.
3. *Le Menteur* to *Nicomède:* the hero as *ambitieux*.
4. *Pertharite* to *Psyché:* the hero as *amoureux*.
5. *Pulchérie* and *Suréna:* the hero as *généreux* once more.

I have already defined the term *généreux,* but I would remind the reader that I am using it in its particular seventeenth-century sense. This is, of course, the connotation which is used in French criticism of the Cornelian hero (Nadal, Bénichou, *et al.*). The remaining terms are more obviously my own designations. *Ambitieux* and *amoureux* I intend in their current and most obvious connotation, and, through their cognates, this connotation should be apparent in English. *Damoiseau* I intend in its double sense as given by Hatzfeld and Darmesteter: "1. Au moyen âge, jeune gentilhomme qui n'était pas encore chevalier. 2. Jeune homme qui ne s'occupe qu'à courtiser les dames." [2] As will be obvious from my discussion, it is the second sense which best characterizes the heroes in question. However, because the term has a pejorative sense in modern French, I would insist on the first sense as I apply the term to Corneille's early heroes, seeing in the Cornelian *damoiseau* a true *gentilhomme*—that is, a wellborn person who behaves "gently" precisely because he is wellborn. The connection between *gentilhomme* and *généreux* is more than etymological.*

Although my division of the canon is chronological, it is not my purpose in this book to relate these renewals to those pressures in public taste or political history which the plays of a given division reflect (and to which the dramatist, ever sensitive to the demands of the spectator and eager to succeed, might have "opportunistically" responded). Such concerns would easily require a volume the length of this one. I am concerned chiefly to *describe* each of the tendencies cited in the Cornelian canon. On the other hand, certain esthetic and moral questions do inevitably follow from my description—particularly the dramaturgy of these differing tendencies, and the conception of the tragic in each. I attempt to reply to these questions in the analysis of individual plays and in the conclusions in my final chapter.

Of these questions, the conception of the tragic seems

---

* "*Gentilhomme:* N. m. 'Homme noble d'extraction, qui ne doit point sa noblesse ni à sa charge, ni aux lettres du Prince. (F. 90).'" G. Cayrou, *Le Français classique: Lexique de la langue du dix-septième siècle.*

especially important in a study of the "Cornelian hero."
More than one critic has wondered whether the hero—or
heroes—of "The Father of French Tragedy" can properly
be called "tragic heroes." However, if there is more moral
than esthetic concern in the pages that follow, it is certainly not due to my presumably low opinion of
Corneille's talents as a craftsman. I have already recorded
the opposite opinion in a close technical study of one
play.[3] Yet, I believe that much of the recent criticism,
cited above, either implicity through the nature of its
concerns or explicitly in its judgments, is in danger of
denying Corneille any importance as a "playwright as
thinker." On the contrary, I believe that, with some exceptions, we might extend to the entire canon L. Harvey's
conclusion to a study of one aspect of one play:
". . . Corneille's art is primarily a conceptual or idea-
oriented art. . ."[4] Nevertheless, I trust that, like the perceptive Harvey, I have sufficiently indicated the nature and
value of Corneille's skills as a dramatist.

I have not discussed in detail each of the plays. There
are too many resemblances within a given tendency for
such detail. I have attempted to "place" each play, but
have discussed at length only the following: *Melite, La
Veuve, La Suivante, Le Cid, Horace, Polyeucte, Le
Menteur, Rodogune, Nicomède, Pertharite, Oedipe, Sertorius, Agésilas,* and *Suréna.** As a rule, each choice is

---

* One brief moment of the canon has not been "placed": Corneille's
contribution to *La Comédie des Tuileries* (1635), the play written in
collaboration with Boisrobert, Colletet, l'Estoile, and Rotrou from an
idea furnished by Richelieu. Corneille's small contribution does not
permit of a holistic approach to the play as his. (On the other hand,
Corneille's substantial contribution to *Psyché* does lead me to consider
it to some extent. See below, pp. 242-243). As to the more general
question of the place of the Cornelian canon (or, indeed, of any one play)
in seventeenth-century French dramatic literature, I am far from believing that the Cornelian theatre is either ethically or esthetically
isolated. I trust that my review of Corneille criticism has suggested a

representative of a given tendency, but in order to remind the reader that I am describing *tendencies,* I have included in this list a number of plays of a mixed character. There is always room for doubt in such matters and specialists, in particular, will perhaps be puzzled by various choices or by the relative length accorded to various choices. For example, *Pertharite*'s poor reputation in its own day—and since—might have suggested another choice from among the group in which I place it. However, it seems to me especially illuminating because of the stresses between two tendencies in the canon which Corneille's extensive reworking of the play shows. Here as elsewhere, I can only hope that the analysis will shed new perspectives not only on the play in question but on that which the reader would have considered a "more obvious choice." I also hope that my analyses will be of particular value to students and teachers. May these analyses help to turn what is so often a chore—the "covering" of a great classic—into an interest.

---

numbers of studies to which the interested reader could refer. I would cite in particular: Lancaster *(History)* for a careful, if necessarily concentrated, discussion of these matters for every play; May *(Tragédie cornélienne)* for a keen perspective on Corneille's predilection for little-known subjects; Nadal *(Le Sentiment)* for the literary ambiance of the early plays in particular; Bénichou *(Morales)* for general cultural and social influences upon and of Corneille's plays; Lawrence Melville Riddle *(The Genesis and Sources of Pierre Corneille's Tragedies from "Médée" to "Pertharite")* which, within its limited subject, corrects the Spanish bias of Martinenche *(La Comedia espagnole et France).*

# I

# Melite to L'Illusion comique:

# le damoiseau

Corneille's first hero, the Tirsis of *Melite* (1629),[1] is a familiar figure: the young blade who takes his pleasure where he finds it, an embryonic Don Juan without the malevolence or diabolism we have come to attach to that figure since Mozart. Yet this Don Juan succumbs when he meets Melite. He is dumbfounded by her presence—or almost so. After Eraste's elaborate, typically rhetorical presentation of him as an enemy of love, Tirsis, in a conceit whose subtlety still shows him the master of his tongue if not of his heart, reveals that he, too, has been won over by Melite:

> Si le coeur ne desdit ce que la bouche exprime
> Et ne fait de l'amour une meilleure estime,
> Je plains les malheureux à qui vous en donnez
> Comme à d'estranges maux par leur sort destinez. (I, 2)

In the ensuing rush of sharp exchanges between Eraste and Melite it would not be surprising if the spectator missed the point of this clever compliment. Even to the

26

attentive spectator, the compliment has the ring more of objective generalization than of personal confession. Yet, as Eraste protests his love to the hard-headed if not hard-hearted Melite, we wonder if the silent (strangely so for him!) Tirsis is not allowing Eraste to speak for himself as well. If so, Eraste is thus cast in a role in which we shall find many another secondary character of Corneille: a surrogate for the "off-stage" spectator of the central action.

The central action is the love suddenly born in Tirsis' breast and, very likely, in spite of her witty denigrations of the sentiment, in Melite's as well. When Tirsis seconds Eraste's description of Melite's irresistible charms with

Je me range tousjours avec la verité. (I, 2)

we recall with some irony his final words before meeting Melite:

Allons, et tu verras que toute sa beauté
Ne me sçaura tourner contre la verité. (I, 1)

Yet there is no contradiction. Truth and Beauty are one: to see Melite is to love her:

Si vous la voulez suivre, elle est de mon costé.
TIRSIS: Oüy sur vostre visage, et non en vos paroles:
Mais cesses de chercher ces refuites frivoles,
Et prenant desormais des sentimens plus doux
Ne soyez plus de glace à qui brusle pour vous. (I, 2)

The speech might still be counted an entreaty on behalf of Eraste, but we do not seriously doubt that in this last

line Tirsis means himself. The last shred of doubt is removed when he tells Melite

> J'ay recognu mon tort aupres de vos appas,
> Il vous l'avoit bien dit. (I, 2)

We cannot be as certain that Melite has fallen, but as a
clue, it can be said that she does not reject Tirsis' court
with anything like the scorn and contempt she accords the
bombastic Eraste. She even admits that she enjoys hearing
Tirsis' flattery and, as she beats her sudden retreat, we
wonder if her mother is really awaiting her with such
impatience.

If the encounter between Tirsis and Melite proves posi-
tively for us the validity of the eye as instrument for dis-
covering reality, the scene between Philandre and Cloris,
to which we abruptly switch in scene 4, proves it negatively, as it were. The abruptness of the shift to these
characters—we have heard nothing about them from
Eraste, Tirsis, or Melite up to this point—immediately
distracts our interest from Tirsis' plan to woo Melite
in the name of Eraste. (Such a shift does not bother
most of us in the twentieth century because we have
been too accustomed to them in the movies.) Yet the
distraction reminds us of Tirsis and Melite in a curious way. The scene between Philandre and Cloris is really
the reverse of that between Tirsis and Melite: where in
the earlier scene two people who deny the power of love
suddenly fall in love, here two people who are presumably
in love fall out of love, or at least give that impression.
That is, from their first verses we presume that (1)
Philandre and Cloris are in love with one another and

(2) there is something which has come between them.
There is, then, a kind of mathematical neatness to this
pairing of the couples, which delights the spirit as much
as the anticipation of Tirsis' courtship of Melite delights
the senses.

Of course, the intellectual and dramatic value of the
pairing is greater than this purely formal rapport suggests.
The real interest lies in what the pairing reveals to us
about the relationship of appearance to reality as it is con-
cretely explored in the play in the various love affairs.*
For all his man-of-the-world air, Tirsis is new to love;
Melite is as sweet as honey (remember that if she has
seemed bitter rather than soft and sweet in what we
have seen of her, it is because she has been replying to the
bombastic courtship of Eraste and that we have noted
some softening if not sweetening of her attitude in her
first replies to Tirsis) ; Cloris is really more wordly—like
her "partner," Philandre, who lives up to his name
—a philanderer, a disrupter.[2] Something of Philandre's
superficial, insincere commitment to love can already be
seen in the purely intellectual, precious delight he takes
in protesting his faults in this first scene with Cloris: the
treason he announces in his first long speech is quite unreal. His elaborate conceits are as subtle as any Eraste has
forged so far, yet, lacking the passion which drives the
latter about like a feather in a whirlwind, they seem
sterile, bloodless, self-congratulatory. Philandre's conceits
tell not of his love for Cloris but of his love for Philandre.
(The sensible, down-to-earth Cloris is not unaware of this,

---

* "All literature tends to be concerned with the question of reality—I
mean quite simply the old opposition between reality and appearance,
between what really is and what merely seems." Lionel Trilling,
"Manners, Morals and the Novel," *The Liberal Imagination*, p. 207.

warning him that she may aspire elsewhere). The one-ness which we have observed between appearance and reality in the case of the couple Melite-Tirsis seems broken in various ways in the couple Philandre-Cloris. Philandre's protestations have a hollow ring, a self-indulgent quality such that their sense or appearance (the protestation of love) belies the underlying reality. Now there is a discrepancy between appearance and reality—but by the character's own admission. The hollow ring and the self-indulgent conceits are meant to show forth—Philandre acknowledges that he is playing a game. Furthermore, given Philandre's conduct after he has received the letters supposed to have come from Melite, there can be little doubt that, as in the case of Tirsis, the appearance which the character gives corresponds to the reality, that is, to what he is by nature: the hollow ring and self-indulgent conceits express exactly his fickle, conceited, self-centered nature.

Philandre is obviously the unsympathetic character of the play. How then explain Cloris' early attachment to him? How also explain certain obvious, unflattering resemblances between him and Eraste? True, Philandre's conduct, for all its immorality, has the virtue of consistency, of being the faithful expression of his basically unfaithful nature. But how explain the presumably good Eraste's forging of the letters and how explain Tirsis' intention to deceive Eraste by making love to Melite through letters presumably composed on Eraste's behalf? I do not mean to burden unduly this relatively slight play with these weighty moral issues; the import of *Melite* is other than this: a delight in the immediate, the sensuous, the intellectually novel—in short, a concreteness far removed from the abstractness of such moral issues.

Nevertheless, *Melite* does suggest them and, in its own light-hearted way, does indicate the directions which Corneille will later take as he considers similar questions in different settings and registers. The heroes and heroines do not, of course, specifically regard each other as *généreux*. But certain themes implicit in the latter concept are explicit in the play:

> ERASTE: Ainsi ce coeur d'acier qui me tient sous sa loy
> Verra ma passion pour le moins en peinture.
> Je doute neantmoins qu'en ceste portraicture
> Tu ne suives plustost tes propres sentimens.
> TIRSIS: Me prepare le Ciel de nouveaux chastimens,
> Si jamais ce penser entre dans mon courage. (I, 3)

But if Tirsis is so "pure," is the very Eraste who challenges him here as pure? If Tirsis is noble because he does noble things and Philandre ignoble because he does ignoble things, Eraste is now noble and now ignoble. How explain then that Cloris should accept him or at least his court after his decidedly wicked deed and how explain the even more perplexing fact of Tirsis' and Melite's unquestioning recommendation of him to Cloris? In view of his reprehensible act, he hardly seems to deserve the reward of Cloris' hand. Morality must be related to consistency of behavior: apologies for yesterday's misdeeds can hardly be met with the same rewards one grants for the noble deeds of today.

Yet, the only reproaches Eraste hears are those he addresses to himself. Furthermore, these self-reproaches lose much of their sting because of their evident excessiveness. The character has not been bombastic to no avail: we are accustomed to his rhetoric and his bombast, so we tend to discount most of what he says not as insincere but as irrelevant. Again, the reproaches are spoken largely in madness, that is, in that disordered state of mind in which we can hardly hold the speaker responsible for his words and deeds. Finally, the moral symmetry of the denouement, the proposed and probable engagement to Cloris, justifies Eraste as noble. The noble Tirsis gets the noble Melite, the ignoble Philandre gets the ignoble Nourrice, the noble Eraste gets the noble Cloris. If, with a number of modern critics we are to look for an existentialist precursor in Corneille, it is not to be in his first play. There people do what they do because of what they are.

Seen in this light, Eraste's behavior becomes more readily understandable, as do the perplexing features of that of the other characters as well. Eraste's is, basically, a "generous" or noble nature. We can assume that he has always given this appearance and thereby explain that he should be Tirsis' best friend: the noble choose the noble. But is this not a cruel psychological law? For example, Eraste falls in love with Melite: the noble chooses the noble. But she does not fall in love with him. Why not? Because there are distinctions of degree between Eraste and Melite, between Eraste and Tirsis, between Eraste and Philandre. The distinctions between Tirsis and Philandre are a matter of degree and not of kind. We have a hierarchy of value in *Melite,* which, following the lead of Paul Bénichou, we can see deriving from the feudal structure of medieval society.[3] According to such a hierarchy, Tirsis is of a degree of nobility or *gentillesse* higher than that which Eraste can claim. Corresponding to this highest degree on the male side is the inborn merit of Melite on the female side. From his early remarks we can assume that Tirsis has not been without some success

with the ladies, but he has yet to fall simply because he
has not met his match—in the literal sense rather than the
polemical. Obviously, the same is true—with less of that
compromising success one wishes to attribute to men but
not to women—in the case of Melite. The very notion of
merit, in fact, might as easily have prompted Corneille
to name his heroine Melite as much as any supposed ill-
concealed effort to consecrate an affair with a Mlle Millet
(or Hue, etc.) [4] The rime *Melite-merite* occurs more than
once in the play and in its first use fixes the resonance
metaphorically in our ears:

> ERASTE: Dites à n'aymer rien que la belle Melite.
> MELITE: Pour tant de vanité j'ay trop peu de merite. (II, 2)

Melite is being ironical, here, of course. Nevertheless, lest
we consider the irony as self-directed, let us listen to the
"metaphor" in an affirmative usage:

> *C'est donc avec raison que mon extréme ardeur*
> *Trouve chez ceste belle une extréme froideur,*
> *Et que sans estre aymé je brusle pour Melite:*
>
> *Car de ce que les Dieux nous envoyant au jour*
> *Donnerent pour nous deux d'amour, et de merite,*
> *Elle a tout le merite, et moy j'ay tout l'amour. (II, 5)*

The importance of the *Melite-merite* metaphor in this
extract is all the more undescored for us when we remember that this is the conclusion of Tirsis's sonnet.

To paraphrase a concept from Pascal, there are, then,
orders of merit. Tirsis and Melite belong to one order, the
rest to other orders. Perhaps Tirsis gives more convincing

evidence of belonging to such an order than does Melite, whom we see more often than not in a caustic, haughty mood. But this is because it has been necessary to put Eraste back into his place—or order. That Eraste should have left his order at all is perhaps theoretically impossible, but dramatically necessary if the drama is to get going. Nevertheless, it is even possible to explain his aberration from a theoretical point of view: he is mad not only near the end of the action, but from the very beginning, for it is only due to such an extreme aberration that the orders of merit could break down at all. There is even some poetic justification for describing madness as his condition from the very outset of the action: his excessive language at the height of his madness is really an extension of the high-flown rhetoric in which he first described Melite's effect upon him. His madness from the very outset also explains how he, by nature a *gentilhomme* sincerely deserving of Tirsis' friendship, could be brought to using the ignoble device of forgery. In a sense, Melite is more responsible than he is for this action: her effect has been so powerful upon him as to derange his senses. However, that we are not dealing here with that ancient cliché about the madness of love in general should be evident from the poise with which Tirsis and Melite respond to each other's lovable presence. It is not madness to love Melite, it is madness only for Eraste or Philandre.

Eraste more appropriately deserves Cloris. That Cloris, without being ignoble, is not of the same order as Melite, is evident from her willingness to put up with Philandre's attentions as well as her envy of Melite. Her envy, being essentially innocuous, is less compromising for her honor than her acceptance of Philandre might be. From their first scene together, it is evident that Cloris is not deeply committed to Philandre. Not only does Corneille show her as better than Philandre at his own game of love— she is far wittier than he—but he even hints at the possibility that Cloris had correctly assessed Philandre's unstable nature all along:

> Du moins ne pretens pas qu'à present je te loüe,
> Et qu'un mespris rusé que ton cœur desadvoüe
> Me mette sur la langue un babil affeté
> Pour te rendre à mon tour ce que tu m'as presté:
> Au contraire, je veux que tout le monde sçache
> Que je cognois en toy des deffauts que je cache,
> Quiconque avec raison peut estre negligé
> A qui le veut aymer est bien plus obligé. (I, 4)

At worst, Cloris, as she then allows Philandre to "steal" a kiss, is guilty of a delight in sensual pleasure.

That Philandre does not deserve Melite is so evident as to need little or no demonstration: he is not only a cold-blooded philanderer, he is a coward as well. In this side of his nature, he shows much of the *capitan fanfaron* familiar to us as far back as Plautus and whom we shall see painted in full colors in the Matamore of Corneille's *L'Illusion comique.* He deserves the Nourrice, which goes to explain the denouement of *Melite* in which Tirsis consigns Philandre to the Nourrice and which most critics have regarded as superflous. Lawrence Harvey has seen the role as necessary, though for what I am afraid are the wrong reasons. Harvey believes that the Nourrice, representing as she does the sordid, materialistic values of the world of sense, finds herself excluded from the idyllic world of the perfectly matched lovers at the end of the play. Philandre, also having proved himself to be cut from the same cloth, deserves the same exclusion and the proposal that he take up with the Nourrice only underscores his unworthiness. Now as far as the implied attributions of merit are concerned—particularly in the case of Philandre and the Nourrice—this analysis is accurate. But to put the couples Tirsis-Melite and Eraste-Cloris on the same footing is to misunderstand the essential conflict upon which the play is built. Harvey takes this to be "an opposition between true love and 'false' loves of different sorts. Corneille associates the former with control by reason over the desires of the senses and the latter with the dominance of the senses as motivation for conduct."[5] Harvey misses the crucial role which the *sense of sight* plays in the play. Sensual pleasure and spiritual pleasure are not in conflict (Harvey's analysis derives from the familiar love versus duty conflict which academic French criticism has consecrated as the theme of the great political plays), but are inextricably bound together. Appearance (the impulsion of the senses) and reality (the impulsions of the spirit) are one. Perhaps Philandre's greatest fault is neither his cowardice nor his inconstancy but his readiness to fall in love without having seen the author of the love letters he receives. Eraste does not "earn forgiveness" through his "remorse." He is not so much forgiven as accepted back into the ranks of the true, the good, and the beautiful—into the ranks of the reasonable (and how much more than the intellective faculties we can now see that to include!). If he gives evidence of anything in his "rational match with Cloris" it is that he has "conquered" not his senses but his madness.

I do not mean to suggest that from the very beginning Corneille himself takes this conception of "noble behavior" and "noble pairings" in utter seriousness. At most

I wish to suggest that *Melite* reflects preoccupations which function in varying degrees throughout Corneille's theater more as a body of *idées reçues* than as a didactic system. Even within individual plays we can see that Corneille does not show an unreserved commitment to one part of the system—to the concept of duty, for example. Thus, in *Melite* we might see in La Nourrice's curtain speech an ironical deflation of the naive idealism of such conceptions as "noble to noble according to degrees of nobility." This *terre-à-terre* affirmation of simpler, grosser and more concrete values is Corneille's last word in the play. It may not burst the bubble of this carefree world of fantastical play and counterplay. But it does remind us that the world is a bubble, a fantasy.

From the designation of his next play, *Clitandre: tragicomédie* (1630-31), one would suppose Corneille began to move quite early from the comic to the serious mode in which he is best known. In his "Examen" thirty years after *Clitandre* Corneille claimed that he primarily wanted to embarrass the critics by writing a play observing the unity of time, but one so full of incident that both the rule and the critics would look silly.* As Lancaster and others have noted, the early preface is far too self-indulgent and self-congratulatory for Corneille's motivation to be so negative.[6] Undoubtedly, he wished to reply to the critics to a certain extent and if the implausibility of the action-time relationship helped him to do so, all

---

* "Pour la [*Melite*] justifier contre cette censure par une espèce de bravade, et montrer que ce genre de pièces avait les vraies beautés de théâtre, j'entrepris d'en faire une régulière (c'est-à-dire, dans ces vingt et quatre heures), pleine d'incidents, et d'un style plus élevé, mais qui ne vaudrait rien du tout: en quoi je réussis parfaitement." "Examen," *M-L*, I, 270. Also in Wagner edition, p. 115.

the better, but the first thing was the action itself. The relationships of the five major characters in this play repeat with variations those of the five major characters of the first play.*

As in *Melite,* the major love affair is settled at the end of the first act and a new interest takes over: Tirsis and Melite, the enemies of love, fall in love with one another; Caliste and Rosidor, embroiled by Dorise's false reports of his infidelity, are united more deeply than ever in love.

Eraste and Tirsis love Melite, but Eraste is eliminated; Clitandre and Rosidor love Caliste, but Clitandre is eliminated.

Pymante loves Dorise but Dorise rejects him as unworthy; Philandre loves Cloris but Cloris rejects him as unworthy (we should remember that Philandre tried to come back to Cloris after his infidelity).

In the denouement, the two worthy but unmatched characters are united: Eraste and Cloris, Clitandre and Dorise.

In the denouement, the unworthy character is relegated to some kind of undesirable place: Pymante to prison, Philandre to courtship of La Nourrice.

The ending is a happy one. Generically, the play fits certain conditions of a tragicomedy as Lancaster has derived them from his study of a number of plays of the late sixteenth and early seventeenth centuries. These are: looseness of structure and primacy of interest, rather than respect for the unities; serious subject matter; leading personages aristocratic, but lower classes introduced in subordinate roles; presence of comic passages frequent but not essential; classic form—the predominant use of alex-

---

*"... cette pièce ne doit être considérée que comme une déformation accidentelle du type normal de ses autres pièces." Rivaille, *Les Débuts,* p. 81. In this context, "autres pièces" means the early comedies.

andrine verse, the division into five acts and subdivision into scenes.[7] More specifically, Georges May sees the play as a melodrama in many respects.[8] However, the political realities of *Clitandre* are not so well articulated as they the in later Cornelian "melodramas." The setting of *Clitandre* is closer to that of the comedies on either side of it. The world of *Clitandre* is peopled by men and women who are more *jeunes damoiseaux* and indulgent parent figures than they are *généreux* and *ambitieux*. Its characters are far less assertive than those of the political tetralogy; in the accord of their bodies and their souls, their bodies have more than a slight edge. *Clitandre* does not really change the course of Corneille's early comic stream.

Though a number of contemporary plays as well as *L'Astrée,* Honoré d'Urfé's seminal, multivolume novel, might easily have provided the source for much of what happens in *La Veuve* (1631-32), Corneille's most likely source, as Lancaster has shrewdly observed, was no doubt his own *Melite.* "In both plays the leading characters are three young men, the hero's sister, and the woman he loves, also a nurse who plays the role of go-between. In both a mother, after preferring a *mariage de raison,* yields to the wishes of her child. In both the rival plots to prevent the hero's marriage, a challenge to a duel is refused, and the man who is supposed to love the sister gives her up and marries a different person.... Moreover, just as Eraste repents of his efforts to prevent Mélite's marriage, so Celidan repents of the assistance he has rendered in the abduction of Clarice, and madness, while not real, as in Eraste's case, is at least feigned temporarily by the Nourrice."[9] Not all of the resemblances are as equally crucial as Lancaster's necessarily brief parallel makes them: the challenge refused and the madness are less conclusive than the pattern of relationships among the six principal characters (including the Nourrice and excluding Florange, who appears only as a name). But the parallel is a just one. As with *Clitandre* the resemblances among the characters of the two plays extends to their personalities as well as to the pattern of relationships: Philiste continues the *jeune gentilhomme,* the forthright lover whom we first met in Tirsis (at least in the Tirsis who fell in love before our very eyes) and again in Rosidor; Clarice is an even more essentialized version of the pure-hearted woman we first met in *Melite,* purified of that character's sharper traits even more than the Caliste of *Clitandre;* Celidan, while without Eraste's madness, is led into a misdeed for a reason which we can as easily excuse—his innocent faith in Alcidon—and in fact, that innocence and trust in others makes him a true brother to the wronged Clitandre of the play by that name; Doris rhymes with the Cloris of *Melite* and evokes the Dorise of *Clitandre* in more than her name: she, too, is a shrewd, witty, playful *rusée* whose apparently dishonest means are justified by her fundamentally virtuous ends; Alcidon is a spiritual brother of Philandre, whose hollow rhetoric, insincere courtship, and cowardice he repeats, and of Pymante, whose treachery he even surpasses; finally, the Nourrice of *La Veuve* adds to the base, materialistic motives of the Nourrice of *Melite* her own special brand of deceit and self-interest.

There are differences, of course, but, as with *Clitandre,* Corneille is manipulating the same elements and the new combination is forged not merely to create something new for its own sake, but to create diverse effects upon the audience. In this play the playwright seems to have aimed at sustaining dramatic interest through techniques of suspense and anticipation much more than in the earlier plays. He has shifted from an essentially lyrical to a more genuinely dramatic dramaturgy. The lyrical—both in its purely verbal and its structural manifestations—is still important, of course. Philiste's long and lovely *complainte* at the beginning of Act II, sung in stances of seven-verse octameters interpersed with alexandrines, does little to advance dramatic action—no more than does Clarice's lovely elegy, also expressed in stances near the end of Act III. These lyrical songs create their own immediate effects. Still, Clarice's does have the added dramatic value of increasing our sense of apprehension and ruefulness as we see her so joyously singing of her newly declared love only to have it interrupted by the masked intruders who rush upon the scene to abduct her. There are, too, a number of undramatic speeches, which though hardly lyrical, are merely recapitulative, serving the functions of similar speeches in earlier plays to remind us of the who, what, when, and where in the rapidly succeeding series of scenes we are seeing: thus, we have Celidan's soliloquy (IV, 7) in which, reminding us of his own good intentions, he recapitulates for us the meaning of the previous scene where he duped the nurse. But there is dramatic value in learning that he intends to keep the nurse locked up to keep her from doing further harm, confirming what we had sensed from his proposal to her in the previous scene. Generally speaking, it is obvious that, while the dramaturgy remains largely "defocused," the juxtaposition of scenes is less abrupt than in the earlier plays and the effects are unified in terms of a central dramatic interest rather than left in isolation. Where

*Melite* was a body of lyrics and *Clitandre* a tone poem, *La Veuve* is much more of an action.

How has Corneille managed to maintain interest in the fate of his central characters throughout most of the play? By varying the pattern of relationships among the couples ever so slightly: if Corneille has made the disgruntled lover (Alcidon) unfaithful to the friend's sister as in *Melite,* he has made the intentions of that lover as serious as those of Pymante in *Clitandre.* Furthermore, the first major conflict of the play—between the principal lovers, Philiste and Clarice—is not resolved so rapidly nor so dynamically as in the first two plays. Not, in fact, until the end of the second act. But, no sooner is it resolved in the lovers' mutual declarations, than Alcidon conceives his plan to abduct Clarice, so that the physical danger involved immediately reawakens the spectator's interest in the main couple. Actually, the threat of physical danger is a kind of dramatic *trompe-l'oeil* which distracts our attention from the fact that, as in *Melite,* the true center of dramatic interest has now shifted to the secondary couple, to the moral relationship among Célidan-Doris-Alcidon (in *Melite*: Eraste-Cloris-Philandre). And this second intrigue is resolved in pretty much the same way as it was in the first play: Eraste in his madness undid the harm he had done through the false letters by revealing to Philandre that they were false; Celidan comes out of his own "madness'—that is, his *duperie*—and undoes the harm he has done by a counterscheme. In the denouement there is a momentary final crisis as Philiste, still believing in Alcidon's good faith, refuses to give the deserving Celidan Doris's hand in marriage. But with Alcidon's admission of treachery, all is resolved. Like Pymante in *Clitandre,* only Alcidon remains without a mistress, although, it might be noted in passing, he "deserved" the nurse of this play as much as Philandre did the nurse of the first play.

Alcidon's last-minute admission also points up some puzzling features of the play. Of course, it is dramatically necessary if Corneille is ever to get his machine to stop running. Should Alcidon persist in his perfidy, he might easily persuade the gullible Philiste that Celidan is a traitor and off we would be on another round of adventure. "Gullible" Philiste must be explained in a world in which an Alcidon exists, though his gullibility makes him a very odd hero indeed. For if *Clitandre* brought us to a certain extent out of the idyllic world of *Melite* in which things were what they seemed and handsome did as handsome was except for madness, *La Veuve* has brought us further away from a pastoral idyll. Thus, Philiste has refused to declare openly his love to Clarice for over two years. But why has he not done so and why has she not reciprocated? Indeed, they appear to be playing a most ignoble game of love, one which seems to go beyond even the sincere limits of the shyness which is an admitted trait of Philiste's character and the understandable reserve which any woman must respect—even a woman whose widowhood gives her a certain allowance of boldness. In fact, it is Alcidon who from the very outset of the play speaks up for that forthrightness in the affair of love which we observed in the love at first sight of Melite and Tirsis:

> Mon cœur ne pourroit pas conserver tant de feu,
> S'il falloit que ma bouche en tesmoignast si peu: (I, 1)

Nor does Alcidon's later treachery explain away the difficulty posed by the lack of forthrightness in Philiste and, to a lesser extent, in Clarice.

The first explanation is that Philiste considers himself unworthy of Clarice. But the explanation raises new problems. It is never made clear, for example, whether he does so for reasons of material possession or those of birthright. When the Nurse, who considers the match with Philiste unfavorable to her mistress, says

> La memoire d'Alcandre et le rang qu'il vous laisse
> Voudroient un successeur de plus haute noblesse.

Clarice replies:

> Il preceda Philiste en vaines dignitez
> Et Philiste le passe en rares qualités,
> Il est né Gentilhomme, et sa vertu repare
> Tout ce dont la fortune envers luy fut avare
> Elle et moy nous avons trop de quoy l'agrandir. (II, 2)

We cannot be too sure whether Clarice means that Philiste is noble in spirit whatever his parents' station or that he really was born "gentilhomme," but a poor one. He himself declares himself to Alcidon as "inégal de biens et de conditions." Even if he is a nobleman thanks to his parents' station, is he not still of lesser rank than Clarice? Respecting the same conventions we found implicit in *Melite,* is he therefore without the right to pretend to her hand? Aspiring as he does, however, and finding his aspirations reciprocated, are we to conclude that, in this more real world as opposed to the artificial, idyllic world of *Melite,* historical accidents sometimes prevent *natural* nobility from finding its appropriate place in the *socially* designated ranks of nobility? Clarice finds her match by flying in the face of social conventions, of conventionally determined attributions of nobility. We seem to be on the verge of the great conflicts of the "serious" play of the middle period and, indeed, on occasion, Philiste's sense of honor takes on a character which seems almost tyrannical in this essentially bourgeois world (for example, his reproaches to his sister that, having feigned to love Alcidon, she must now marry Alcidon even though her motives were of the purest: to spare Philiste's own feelings in his great friendship for Alcidon).

Other behavior in the play seems perplexing according to a rigorous application of the ethos implicit in the first two plays. Eraste's immoral conduct and, to a certain extent, even Pymante's could be excused as madness, but no such explanation is offered for the similar conduct of Alcidon and Celidan. Of course, the validity of faith in appearances does seem to be proved negatively in Alcidon's behavior. Once we catch on to his basic disloyalty, we automatically convert his assessments of the behavior and motives of himself and others into the reverse: for example, his frequent accusation of others as cowards and traitors. In fact, this somewhat mechanical presentation of the character robs the play of much interest: where, in the earlier plays, the impassioned declarations of a character might momentarily lead the spectator into emotional involvement with the character if for no other reason than the strength of his accents, with Alcidon his most impassioned declarations are immediately translated by the spectator into their real worth and so lose any emotional impact. But Alcidon is an unsympathetic character. In him, proof of the coincidence of appearance and reality, of the necessity of always acting openly, remains necessarily negative and indirect.

Even so, how are we to assess the behavior of the

obviously sympathetic Celidan—sympathetic from the very first lines he speaks?

> Ce n'est pas que j'excuse, ou la soeur, ou le frere,
> Dont l'infidelité fait naistre ta colere,
> Mais, à ne point mentir, ton dessein à l'abord
> N'a gaigné mon esprit qu'avec un peu d'effort: (III, 1)

Celidan is sympathetic because he is a victim of the treacherous Alcidon, if for no other reason. Again, he unwittingly becomes Alcidon's victim only out of the noblest of motives. Finally, he becomes most sympathetic when he turns on the treacherous Alcidon. But in doing so he uses Alcidon's own means: treachery. The rationale seems to be that the end justifies the means. Now it is not my purpose to argue the rightness or wrongness of this proposition (for those looking for Jesuitism in Corneille, here it is at its purest); but it is obvious that the proposition is impossible—or at least wrong—in a world in which appearance corresponds to reality, where the eye is its own guarantor of what it sees and where it is the mark of an honorable man always to act openly. Philiste himself fulfills all of the stern imperatives which such a morality involves and, to the degree that we accept him as the model hero of play, the conduct of the other characters must remain perplexing: how is an Alcidon possible if madness is to be disallowed as an explanation of his conduct? Can we really condone Celidan's "treachery?" Should we not approve Philiste's stern remonstrances to his sister for her "deceit" with Alcidon? Certain aspects even of Philiste's behavior become questionable: for example, how can he approve of using the nurse's wiles to win Clarice to him and how in the Lord's name did he ever get mixed up with such a thoroughgoing scoundrel as Alcidon? Philiste seems to have inherited everything from Tirsis except his intelligence—most of that seems to have gone, however belatedly, to Celidan.

The fact of the matter is that we should be perplexed by various aspects of Philiste's behavior alone—and then, even there, not too seriously. For as the subtitle of the play indicates, the center of the action is not Philiste but Alcidon, *le traître trahi*. And, as the instrument who brings about the betrayal of the traitor, Celidan is the model hero and not Philiste. The latter seems to realize this himself in his finicky doubts about Clarice's ability to be completely his own, now that she is indebted to Celidan for saving her from her abductors. In fact, throughout the play Philiste is cast in an almost comical light: for his naive trust in Alcidon, his petulant retorts to his mother, his tyrannical disposition of Doris' hand, his excessive shyness, his elaborate refusal to believe in his own happiness when Clarice openly declares her love for him. Marty-Laveaux and others have noted the allusion to *Melite* (III, 3)[10] which Alcidon makes by way of accusing Doris of infidelity to himself (when he identifies himself with the Cloris of that play in her awareness of Philandre's treachery, we automatically identify him with Philandre). And Corneille has *Melite* in mind, as we have seen, in the very patterns of his play. But it is not a lack of imagination which makes him return to that first play. No, if he "redoes" *Melite* it is for much the same reason that he "redoes" the theme of the magician in *L'Illusion comique* after using it in *Médée*. More precisely, for the reason that he wishes to "undo" the play: *La Veuve* stands as a caution that we should not take the world of *Melite* so seriously that we miss its fun.

Corneille himself underlines his intention to bring this play "down to earth:" "Si tu n'es homme," he writes in his preface to the reader (1634),

à te contenter de la naïveté du style et de la subtilité de l'intrique, je ne t'invite point à la lecture de cette pièce: son ornament n'est pas dans l'éclat des vers . . . Ici donc tu ne trouveras en beaucoup d'endroits qu'une prose rimée, peu de scènes toutefois sans quelque raisonnement assez véritable, et partout une conduite assez industrieuse.[11]

If *La Veuve* is structurally a repetition of *Melite*, texturally and thematically it is a reversal of that world, an ironic commentary upon it. Philiste is a quixotic hero, ever ready to do battle for his lady love, but prevented from doing so by circumstances. Without making him out to be the fool in essence, Corneille nevertheless shows him to be more often a fool than not. But the play does end with an emphasis on the pleasant rather than the sombre and, in fact, as he at last gives Doris' hand to the deserving Celidan and otherwise disposes of his little band of "courtiers," Philiste even takes on some of the majesty and *éclat* of the king, Alcandre, who performs a similar adjudicative function at the end of *Clitandre,* and of Tirsis at the end of *Melite*. Corneille's self-conscious critique of his first creation, that is, is not a reversal, his irony is not "sincere." In "taking back" *Melite* he does not wish us to sympathize with the outcast Alcidon (in a modern version of *La Veuve,* Alcidon would figure as the rogue as hero) or to prefer decisively Celidan's pragmatism to Philiste's idealism. We are called upon to judge characters not ethically but esthetically. True, we delight in seeing the fooler fooled for a very profound reason which goes to the heart of the very idea of morality:

an ineradicable belief in the idea of justice such that, as Plato says, even the wicked man tries to *justify* his acts. (See, in our day, the judges of the Moscow purge trials or Nazi justifications of genocide). But it is not this idea of the impulse to justice that Corneille is trying to dramatize in his play. Rather, he counts upon this as an assumption and then proceeds to create a variety of means which will give rise to the pleasure we feel in the demonstration of the assumption. Celidan is a better actor than Alcidon and, it goes without saying, than Philiste. The latter, in fact, is the only character of the play who does not play a role—a stage notion which becomes explicit on the lips of both sympathetic and unsympathetic characters:

> LA NOURRICE: Sortons de pasmoison, reprenons la parole,
> Il nous faut à grands cris joüer un autre roole, (III, 10)

> CELIDAN: Je joüerois à ce conte un joly personnage, (IV, 5)

and the same character:

> Et que depuis qu'on joüe à surprendre un amy
> Un trompeur en moy trouve un trompeur et demy. (IV, 7)

Thus, if Alcidon's confession is perplexing from a moral point of view (if not due to madness, how explain this corruption of a *généreux?*), from the theatrical or esthetic point of view, it becomes clear: he has been outwitted, his ingenuity can do no more—except, perhaps, in a parting shot to try to implicate Celidan in his intrigue. He has been a hypocrite only etymologically, that is, an actor. And, a bad one at that, he deserves to be cut out of the happy denouement. One senses too that La Nourrice has been cut out not only for the reason Corneille gives: that such characters aren't of sufficient important to wonder about and once their role is finished there is no need to bring them back. Indeed, good actor that she has proved herself to be, it might be dangerous to bring her back on stage!

No more so, then, than the first two plays does *La Veuve* appeal primarily at the moral level.[12] To take either *La Veuve* or *Melite* too seriously, to seek in them lessons for life, is not only to put upon them an impossible burden: it is to become the victim of an illusion, to be carried away by the effects which these appearances of appearances create in their little moment of time.

In *La Galerie du Palais* (1632) the most schematic and stylized of the plays thus far, the specifically intellectual appeal is minimized for the sake of emotional impact. Obviously, the central theme is once again the relationship of appearance to reality. But here there is no conflict between the two which we found implicit in the study of character in each of the three preceding plays. Paradoxically enough, in this play where everybody but Dorimant acts or gives an appearance the opposite of his intentions, it is possible to claim that the equation between appearances and reality has never been more unquestionable. For here, with the possible exception of Hippolyte, no one really acts out of evil intentions; there are no Philandres, no Pymantes, no Alcidons. The "base types"—Florice and Aronte—are not banished from the scene of idyllic reconciliation which terminates the comedy, but are absolved of all possible guilt and invited to participate in the cheerful denouement.

A less cheerful denouement characterizes Corneille's

next play, *La Suivante* (1633). The play is written with a cold, hard hand. Each act contains exactly the same number of verses.* Again, it is superficially the most regular of the plays Corneille has written thus far: the unities of times and place are very strictly observed and the unity of action has at least the technical coherence which a genuine linkage of scenes gives. The fact of the matter is that, in spite of the skillful *liaisons de vue,*‡ the play actually suffers from a certain dispersal of dramatic interest, as Corneille readily admits in his "Examen." The Théante-Clarimond-Florame relationship is no more than the basis for "un agréable épisode de deux honnêtes gens qui jouent tour à tour un poltron et le tournent en ridicule."[13] But the episode is a rather lengthy one and its effect is to arrest dramatic interest in very much the manner of the lyrical emphasis of the dramaturgy of the first plays. Corneille has also repeated other devices from those plays. The misunderstandings give rise to a number of fearful threats and internal conflicts which evoke tragic anxiety in the spectator's breast for no really good reason: Géraste's reversal on his choice for Daphnis' suitor actually enables the lovers to wed as they wish, but, given their misunderstanding of Géraste's first choice, Florame threatens to kill the "treacherous" old man and Daphnis is torn between filial loyalty and

---

* In the original as well as in the definitive version. Corneille himself takes pains to point to this unique feature of the play in the dedicatory preface to the original edition, M-L, *II*, 118-119.

‡ Corneille's term for those transitions "quand l'acteur qui entre sur le théâtre voit celui qui en sort, ou que celui qui sort voit celui qui entre; soit qu'il le cherche, soit qu'il le fuie, soit qu'il le voie simplement sans avoir intérêt à le chercher ni à le fuir." "Examen," M-L, *II*, 124. Certain critics had denied the legitimacy of this kind of transition, demanding that characters actually speak to each other. Corneille typically rejects the "advice" of his critics.

amorous inclination. Tragic emotion is created only to be dissipated. Again, we have once more the pattern of the five principal characters: three men (Théante, Florame, Clarimond) and two women (Amarante and Daphnis) with the first suitor (Théante) being forced out of contention. But beyond this initial *donnée* Corneille has not really worked out the resolution among the remaining four characters. Rather, he has worked it out among the major characters (Florame, Armante, and Daphnis) and Géraste, the father-type whose role heretofore has been merely that of guarantor of the situation worked out independently of him. Corneille might as easily have used him as a mere name, as he does Florise, the sister one never sees. Thus the relatively intense concentration of dramatic interest upon Clarimond must also be regarded as structurally unimportant, lyrical in its effect.

Yet, the lyrical effect is far more sophisticated here than in its earlier usage. Much of the bombast and flourish is gone and the soliloquies do not merely recapitulate events or remind us of a character's role in a rapidly developing action, but serve rather to develop the character himself. The lyrically isolated events also serve this function of characterization, so that we can say that in *La Suivante* the characters are far less schematic than in *La Galerie*. However, events are still determined from without—by chance and by circumstance, so that *La Suivante* represents a curious mixture of the *comédie d'intrigue* and the *comédie de caractère*, an "essai" in which as Lancaster puts it, Corneille shows "a desire to try out all sorts of dramatic suggestions."[14]

If *La Galerie du palais* had some of the cruel funmaking of a Marivaux comedy (of *L'Epreuve*, for example, another plot based on a "love test"), it nevertheless stayed within the domain of comedy both texturally and structurally: literally nobody is left to "hold the bag" in the playlike happy ending of absolutions and marriages. In *La Suivante,* however, the funmaking takes a grim turn and the play takes on some of the sombre aspects of Shakespeare's problem comedies (*All's Well That Ends Well* or *Measure for Measure*).

Obviously, as in *Melite,* we have an old dramatic relationship among Théante-Daphnis-Florame: the lover who loses his mistress by introducing his friend. This time, however, Théante resembles more Philandre than he does Eraste, for his motives are ignoble where Eraste's were not. Again, in Amarante we have a successor to the shrewd and cunning Cloris of the first play: as readily as her prototype, she can see into the "philandering" intentions of Théante. But her own intentions are less commendable than those of Cloris when she is dealing with the equally double-dealing Florame, who is also using her as a means of getting close to her mistress. The relationship between the two women is no more wholesome than that between Amarante and her "suitors": Amarante consciously deceives her mistress and the mistress, though she never comes to this kind of deceit (for want of opportunity, one feels) treats her *suivante* in an unkind, mocking, and vindictive way which is hardly becoming in the successor to the spirited but honest Melite of the first play. The blacking of character extends to secondary as well as minor characters: Géraste is a scheming old man little better than a procurer in the bargaining away of his daughter's hand for the young Florise he unashamedly desires; of the two characters from whom the confidante Célie is drawn, she resembles more the infamous Nourrice of *La Veuve* than the generous Chrysante of *La Galerie;* Damon is a double agent of Iago-like duplicity.

Only Clarimond is a character of unquestioned virtue. Significantly, unlike his prototype in *La Veuve,* Celidan, he finds no means to undo the pretense in which he has been involved. His virtue is passive. In fact, from *La Veuve* through *La Galerie* and into the present play, we can trace the gradual "deactivation" of the type: Celidan upsets Alcidon's plan and, in an implicit parody of the supposed hero of the play, must really be considered as the model hero. But Dorimant, though wishing to do his share and certainly ready for action, as we see in his duel with Lysandre, really had no share in the undoing of his enemy's intrigue. Too virtuous to resort to ruse, he was somewhat out of place in the world of *La Galerie.* The world of *La Suivante* is even more thoroughly one of ruse and pretense, the virtuous Clarimond's honesty being an idyllic construct from the world of *Melite.* He can do no more than we see him do: serve his lady love by "generously" accepting his dismissal. It is conceivable that he would be as ready as Dorimant to duel if provoked, but Corneille never allows this circumstance to arise and it is more likely that we would have found sincerely expressed on *his* lips the arguments which the insincere Théante invokes to fend off a duel with Florame: to slay the man Daphnis loves would be only to offend the mistress and to compromise his own position with her.

Though the familiar tactics of teasing and surprise are as numerous in this play as in *La Galerie,* their effect is not so securely anchored in the reassuring moral framework of the earlier plays. Curiosity tends to become anxiety in *La Suivante* and surprise to become shock. We cannot take as great delight in seeing the fooler fooled.

The characters do not act out of the best motives; intentions are relatively rather than absolutely distinguished. Both Théante and Florame use Amarante in an indecent way to gain access to Daphnis and this immorality is no more excused in the case of the "hero" of the play, Florame, than in the case of the "villain." Brave in the face of physical danger Florame always is, and this irrelevant *vertu* or courage makes him seem more morally virtuous than the cowardly Théante. But Florame becomes morally virtuous only when he sees fit or when pretense will no longer serve his ends. Fundamentally more compromising than his resort to pretense is his unabashed bartering of his sister in his dickering with Géraste for Daphnis' hand. As with his use of pretense, the immorality of the act is lost sight of in the dazzle of the virtuous glow in which the act takes place: there his courage, here his love for Daphnis. In a similar way Daphnis's own deeply felt love and her noble fidelity to her lover in the face of what seems to be her father's opposing choice blind us to the fact that she is really very cruel and vindictive in her attitude to her "poor relation," Amarante.

When we turn from the principal lovers of the play to the characters surrounding them, we do not even find the compensatory glow of virtuous commitments which blinds us to their basic cruelty and viciousness. Géraste is a familiar type in old comedy: the rich old man in love with the young girl whom he usually loses to an adroit young suitor. He is a schemer and a panting old sensualist, but he does have his way in this play. Théante, being endowed with none of the saving comic pomposity of the *capitan fanfaron,* strikes us as a coward pure and simple. Damon is very much of a devil (*daemon*), but painted in cool colors, he lacks the comic verve of a Scapin, so that his daemonism strikes us much more as treachery than as *diablerie*. Indeed, of all the characters it is most difficult to decide what his ends are. The double agent is by definition a slippery character: we never know whether he will turn out to be a triple agent, a quadruple agent, etc.

With the exception of Amarante and Clarimond each of the characters is either social climbing or self-seeking in such a way as to make a mockery of the ethical premises and social conventions of the world of *Melite*. Appearances belie reality. The abuse of Amarante by Théante and Florame makes this apparent enough, but there exists as well a certain amount of doubt about Florame's intentions even in marrying Daphnis:

> Sa richesse l'attire, et sa beauté le blesse;
> Elle le passe en biens, il l'égale en noblesse,
> Et cherche ambitieux, par sa possession,
> A relever l'éclat de son extraction.
> Il a peu de fortune, et beaucoup de courage;
> Et hors cette espérance, il hait le mariage.
> C'est ce que l'autre jour en secret il m'apprit;
> Tu peux, sur cet avis, lire dans son esprit. (I, 1)

This, of course, is the assessment of Damon, hardly reliable as a fair judge of others motives. But the Florame who is ready to barter his sister in marriage is also ready to count on his birthright as a lure which will prevent his mistress from resisting his offers of marriage:

> Elle [Daphnis] a trop de bonté pour me vouloir du mal;
> D'ailleurs sa résistance obscurciroit sa gloire; (III, 1)

His assessment of Daphnis's motives cannot be proven

from anything she herself says in the play. In fact, in her attribution of the noblest virtues to Florame and in her confidence in her father's early approval of "Florame" (really of Clarimond) as a demonstration of the power of *mérite* over *biens*, she is as ridiculous as Philiste in her naive idealism. But her idealism, as we have seen, is limited only to Florame and her father; with Amarante she is quite pragmatic. The spirit of absolution which obtained between Clarice and Dorise in *La Veuve* and Célidée and Hippolyte in *La Galerie* is missing at the end of *La Suivante.*

Not even in *La Veuve*, the explicit parody of *Melite*, did we have such a thorough breakdown of the hierarchical relationships of a society whose principal rule of action is sincerity. Excuse for pretense by madness is completely out of the question here. And the notion of like choosing like and social station reflecting individual merit is nowhere observed. Florame and Florise, better born than Daphnis and Géraste, marry them nevertheless, and the very fact that Florame *forces* his sister into the marriage indicates the corruption of the ideal as much as the marriage itself.

In such a corrupt world, Amarante appears as a sympathetic character. Judged on purely moral grounds she and Clarimond alone act only out of the best of intentions. Judged on purely esthetic grounds, she is even more sympathetic than the passive, ineffectual Clarimond: she is a better player than he. She is probably an even better player than any of the others except Damon, whose complete lack of scruple gives infinite extension to his talents as an actor. But the cards are stacked against her: she is playing only for love and is using the player's tricks of that relatively unserious game; the others are playing the serious game of social ambition where the stakes are higher and the tricks more complicated. We might describe the play as a comi-tragedy in which Amarante is the "tragic hero." There is some doubt, however, about the degree to which we can consider Amarante as *the* principal character. Though he has moved a traditionally secondary character to a primary place in the play, Corneille has, following a practice of all his early plays, divided dramatic attention about equally among the principal characters. Whatever we may think of it morally, the fact of the matter is that the affair between Florame and Daphnis occupies our attention throughout most of the play. In this respect, *La Suivante* repeats the dramaturgy of various of the early plays: of *La Galerie* and *La Veuve* where the problem was not to unite the two lovers but to reunite them; of *Melite* and *Clitandre,* where the center of interest shifted after the first act to a different set of relationships (here: from Théante-Amarante-Florame to Amarante-Florame-Daphnis). On this latter resemblance, Corneille has dispersed dramatic interest even more by creating the new relationship of Florame-Daphnis-Clarimond. And in the midst of these changing relationships he has still managed to keep Théante in the spectator's eye, apparently for no other reason than to expose him as a coward. His refusal to second Florame in a duel with Clarimond only precludes a duel which, given Clarimond's absolute fidelity to his mistress, would never have taken place. Amarante herself is brought on stage in this crisscross of motives only to make her undoing the more ironic. True, she does complicate things by telling Géraste that Daphnis really loves Clarimond, but a combination of chance (Daphnis's misunderstanding of her father's meaning) and purpose (Géraste's reversal for reasons of self-interest) only raises her hopes finally to dash them down in the cruel denouement.

Her fate thus responds in some ways to that of the tragic hero: the belief that she can manipulate reality as given, control circumstances at will, is proven to be an illusion. But her reaction to this "lesson" of the play hardly shows that spirit of acceptance characteristic of "tragedy." As Amarante vindictively wishes revenge upon Géraste we see that she lacks any genuine insight into the inevitability of her fate, the impossibility of reversing it or of redeeming it through revenge. Neither in the structure of events nor in the characterization is there any implication of the metaphysical necessity of Amarante's fate. The solution or denouement of the play is not inevitable within the terms of the ethical system and social conventions it implies. As Géraste and Florame "break the rules" of sincerity and hierarchical order we are not led to believe that the rules are impossible to keep, given the realities of human nature (the tragedy of idealism); nor are we led to believe that in doing so they represent the abstract force of pure evil in a Manichean struggle with the forces of good. It is not inconceivable that Amarante be "rewarded" with Clarimond in the same way that the "losers" in all of the previous plays have been rewarded. That she is not makes the point of view cynical, but hardly tragic.

In fact, a genuine tragic conflict is much more evident in the predicament in which Florame and Daphnis find themselves after Géraste has taken back his word: Florame is torn between a desire to revenge his sullied honor and the fear of offending his mistress by slaying the author of her life; Daphnis is torn between a desire to obey parental wishes and the sense of honor which dictates that she keep her pledged word to her beloved. And as the lovers vie with each other in protestations of fidelity we have the first of those Cornelian *combats amoureux* which make later plays so memorable. But the tragedy is without basis, there is no real tragic dilemma, since Géraste has changed his mind in such a way as to make his daughter's original misunderstanding and his present intentions coincide. We have, as earlier in *Melite* and *Clitandre*, the evocation of tragic effects only for the sake of dissipating them.

In its ideas, *La Suivante* is best described as an *"anti-thesis play."* In this satire of the idyllic concepts of the world of *Melite*, *La Suivante* does not merely reproduce the point of view of *La Veuve*. Here the model hero who casts the conventions aside is no Celidan acting out of the best of intentions, seeking to restore order and punish an Alcidon derelict in his sense of honor as a *généreux*. In *La Veuve*, Philiste, parodistically displaced as hero by Celidan, is nevertheless restored to his function as quasi-ruler of the little band of courtier types who make up the cast. In *La Suivante* Clarimond, the ideal hero, is permitted to achieve prominence neither at the beginning nor the end of the action. Yet Corneille may have been "negatively" aristocratic in this play. There is an anti-bourgeois bias in casting Géraste as the villain of the piece: he *buys* Florise. Furthermore, it is also possible to see a similar bourgeois vice in the nobly born Florame: he *sells* Florise. In fact, the brunt of parody and satire is not principally directed at Géraste whose self-interest takes a sensual rather than a financial turn or at Daphnis whose self-interest might be a vicious social climbing through wealth but who somewhat naively expresses the ideals of *générosité* that her lover cynically abuses to suit his ambitions. Rather, the satire is of the *généreux* types who derogate from expected standards of conduct.

Thus, it is less his futility than Florame's cynicism which commands our attention. In the world of *Melite* the nobly born acted only out of the best intentions and in a noble manner and their actions were effective (it should be remembered that [1] Tirsis never actually deceives Eraste or Melite with the sonnet on behalf of Eraste; [2] that the intention to deceive Eraste must be judged esthetically rather than morally as a stratagem in the game of love). In the world of *Melite* parodied in *La Veuve* the nobly born who acted in a noble manner and out of the best of intentions were ineffectual. In the world of *La Suivante,* the nobly born act out of the worst of intentions and in an ignoble manner and *their* actions are effective. The *damoiseaux* and *demoiselles* are rakes and *rouées.*

In the relatively slight *La Place Royale* (1633-34) Corneille has created the first example, although a bizarre one, of that dynamic, morally serious figure whose contradictory critical fate it has been to be cast in the rigid mold of critical thought: the Cornelian hero. But the dramatist has not created him in one piece: Alidor is really a patchwork of the *damoiseau* hero of the preceding comedies and the *généreux* types of the later plays. Indeed, much more consistent heroism stands forth in the character of Angélique, who, though she too derogates from the code of honor in her consent to Alidor's betrayal of Doraste, castigates her derogation from the code and commits herself to a convent in a noble renunciation of the world. I do not mean to imply that the *damoiseau* in him prevents Alidor from being a *généreux*. A *généreux* Alidor certainly is, in all that the word in its seventeenth-century usage comports of fierce pride, self-esteem, strength of will, and sense of personal honor. Alidor's fierce devotion to himself as a superior man cracks the fragile pastoral mold of *La Place Royale*.

> Comptes-tu mon esprit entre les ordinaires?
> Penses-tu qu'il s'arrête aux sentiments vulgaires? (I, 4)

"Alidor," writes Octave Nadal, "annonce Rodrigue, Polyeucte, Suréna."[15] Given this essence, all of Alidor's actions should only be the expression of it. Yet obviously they are not. A true *généreux*—the hero whom we shall find in the political tetralogy—would never think of expressing noble intentions in an ignoble deed, of deceiving a mistress in order to be rid of her. The noble thing to do is to admit the change of heart to the mistress. More consistently, it is inconceivable that a true *généreux* would or could know a change of heart.

Yet we should not lean too hard on this "precursor" of the "Cornelian hero." Alidor's instability is a dramatic rather than a psychological necessity, like that of the heroine of *La Veuve*. It keeps things going and in the blur of events we have little time or inclination to reconcile deeds and intentions. The intrusion of Alidor's emphatic heroism is not so much morally disturbing as it is esthetically inappropriate. It is not difficult to understand why Alidor should strike us so much as a patchwork character, for *La Place Royale* is a reworking of so many of the themes and situations of the first five plays. Having tried a character who unwillingly loses his mistress by introducing her to his best friend, Corneille now tries one who willingly loses her to his best friend; having tried a character who falls out of love unwillingly (the heroine of *La Galerie*), he now tries one who falls back into love unwillingly; having created a number of well-intentioned but ineffectual heroes, he now creates a well-intentioned but effectual hero; etc. Like all its predecessors, including the partially "romantic" *Clitandre, La Place Royale* is not a moral drama, but a game. However, still aiming at excitement rather than anxiety, yet at the same time intent on not repeating himself, Corneille is beginning to find that the pastoral-bourgeois setting of his manipulations is wearing thin.

In creating the heroine of his next play, *Médée* (1634-35)* Corneille is obviously not playing games. The seriousness of his purpose is evident in the fact that this is the first play he calls *"tragédie."* Yet, as one watches this serious heroine at work in a world where others seem at play, one wonders if it can really be described as a tragedy.

One of the most persistent strains in tragic theory from Aristotle's day to our own is that the tragic is the loss of value. As Richard Sewall has put it recently: tragic stories such as those of Job and Oedipus make us wonder if there is "justice in a world where, for no reason clear to the ethical understanding, the worst happens to the best." [16] For many a student of the form, the very designation of a play as either "tragedy" or "comedy" predisposes the spectator to expect such final moral and metaphysical assessments of the human condition. But for Corneille and certain of his contemporaries, the term *"tragédie"* in particular did not automatically involve these final "negative" assessments. With certain modifications, Lanson's excellent history of the concept is to the point here. The

---

* For the dating of the canon beyond this point I have relied on the studies of Couton: *Corneille* and "Comment dater les grandes pièces de Corneille," *Revue d'Historie du Théâtre,* VIII, 15-23. Double dates refer to theatrical seasons.

critic first states a morally more neutral definition of the tragic: "Le tragique est la manifestation, dans un cas douloureux, des limites de la condition humaine et de la force invisible qui l'étreint." [17] Lanson then traces the history of the tragic. In the Middle Ages, he notes, "on appelle *tragédie* ou comédie toute narration mêlée de dialogues" and he cites four characteristics of tragedy at the time: "Historique—Royale—Sanglante—Elevée de style." [18] In the Renaissance, particularly the late sixteenth century in France, he notes that "la notion médiévale s'affirme et s'enrichit," but that "l'impression que la tragédie représente l'instabilité de la grandeur et de la félicité humaines, qu'elle veut des spectacles cruels et pitoyables, se confirme." [19] In the seventeenth century, Lanson finds that a major shift in conception occurs. There is still some hesitation and irregularity, but there is "détermination sur l'essentiel: La tragédie est dans les âmes." [20] Now, we may agree with Lanson that this psychological definition of tragedy is the ascendant conception of tragedy both among dramatists and critics in Corneille's time. But it should be noted that it does not *necessarily* involve those final assessments which we tend to associate with the term. True enough, Corneille and Racine represent seventeenth-century French tragedy with its concern for definitions of the self. But comparison of these two leads to a contrast between the kinds of selves or *"âmes"* and the fate which they meet in each. Internal laws of necessity lead to disaster in one, triumph in the other. Defined in a psychological way, *"tragédie"* covers a multitude of outlooks which can very easily go counter to moral definitions of the form—as Corneille's *Médée* obviously does.

What then can we call this play, if not a tragedy? To the extent that we do take Médée as a representative of the human, it emphasizes the very opposite of *"le tragique."* The action of *Médée* is a progressive justification of Médée in which her single-minded dedication to the worthless Jason in its very intensiy and purity places her in sharp relief to the piddling creatures who surround her. In his reflections on this play, Thibaudet believes that *Médée* and *Le Cid* stand in Corneille's artistic and moral development in about the same relation as the first *Tentation de Saint Antoine* to *Madame Bovary* in Flaubert's: "un certain plan de littérature personnelle est abandonnée, de façon en somme définitive."[21] And to Emma bargaining with Lheureux, Thibaudet compares Créuse bargaining with Jason for Médée's dress. Yet a still closer comparison of the novel and the play would reveal a closer resemblance between Emma and Médée, both demonic personalities surrounded by conservative, cautious, and caviling lesser personalities willing secretly to use the force of an Emma or a Médée, but fearful of that total commitment which open collusion with her demonic personality represents. But where Emma suffers defeat in her piddling world, Médée escapes hers. She quits that world of broken marriage vows and scheming parents—and probably more to the relief than dismay of its people. When Créon reproaches Médée—fearful, surprised that she has not yet gone into exile—he is in effect telling her that she "plays too rough" for his world of fantasy. Though she is far more *engagée* than the Alidor who is her prototype in *La Place Royale,* Médée, like him, is out of place in the world of the play in which she figures: she is too big, too overwhelming for the relatively trivial world in which Corneille has forced her to function. This relation between hero and world should be especially illuminating when we turn to the plays with which Corneille is said to have founded French "tragedy."

However, before he began those plays, Corneille brought the series of plays which began with *Melite* to an appropriate close in *L'Illusion comique* (1636), his eighth play, a kind of *"prise de conscience théâtrale."* He has included within the structure of *L'Illusion* esthetic considerations which usually remain external to the work of art. He has, so to speak, dramatized his dramaturgy. In this play, the literary self-consciousness which Nadal has seen as characteristic of all of the early plays of Corneille reaches its greatest intensity.[22] The magician is a convention of the dramatic literature of the period, Corneille having used one in the play immediately preceding this one, *Médée*. In this connection, A. Donald Sellstrom has properly seen that the substance of the inner play here constitutes a parody of the preceding play about the *magicienne*.[23] I also suggested in an earlier work that "it is as if Corneille wished to reassure us in *L'Illusion* that even Médée's magic, however malevolent it may have seemed, was really stage magic, too, harmless and only '*pour vous faire plaisir.*' In Eric Bentley's careful distinction between the serious and the playful use of magic, Corneille's is a magic of *as if*—'as if real contact were made with another realm.' "[24] Other conventions both from the literature of the time and from Corneille's own theater both before and after this play also figure prominently in it. The names of the principal characters are stock names in the plays of the time and are used frequently by Corneille: Alcandre (*Clitandre*), Dorante (*Le Menteur* and *La Suite du Menteur*), Isabelle (*Le Menteur*), Lyse (*La Suite du Menteur*), Hippolyte (*La Galerie du palais*), etc. Nor was Corneille the first to use the relatively new convention of the inner play, Baro, Gougenot, and

Scudéry all preceding him in its use. Again, the *"comédie imparfaite,"* as Corneille described the play about Clindor's adventures, when taken in isolation resembles many another *tragi-comédie,* the dominant genre of the period.

Yet, this tragicomedy is set within a larger structure which more resembles the plays on its hither side. The play is a comedy, one which epitomizes many of the characteristics of that form as already practiced by Corneille. Thus, the world of the play is fantastical, a realm of appearances: a *"grotte obscure,"* the stage of a theater. These people are specific continuations of many of the types of the earlier plays: the *jeune premier* and the *jeune première* are drawn from the clever *damoiseaux* and *demoiselles* of those plays; Pridamant (like Alcandre to a lesser extent) resembles the indulgent parents of the earlier plays, while Lyse recalls the *suivante rusée*. The only ones to suffer in this realm are the wicked (Matamore, Géronte, Adraste, Théagène, Rosine) but their wickedness is not a manifestation of cosmic imbalance or metaphysical evil—it consists simply and superficially in their opposition to the wish fulfillment of the principals. This opposition is not really significant; there is no real conflict. All that we and the hero wish were so, proves to be so, for, being *basically* good *(gentils)* their dreams of success and wealth and blissful love are bound to be fulfilled.

# 2

# Le Cid to Pompée
## le généreux

As the cause of one of the great quarels of French literary history, *Le Cid* (1636)* tends to be subordinated to the documents which have accumulated around it. In approaching the play, many scholars and critics are carried away by the purely personal aspects of the "Querelle du *Cid*." Others, taking their cue from Scudéry's *Observations* or the *Sentiments de l'Académie*, become involved in a theoretical discussion of esthetic or ethical matters. Critics of both tendencies forget that the play is, after all, the primary "document." Corneille wrote it not to air any grievances or to comply with any doctrines, but to please his spectators. I would like to turn to the play in this particular context, treating it not as a document but as an unfolding drama. In this emphasis I do not mean to imply that documentary matters are irrelevant. But I do believe that only by studying *Le Cid* in its developing action can we see the relevance of certain aspects of the

---

*I give the date consecrated in literary history, but Couton gives January of 1637. *Corneille*, p. 42.

play which have puzzled documentary critics from
Corneille's day to our own: the "morally inconsistent"
behavior of the principals, the role of politics, the dramatic value of various secondary characters (particularly
l'Infante), etc.

Accustomed by centuries of criticism to the image of
the "Cornelian hero" in *Le Cid* we are liable to forget that
the heroes of the play, Rodrigue *and* Chimene, are presented to us primarily not as heroes but as lovers. They
are so presented especially in the first version of the play,
as the second scene in that version shows:[1]

> ELVIRE (seule): Quelle douce nouvelle à ces jeunes amans!
> Et que tout se dispose à leurs contentemens!
> CHIMENE: Et bien, Elvire, en fin, que faut-il que j'espere?
> Que dois-je devenir, & que t'a dit mon pere?
> ELV.: Deux mots dont tous vos sens doivent estre charmez:
> Il estime Rodrigue autant que vous l'aimez.
> CHIM.: L'excez de ce bon-heur me met en deffiance;
> Puis-je à de tels discours donner quelque croyance?
> ELV.: Il passe bien plus outre: il approuve ses feux,
> Et vous doit commander de respondre à ses voeux.
> Jugez apres cela, puis que tantost son pere,
> Au sortir du Conseil, doit proposer l'affaire,
> S'il pouvoit avoir lieu de mieux prendre son temps,
> Et si tous vos desirs seront bien tost contents.
> CHIM.: Il semble toutefois que mon ame troublée
> Refuse cette joye & s'en trouve accablée.
> Un moment donne au sort des visages divers,
> Et dans ce grand bon-heur je crains un grand revers.
> ELV.: Vous verrez vostre crainte heureusement deceuë.
> CHIM.: Allons, quoy qu'il en soit, en attendre l'issuë. (I, 2)

In the original version the accent is already familiar to

us from the early comedies: the tone is utopian rather than imperative, the emphasis upon young love's bliss. Chimene might be said to be anxious and she does express this anxiety in the same terms ("Et dans ce grand bon-heur je crains un grand revers"), but in the first version her excitement and hope are allowed to stand as freely as her anxiety. In the familiar final version, Corneille has indirectly compressed into the first scene what had transpired in the first scene of the original: the father's assent to the marriage with Rodrigue. And in doing so he has introduced an ominous tone, adjusting all of his characters—the father by report and Chimene and Elvire directly—to that tone. Thus, where Elvire had sounded like the *suivante* she was called in the *dramatis personae* of the first version, she sounds in the final version more like the *gouvernante* which she is in fact called in the *dramatis personae* of that version. Gone are her ecstatic and exalted accents, to make way for more sober ones. The same change can be seen in Chimene herself. Where in the first version Corneille underscored in her very first reply the note of youthful expectancy and placed her anxiety in rather vague terms, in the final version her mood is imperative rather than interrogative ("dis-moi donc . . .") ; and when she does ask questions in the final version, they are edged with an anxiety with a specific source (the questions about the relative merits of Rodrigue and Sanche). Where in the first version Elvire attributed the expected delight of the senses to her mistress ("tous *vos* sens doivent estre charmez"), in the final one this delight is attributed to Elvire directly ("Tous mes sens à moi-même en sont encore charmes"), and only by imputation (in the "à moi-même) to her mistress. Again, in the final version the hoped-for bliss of the sweet, young lovers

("Quelle douce nouvelle à ces jeunes amans!") comes up harder from the very outset against the political realities which will indeed complicate their lives. But in the original version the question which immediately intrigues us is not "will Rodrigue be forced to forego Chimene because of these political realities?" but the more general one: "will the lovers be united?" As Faguet saw some time ago, the first question is answered by the end of the first act. As for the second, its answer would be quickly: yes— were it not for Chimene. This fact led Faguet to retitle the play *"Chimène,"*[2] but even in *"Chimène"* the basic question is not "will she defend her honor?" but "will the lovers never find a way to reconcile love and honor?"—in short: "will they be reunited?"

Throughout the play the dramatist maintains in the spectator's breast a contrapuntal effect between the amorous and the moral in which the amorous is the dominant motif. Her father having approved of Chimene's preference for Rodrigue over Don Sanche, what is the meaning of Chimene's unspecified anxiety when we first meet her? In what we would nowadays call the "subliminal" areas of the psyche it finds specific meaning in the political matter of the preceptorship which has been hastily and "incidentally" mentioned by Gormas in the first scene of the original version (I shall comment on the matter of the more "knowledgeable" contemporaries of Corneille in a moment). What of l'Infante's inclination toward Rodrigue? Will she cast aside her scruples about his inferior station and even possibly use her own station to usurp Chimene's prior claim? The political quarrel between Gormas and Diegue only intensifies the spectator's curiosity about the love affair: does it not mean the separation of the lovers? And will l'Infante attempt to profit by this separation? Even when the action becomes overtly "moral," it is the love tie between the characters which provides the shudder of interest: what more pathetic than the mistress forced to demand her lover's head or the lover willing to die by his mistress' hand in order to satisfy her honor? Never has Corneille used dramatic suspense (his principal "artifice" according to May)[3] to greater effect. A performance of the play is the best answer to Scudéry's theoretical observation that Corneille sacrificed all possibility of suspense in choosing such a well-known subject.[4] There is even some doubt that the subject was so "well known"—at least, to a wide public. But even granting Scudéry the point, such a limitation could only stimulate Corneille in his benevolent assault upon the spectator. This spectator-conscious manipulator of theatrical effects knew that before the unfolding drama, the spectator's foreknowledge is quickly diluted in the excitement of his blood.

Realistic criticism like Scudéry's* or moralistic criticism like that of the Académie only stresses the dramatic vitality of Corneille's characters. Rodrigue and Chimène are not *généreux* dropped "full-blown" into the crisis which confronts them. As Nadal has said, when Rodrigue is confronted with the terrible implications of Gormas' insult, the image of his beloved comes to him "non comme un objet d'estime et d'adoration, mais comme une promesse de jouissance."[5] The language of the famous *stances* is affective rather than analytical. The tone is essentially plaintive in the first stanza—*percé, coeur, mortelle, miserable, injuste rigeur, abattuë, tuë, peine* are the key words. The tone remains plaintive throughout the next stanza. In the third, it shifts to the hallucinatory, as

---

[5] Scudéry also objects violently to the compression of action in the play, especially in the fifth act.

Rodrigue's emotional dilemma is conveyed by a series of oxymorons—*illustre tyrannie, adorable contrainte, cher et cruel espoir*. The tone of the fourth is more coherent, but is again not essentially analytical as Rodrigue exhorts himself to suicide. The fifth remains hortatory as the shameful meaning of suicide forces itself upon Rodrigue and he resolves to save his honor. True, the end of the fifth and the beginning of the sixth show some "reflection" ("Ouy, mon esprit s'estoit deceu. / Dois je pas à mon pere avant qu'à ma maistresse"—I, 7), but it is diluted in the exalted accents with which the speech concludes. In all this one can hardly speak of a process of reasoning, at least in the Cartesian sense of a deductive chain. True, there is a glimmer of the later complexities of honor which the lovers work out as the action develops: Rodrigue "reasons" that "Qui vange cet affront irrite sa colere, / Et qui peut le souffrir ne la merite pas" (I, 7). But at this juncture, his first reaction to this dilemma is to commit suicide. And when he rejects suicide it is not because in avenging his father's honor he will be paradoxically respecting Chimene's choice of him in the first place—the paradox of love as honor. Rather, at this moment Rodrigue simply chooses his father over his mistress. The process is dramatic, a conflict between two emotionally charged choices.

The process is the same with Chimene. She, too, chooses the father over the beloved—instinctively, not analytically. In the "justice" she demands of the king, she seeks more revenge than justice. In all justice, Rodrigue only obeyed the very code his mistress now invokes against him. Though she may love Rodrigue at this point, it is because he behaved as a man of honor in slaying her father. Her father's blood is too fresh for that, so much so that in her case we get no scene of inner conflict. Her tone is at once plaintive and imperious as she appears before the king demanding justice. Her father's blood flows in her verses; in it she unhesitatingly reads her duty ("Son sang sur la poussiere escrivoit mon devoir"—II, 7). Even in the third act, before the confrontation with Rodrigue, she has not gotten much further than he in her "analysis" of the solution to their dilemma: once she has had her revenge on her beloved enemy, she will take her own life: "Pour conserver ma gloire & finir mon ennuy" she tells Elvire, she can only "Le poursuivre, le perdre & mourir après luy" (III, 3).

However, in the first confrontation scene, the lovers teach each other that the very code they would uphold forbids such a solution to their dilemma. Here is the paradox of love as honor stated explicitly. At first, Rodrigue repeats his major motive in taking her father's life: "J'avois part à l'affront, j'en ay cherché l'auteur, / Je l'ay veu, j'ay vangé mon honneur & mon pere" (III, 4). But now that the deed is over and he has had time to reflect, he sees the full implications of the code of honor:

> Et ta beauté sans doute emportoit la balance
> Si je n'eusse opposé contre tous tes appas
> Qu'un homme sans honneur ne te meritoit pas,
> Qu'apres m'avoir chery quand je vivois sans blasme,
> Qui m'ayma genereux me haïroit infame,
> Qu'écouter ton amour, obeïr à sa voix,
> C'estoit m'en rendre indigne & diffamer ton choix. (III, 4)

As parts of the *stances* show, this paradox is implicit in the code of honor. But we remember that in the *stances* Rodrigue chooses to duel Chimene's father not because of Chimene but in spite of her. In the present speech,

the tenses of the verbs might be taken as signs of ration-
alization by Rodrigue. Actually, the difference between
the two speeches is not one of personal sincerity, but of
dramatic timing. Rodrigue may be deluding himself as to
his motives before he acted, but in this very delusion we
see that the dramatic conflict has deepened.

Reminded of the demands of Rodrigue's sense of honor,
Chimene remembers her own: "Tu t'es en m'offençant,
monstré digne de moy: / Je me dois, par ta mort, monstrer
digne de toy" (III, 4). She is deaf to his demands that she
take his life to save her honor and she is indignant at his
invocation of the *qu'en-dira-t'on* ("Quand on sçaura mon
crime & que ta flame dure, / Que ne publieront point
l'envie & l'imposture?"—III, 4). She will save her honor
in refusing his self-sacrifice and she wishes "que la voix
de la plus noire envie / Esleve au Ciel ma gloire & plaigne
mes ennuis / Sçachant que je t'adore & que je te poursuis"
(III, 4). *Générosité* demands an absolute identity between
appearance and reality, a lesson which Chimene understands far better than her lover. Actions show the man.
Any derogation from this noble code is hypocrisy.

Now, hypocrisy is the charge of the Académie in blam-
ing Rodrigue for asking Chimene to take his life instead
of taking it himself—that is, if he is really determined to
die.[6] And the Académie comes close to this charge again
when it blames Chimene for dissimulating her love for
Rodrigue, after she learns that the news of his death—to
which she had reacted as true mistress—is false.[7] But in
each instance where the Académie would have a monster
of reflection we have only a dramatic character. The
Académie demands too much presence of mind from the
distraught Rodrigue and it almost goes without saying
that it has failed to grasp the dramatic excitement of his

symbolic gesture (we post-Freudians and devotees of the Metaphysicals know all too well the strange alliance between Eros and Thanatos). Similarly, with Chimene's "dissimulation" the Académie has taken it out of its dramatic context. When Chimene tells the king at the end of the play "il n'est plus besoin de vous dissimuler" (V, 6), she does not inadvertently admit to hypocrisy earlier. Commenting on his heroine's behavior in this respect, Corneille quotes from Guillén de Castro's *Engañarse engañando*:

> A mirar
> bien el mundo, que el tener
> apetitos que vencer,
> y ocasiones que dexar,
>     Examinan el valor
> en la muger, yo dixera
> lo que siento, porque fuera
> luzimeiento de mi honor.
>     Pero malicias fundadas
> en honras mal entendidas,
> de tentaciones vencidas
> hacen culpas declaradas:
>     Y asi, la que el desear
> con el resistir apunta,
> vence dos veces, si junta
> con el resistir el callar.

"C'est, si je ne me trompe," writes Corneille, "comme agit Chimène dans mon ouvrage, en présence du roi et de l'Infante." [8] Chimene was not "dissimulating" her love, but overcoming it. As for the nearness of this dissimulation to her fainting at the news of Rodrigue's death, nothing could dramatize for us more fully the terms of the basic conflict of the play between two sets of values. To borrow Nadal's analysis of Rodrigue's earlier conflict, Chimene faints at the news of Rodrigue's death because she has lost not the *"objet d'estime"* but the *"promesse de jouissance."* Learning that he is still alive, she sees him once again as the *"objet d'estime"* she is bound to destroy. Of course, she then claims that she fainted at his death because "une si belle fin m'est trop injurieuse" (IV, 5). But like Rodrigue in the first confrontation scene, she is not consciously rationalizing (in the pejorative sense): this is the way a woman of honor should view the heroic death of her beloved enemy, it is the only way a woman of honor can prove her love for that enemy.

At the successive moments of the action, Chimene and, to a lesser extent, Rodrigue, are striving to make a choice not between love and duty, but between two kinds of love. To state this conflict in the familiar terms of love and duty robs the play of much of its dramatic vitality. Duty evokes certain supraindividual concepts: the state, the party, etc. Emotionally, duty has the static quality of these institutions; dramatically, it is the immovable object against which the dynamic force of love unsuccessfully (it is usually said) hurtles itself. Yet, if anything, the only duty involved in the complex character of the "Cornelian hero" is the duty to his derived sense of self. Furthermore, as I have tried to show, this duty is not whole at the outset of the action, but is a growing force. In fact, it is its very growth which sharpens the conflict of the play. As the demands of love as honor become clearer and greater, they force the individual deeper and deeper into himself and away from natural love (the really "constant" force). Natural love obliterates the self-consciousness which is the essence of love as honor.

So when Chimene "yields" to her love in telling Rodrigue that she is the prize of the combat, she is literally and passionately forgetting herself (V, 1). Actually, the drama could be said to end here. The conclusion of the act functions very much like the coda of a symphony (although it serves another purpose, as I shall show): it recapitulates the major movements. Thus, Chimene's "re-dedication" to her father's honor in V, 4, is followed by her avowal of love for the "dead" Rodrigue in V, 6. And when the king commands Chimene to accept the live Rodrigue, he is only confirming a *fait accompli*. Now it has been said that Chimene obeyed his command only grudgingly. Years later, still piqued by the Académie's reproaches, the polemical Corneille himself implied that Chimene does not really accept Rodrigue, but simply buys time in which something can develop to prevent the marriage. Perhaps. But the text of the first version suggests something else:

> Releve toy, Rodigue. Il faut l'advouer, Sire,
> Mon amour a paru: je ne m'en puis dédire.
> Rodrigue a des vertus que je ne puis haïr,
> Et vous estes mon Roy: je vous dois obeïr.
> Mais, à quoy que desja vous m'ayez condamnée,
> Sire, quelle apparence, à ce triste Hymenée,
> Qu'un mesme jour commence & finisse mon deuil,
> Mette en mon lict Rodrigue & mon pere au cercueil?
> C'est trop d'intelligence avec son homicide,
> Vers ses Manes sacrez c'est me rendre perfide
> Et souiller mon honneur d'un reproche eternel
> D'avoir trempé mes mains dans le sang paternel. (V, 7)

According to Lacy Lockert, the King's "Laisse faire le temps" is a direct reply to Chimene's "un mesme jour,"

that is, Chimene is shocked not by the marriage in itself
but by the fact that it is sealed on the very day of her
father's death.[9] And the whole speech suggests less resolution than confusion and hesitation. The nearness of her
father's grace to her conjugal bed does not so much renew
her enmity towards Rodrigue as embarrass her ("Quelle
apparence...."). Even in invoking her honor in the last
two verses she emphasizes less the moral aspects than the
feelings it arouses in her. Finally, even taken as "reasoned"
objections and not emotional reactions these lines are
confusedly stated *after* she has given two reasons for accepting Rodrigue: his own *"vertus"* and the King's word.
Phrased as a question, these are objections about which
Chimene wants to be reassured. The King's reply accom-
modates her.

Love triumphs—although Nadal would have us believe
otherwise. In Rodrigue's "Ma teste est à vos pieds" this
critic would have Corneille forever alienating the lovers.

Cette lassitude de Rodrigue est bien remarquable. Elle
s'exprime dans le même moment où la gloire de Chimène est
sauvée, où tous les obstacles sont levés, l'héroïne forcée au
silence, et, semble-t-il, conquise; dans le moment où il aurait
le plus de raisons d'espérer. Or, jamais Rodrigue ne paraît
aussi distant d'elle, aussi désespérément écarté. C'est qu'il
garde le sentiment que l'irrémédiable a été accompli, qu'il ne
peut plus être pour elle qu'un grief et un désir, qu'une
tentation et un tourment. Aussi pressent-il déjà qu'elle l'a
banni loin d'elle, sinon de coeur, qu'ils vont retourner tous
deux à leur solitude, à la fois emplis et privés l'un de l'autre.[10]

But this is to treat Rodrigue's speech as if it were not only
his last but the last of the play, not followed by Chimene's
acceptance with its strong sensual accents. As for

Rodrigue's actual last speech, it is far from the pessimism
Nadal attributes to him:

> Pour posseder Chimene & pour vostre service,
> Que peut on m'ordonner que mon bras n'accomplisse?
> Quoy qu'absent de ses yeux il me faille endurer,
> Sire, ce m'est trop d'heur de pouvoir esperer. (V, 7)

Even were we to grant Nadal's interpretation of the
denouement, would the separation of the lovers be truly
tragic? The paradox of love as honor is that in the beloved the lover is only seeking an image of himself. Possession—of the self—is the very essence of love-as-honor.
Renunciation in Corneille, far from being a "tragic
focus,"* is the focus of a far different vision.

Renunciation is the wrong category for discussing *Le
Cid* in particular. Natural love, not love as honor
triumphs. This is the love which we see triumph in almost
all the early plays of Corneille To appreciate the strength
of the sensuous strain in these plays we have only to read
them in the first versions. (The bedroom scene between
Rosidor and Caliste in Corneille's first tragicomedy,
*Clitandre,* is especially revealing in this respect). The
strain persists in *Le Cid* as both language and structure
indicate. Though, as we have seen, Corneille attempted
to "take back" this strain in his revisions years later, its
significance in the first version of the play cannot be
denied. At the beginning of the fifth act, love-as-honor
has been fully developed. Rodrigue has been well schooled
by Chimene: he subtly proposes to use Don Sanche as

---

* The thesis of *Renunciation as a Tragic Focus* (1954) by Eugene H.
Falk. I hasten to add that Falk applies the thesis to Corneille in
*Polyeucte.* I shall consider the applicability of this thesis to Corneille
at greater length in my essay on that play.

Chimene's surrogate, through her champion he will die at her hands, and far from reproaching him for his "suicide" people will admire him for it. This is *"estime"* in its most frightening refinements. To Rodrigue *"objet d'estime"* Chimene finally prefers Rodrigue *"promesse de jouissance."* In doing so, she does not show herself heroic enough—or what we would call "Cornelian" enough—for the Académie: ". . . nous trouvons qu'il lui fait faire une bien plus remarquable [than her "dissimulation"], en ce que, sans autre raison que celle de son amour, elle consent à l'injuste ordonnance de Fernand, c'est-à-dire à épouser celui qui avoit tué son père." [11] But Corneille himself would not have her so "Cornelian" (at least in the first version).

It is time we stopped treating Corneille as the most simple-minded of geniuses, seeing in him a lack of irony which makes him the least French of Frenchmen. He has written one of the slyest pieces of dramatic self-consciousness ever—*L'Illusion comique.* The benevolent magic of that play "takes back," I maintained above, the malevolent magic of the play before it, *Médée.* And in *Le Cid,* as in all three plays before it the setting serves as a constant check to the heroic subject; the secondary characters give special meaning to the unfolding drama. In fact, we saw that most of the secondary characters in these plays do not seem to belong to the same world as the main characters. In *La Place Royale* this relationship was expressed in the central character himself: Alidor is half *généreux,* half *jeune damoiseau.* He does and does not belong in the world of the "one-dimensional" types who make up the world of Corneille's early plays. The mood of these plays, for all the vaunted realism of many of them, is, as we have seen, idyllic rather than realistic. For example, it was the clash between this mode as it is represented in the secondary characters and the heroic as it was represented in Médée which made the play by that name seem unfused. Moreover, not only were Médée's heroic traits more consistently developed than Alidor's, but they were also magnified in her mythological character so that her presence in the flimsy world of the play seemed doubly inappropriate. In *L'Illusion comique* Corneille had, so to speak, spelled this structural relationship out as he separated the secondary characters and the main characters into spectators and actors. One of the delightful ironies of that play was that it taught us not to take the "hero" any more seriously than the spectator of his deeds. In *Le Cid* Corneille comes closer to a balance between these elements of his structure: the heroes—Chimene and Rodrigue—are the most consistently developed to date and the setting more sophisticated, being a royal court threatened from within by unruly barons and from without by ancient enemies. Nevertheless, we perhaps err in taking the politics of *Le Cid* too seriously. Croce believed Corneille turned to politics because it offered the readiest occasions for the expression of "deliberative will." [12] Yet it is also quite possible that purely technical considerations led Corneille to the political setting of *Le Cid*. Having exhausted the familiar devices of interfering parents, clever rivals and misunderstandings in his plays thus far, Corneille, who did not like to repeat himself, might have turned to politics for a new and more exciting source of complications for the love intrigue which had been his principal subject ever since *Melite*. We should, therefore, study the "politics" of the play in their dramatic rather than historical context.

Dramatically, politics is subordinated to love. The

action is framed, as it were, by two political events: at the beginning by Diegue's "rebellion," at the end by the threat from without. But neither of these events presents any real problem in itself. To no one's real surprise, Rodrigue quickly settles each of these problems. The real value of these events or settlements lies in the fact that they complicate the love intrigue: Rodrigue is torn not between his duty to the cause of the barons and his duty to the King, but between his duty to his father and his love for Chimene. In fact, the basic political problem of king-versus-unruly barons is never really resolved in the play. As for the external problem, its quick solution only dramatizes the inconclusiveness of the internal problem. Politically, *Le Cid* is the story of Rodrigue's ascension to kingship ("Ils t'ont nommé Seigneur & te voudront pour Roy"—V, 7). Don Fernand, a pusillanimous monarch in the eyes of his creator turned critic, enters into an alliance with an equal after his great victory. But Rodrigue's rise to power only serves the non-political purpose of making him at once more desirable and more detestable to his beloved enemy. Indeed, Rodrigue goes off to combat in the play only to provoke Chimene to a display of natural love at the reports of his "death."

Is it any wonder, then, that the secondary characters of the play seem so conventional? They are mere pretexts to bring out fully the conflict between the heroic lovers. The weak King is in the line of those opportunistic parents of the early comedies who used their children to shore up their own fortunes. Gormas continues the line of the *fanfarons* of the comedy of the period, one of whom Corneille had pictured in the Matamore of *L'Illusion*. Of course, he is not the absolute coward Matamore was, but his promise is less than his performance: in the play he defeats only an old man and is defeated by a younger, untried one. Similarly, Elvire, as we saw above, recalls the one-dimensional *suivantes* of the early comedies and Don Sanche the ineffectual suitor who seems to exist only to take second place to the hero (Dorimant in *La Galerie*). Traces of the old comic setting thus persist in *Le Cid,* a fact which undoubtedly led Croce, in part at least, to regard the play as transitional.[13]

But what of the one role in the play which critics almost without exception have condemned as useless: L'Infante? How does she fit into the unfolding drama of *Le Cid*? I have already pointed to the dramatic purpose she serves in the first act. But what of her role beyond this? With profound insight Jean Boorsch has said that "si l'on regarde de plus près, on s'aperçoit qu'elle est toujours dans une scène contiguë à une autre où parait Chimène: c'est exactement comme si elle reprenait en mineur, et sur un thème alterné, les motifs d'émotion que vient de développer Chimène."[14] I would go even further: the role constitutes a dramatic as well as a lyrical echo of the main plot. It is a sort of play-within-a-play functioning as a "mirror," like the Shakespearean subplot. The outcome of this play-within-a-play is, of course, the opposite of that of the main play: l'Infante does choose heroic renunciation over natural love. At first, we might read this outcome as if Corneille were implicitly reproaching Chimene. But the sequence of action in the fifth act suggests that l'Infante only deludes herself in her "choice." In V, 1, Chimene gives in to natural love; in V, 2, l'Infante renounces Rodrigue in lyrical *stances* and in V, 3, announces her decision to Leonor. The delicate political problem of Rodrigue's status has been resolved in his accession to power: he is now more than a "simple Gentilhomme"—he is "le maistre de deux Roys." But, l'Infante tells Leonor:

Je me vaincray, pourtant, non de peur d'aucun blasme,
Mais pour ne troubler pas une si belle flame,
Et, quand pour m'obliger on l'auroit couronné,
Je ne veux point reprendre un bien que j'ay donné.
Puisqu'en un tel combat sa victoire est certaine,
Allons encor un coup le donner à Chimene.
Et toy, qui vois les traits dont mon coeur est percé,
Viens me voir achever comme j'ay commencé. (V, 3)

When did she really ever possess Rodrigue to be able now to give him "encor un coup?" And does not her gesture strike us as altogether too convenient, particularly ironic coming as it does upon the heels of the scene in which Chimene has taken Rodrigue back very much on her own? In this empty gesture, l'Infante is only making an accommodation to reality. In a certain sense, Chimene also gives Rodrigue away in order to accommodate to reality, but it is only to get him back in a much more real sense. Chimene's accommodation is filled with the promise of fruitful union, l'Infante's with solitude and vainglory. In bidding Chimene to dry her tears and take back "Ce genereux vainqueur des mains de ta Princesse" (V, 7), l'Infante only confirms a *fait accompli*. In giving away what is not hers to give, she reminds us of those ineffectual idealists whom Corneille had parodied in previous plays (for example, Philiste in *La Veuve* and Célidée in *La Galerie*). Corneille is perhaps only being cruelly kind (and, incidentally, perhaps, politically shrewd) in allowing l'Infante this final gesture of idealism: it does save face for the unloved Princess. Like all of the roles of the play, then, that of l'Infante is admirably appropriate in *Le Cid*. In its unfolding it illuminates the unfolding drama of the major roles. It may also show the parodistic spirit which has marked all of Corneille's work up to this time.

Like *Médée*, then, *Le Cid* emerges from the comedies which had immediately preceded it. Particularly in its secondary characters, it has many of the characteristics of the early comedies. But it would be foolish to deny that on balance it shows much more the characteristics of another form. As indicated, for Croce *Le Cid* marks a transition to the series of plays which immediately follow it, in which the hero is a *généreux*. However, it actually looks beyond the great political tetralogy to those plays in which the hero is both *généreux* and *amoureux*. Time will bring the protagonists together as both lovers *and* heroes—as *amoureux* and *généreux*, rather than as *amants généreux*. The paradox of love-as-honor is not defeated in the play, it is simply split into its two components. The connotations of the separate terms are simpler than they are in the paradox: the *généreux* is a political or military concept, *amoureux* a psychological one. Now, as Nadal has maintained, quoting from the final speech of Suréna, Corneille's last hero, "La tendresse n'est pas de l'amour d'un héros." [15] But this is so only when the political realities of a given play do force a choice upon the hero. The relatively unstable political realities of the world of *Le Cid* do not really force this choice upon the hero and the heroine. In its very instability that world allows for the fulfillment of one of the conditions which will allow the lovers to be reunited: that Rodrigue ascend to political supremacy, to kingship. In the end Chimene will marry not the slayer of her father, but one king upon the command of another king. Rodrigue is the slayer of her father, of course, but the "éclatante vertu" of the victorious Cid operates as the ultimate expression of what Henry James calls in his remarks on romance "a medium which relieves the total experience in a particular interest, of the inconvenience of a *related,* a measurable state, a state subject to our vulgar communities." [16] The suspension of these communities is summarized in the final verse of the play:

Laisse faire le temps, ta vaillance & ton Roy.

Neither tragicomedy nor tragedy, *Le Cid* is a romance.

*Horace* (1640), not *Le Cid,* marks a clear break with the comedies in many significant ways. Both in subject matter and technique it maintains throughout that tone of "serious" self-justification which has been traditionally associated with "Cornelian tragedy." It is the first of the great "Roman" plays—*Horace, Cinna, Polyeucte, La Mort de Pompée.* More pertinently, in the light of my analysis of *Le Cid, Horace* is really the first of Corneille's "political plays." Corneille's very choice of subject matter betokens a shift of interest. To be sure, we are still in the domain of legend, as in *Médée* and *Le Cid.* But where Médée and, to a lesser but still significant extent, Rodrigue and Chimene were obliged to function heroically in a quasi-pastoral setting, the world of the two Horaces is a more fully realized, highly civilized world peopled almost without exception by characters with depth as well as surface.

Yet this world is not realized without some ambiguities. Corneille himself pointed to one of the essential weaknesses of the play: its duplicity of action.[17] The modern critic, Georges Couton, may graciously try to save Corneille's face in this connection by speaking of the two actions of the play as successive steps of a single action.* Corneille knew better: we have one plot concerning young Horace's heroism and the conflict it sets up between two houses—whether, bound to each other by actual and potential marriage ties, they are to battle one another; we then have a second plot, born of the resolution of the first undoubtedly, but still unique and not really necessary to the play—young Horace's murder of his sister and the dilemma this poses for his house and the Empire.

The play's ambiguous structure is perhaps implicit in its very title: *Horace*. Which Horace, one might ask, young or old? In the first four acts, father and son share the center of the stage equally, with young Horace being more in the limelight in the early part of the action and his father in the later part (stopping the action, of course, just short of the murder of Camille). Each may be said to "demonstrate" his heroism in that part of the play he occupies, with no real doubt ever arising about the outcome of the challenges to which he is subjected—challenges more physical than moral in the son's case, exclusively moral in the father's. Indeed, the son may be taken more for granted than the father: there never is any doubt that young Horace will defend his honor. He is deaf to the demands of the "heart" represented by his wife and his sister. It is not his moral courage, but his courage in battle, which is brought into doubt. Young Horace might

---

*"Quant à l'unité de la pièce, l'impossibilité même du jugement la scelle. Le Héros veut vivre devant le spectateur une journée, qui est toute sa vie: il n'y a pas deux actions d'Horace, mais les deux épreuves de plus en plus difficiles d'une crise qui déchire et révèle une âme." *Corneille,* p. 62.

even be regarded as a pretext, a lever for the real conflict between the women on the one hand (first Sabine and then Camille) and old Horace on the other.* (The so-called Cornelian conflict between love and duty exists only in the secondary characters of Sabine and Camille, an aspect to which I shall return.) Old Horace is a Don Diegue who does not lament a lost prowess. Indeed his prowess is never in question—not tested in the play and not to be tested, because he occupies too exalted a position. The position he occupies is, in fact, that of king in the first four acts, and if the play were to end where its creator indeed says it ends—at the end of the fourth act before the murder of Camille—we would have a perfect resolution of the conflict which is ambiguously resolved in *Le Cid*: the relation between king and powerful subject. In the best monarchic tradition, the king, old Horace, would be or could be expected to be succeeded by the new king, young Horace. The solution is as satisfying psychologically as it is politically.

If old Horace's prowess is not challenged, his moral courage certainly is, and the challenge leads to one of the great moments of the Cornelian theater. Young Horace having been reported as fleeing the Curiaces after the latter have triumphed by slaying his two brothers, old Horace heaps praise upon the dead sons and opprobrium on the "cowardly" survivor. Julie, confidante of the grief-stricken Sabine and Camille, would defend the survivor:

---

*Reproaching Faguet for designating old Horace as the hero, Couton cites Corneille himself as designating young Horace the hero (*Corneille*, p. 58). But citing the dramatist as critic can be a dangerous game, as we have noted with Couton justifying the unity of the action in *Horace* in spite of Corneille's own admission to its doubleness. Each critic must come to his own conclusion—which may or may not coincide with Corneille's.

Que vouliez-vous qu'il fît contre trois? (III, 6)

To which old Horace, father of the beleaguered warrior so sympathetically and reasonably defended, replies:

> Qu'il mourût,
> Ou qu'un beau désespoir alors le secourût.
> N'eût-il que d'un moment reculé sa défaite,
> Rome eût été du moins un peu plus tard sujette;
> Il eût avec honneur laissé mes cheveux gris,
> Et c'étoit de sa vie un assez digne prix. (III, 6)

Here death does not figure as the sign of man's tragic limitation. Whether we designate father or son by the term, the hero of this play looks upon death in very different terms: as an *instrument* of human possibilities. As he had the possibility to flee, so young Horace had the possibility to die. Neither necessary nor an evil, death for him was a matter of choice—something to be *used* by man, not *suffered*. And something to be used in the name of values which neither father nor son ever question: their derived sense of honor. So much alike are they in this respect that it is perhaps best to resolve the question of the play's title as it was by some of Corneille's contemporaries: it is called *"Les Horaces."**

However, this will not resolve the "duplicity" to which Corneille and others after him have pointed in the play. To the play in which both Horaces respond to external challenge, Corneille has added, in the inadequate compression of one act, a play in which the challenge is internal. The very act of virtue by which young Horace defines

---

* By Chapelain, for example, in a letter to Balzac (November 17, 1640). Quoted in M-L, *III*, 255.

himself puts him on trial not only before his father, but before his king: he slays his own sister. Yet this "new" play is resolved according to the same code and in the same way within that code as the "first" play in *Horace*:

C'est trop, ma patience à la raison fait place;
Va dedans les enfers joindre ton Curiace. (IV, 5)

says young Horace as he dispatches his sister to the shades. In reading such lines one cannot but recall the plaints of the distraught queen and her stepson in Racine's *Phèdre*: ". . . la raison cède à la violence" (II, 2) laments Hippolyte as he confesses as much to himself as to Aricie his love for her; "Où ma raison se va-t-elle égarer?" (IV, 6) asks Phèdre. Incest, illicit love, sororicide—the universally suspect deed goes against reason in Racine; it is performed in the name of reason in Corneille. Reason leads (or *would* lead) to disengagement in Racine; it leads to engagement in Corneille. The concept of passion is close to its etymological source in both dramatists: *patior* is to suffer, to endure, and is the opposite of *agere,* to do, to act. Yet Racine is much closer to the present-day connotation of passion, that best grasped when we use the adjective form, passionate: emotionally wrought or, in one of the great ironies of semantic change, agitated. Passion in Racine is anything but passive. I do not mean to imply that Corneille's men and women are not "passionate," that is to say, capable of emotional excitement or agitation. Passion, in this sense, there is, but rather than opposed, it is joined to reason—as in young Horace's slaying of his sister and in his father's defense of the deed before the king.

It is, then, in the name of his high conception of himself that young Horace slays his sister. More importantly, this sense of self derives from the fact that he is the son of old Horace. At the "trial" of young Horace, where, in a curious psychological reversal the father is surrogate for the son, old Horace justifies his own "failure" to punish the sororicide as follows:

> ce bras paternel
> L'auroit déjà puni s'il étoit criminel:
> J'aurois su mieux user de l'entière puissance
> Que me donnent sur lui les droits de la naissance;
> J'aime trop l'honneur, Sire, et ne suis point de rang
> A souffrir ni d'affront ni de crime en mon sang. (V, 3)

And later in the same speech:

> C'est aux rois, c'est aux grands, c'est aux esprits bien faits,
> A voir la vertu pleine en ses moindres effets; (V, 3)

The virtue he is speaking of is young Horace's, of course —his son's virtue, a Horation virtue. It is true that the king defends young Horace's virtue more cynically:

> Sans lui j'obéirois où je donne la loi,
> Et je serois sujet où je suis deux fois roi. (V, 3)

Such a view of himself obviously places Tulle in the line of the weak king figures who began with the king in *Médée* and who will continue through to the Félix of *Polyeucte*. Indeed, they will not be vindicated till we reach the Auguste of *Cinna*. Nevertheless, Tulle's weakness does not obscure the fact that the strength of the Horaces lies in their view not of what they do but of what they are, or more precisely, that they do what they do because of what they are.

*Horace* is a *"tragédie"* in which the "tragic hero" learns no tragic lesson— he is unilluminated in the end. This is to say that he retains the values with which he began. His trajectory—"his" referring to either of the Horaces—is the realization of the values of the *généreux*. Yet it is obvious that the concept of *générosité* is developed, however deeply, primarily around the political-military connotation of the term. The paradoxes of love-as-honor are maintained as if by formula only in the case of young Horace. The call of the heart—much more the call of the flesh—is easily muted by his exalted sense of responsibility. The other "lover" does not maintain the paradoxes—or "lovers", if we include in the term all those who stand for a set of private values, thereby encompassing Horace's sister Camille as well as his wife Sabine. They refuse to follow the Horaces in the latter's obedience to the injunctions of the code of *générosité;* their idealism is of a more humane kind. But it is defeated in the play—defeated and not merely put aside, as in the romance of *Le Cid*. To the extent that this is so, we have a demonstration of the tragic in *Horace*. Especially in the case of Sabine:

> Approuvez ma *foiblesse,* et *souffrez* ma *douleur;*
> Elle n'est que trop juste en un si grand *malheur:*
> Si près de voir sur soi *fondre* de tels *orages,*
> *L'ébranlement* sied bien aux plus fermes courages;
> Et l'esprit le plus *mâle* et le moins *abattu*
> Ne sauroit *sans désordre* exercer sa vertu.
> Quoique le mien *s'étonne* à ces *rudes alarmes,*
> Le *trouble* de mon *coeur* ne peut rien sur mes *larmes,*
> Et parmi les *soupirs* qu'il *pousse* vers les *cieux,*
> Ma *constance* du moins règne encor sur mes yeux:
> Quand on arrête là les *dèplaisirs* d'une âme,
> Si l'on fait moins qu'un homme, on fait plus qu'une femme.
> Commander à ses pleurs en cette extrémité,

C'est montrer, pour le sexe, assez de fermeté.
(I,l; My italics)

These tragic presentiments are realized in Sabine's case. In her we find a character who runs into irreconcilables: she must yearn for the victory for her brother only at the expense of the loss of her husband; she must yearn for the victory of her husband only at the expense of the loss of her brother. She loses the brother; private value is sacrificed to public value.

But it is so sacrificed only in the case of a secondary character, or, if one wishes to raise her to full dramatic status, the sacrifice occurs in only one of the two principal characters involved in the love-duty relationship. In either view, the tragic is realized in an incomplete manner in the play. Furthermore, in the king's final imperative to Sabine:

Sabine, écoutez moins la douleur qui vous presse;
Chassez de ce grand coeur ces marques de foiblesse:
C'est en séchant vos pleurs que vous vous montrerez
La véritable soeur de ceux que vous pleurez. (V, 3)

we anticipate the resolution of *Suréna*. Sabine is being told not to conceive of love and duty as separate. Rather, she is being told to return to the injunctions of love-as-honor according to which she may be presumed to have first of all been drawn to young Horace. Tulle's imperative is designed not to consecrate the split between love and honor in the name of honor, but to restore the paradoxical fusion of the two in her breast. The death of her brother and her sister-in-law was necessary in a world governed by the code of honor.

Tragic presentiments of the beginning do not clearly

issue in tragic illumination. True, Herland discusses Camille under the rubric *"tragédienne ingénue,"* and describes her fate in these terms: ". . . faite pour la joie, le rire, le bonheur, . . . c'est pourquoi la tragédie qui s'abat sur leur maison va la tuer." [18] But it seems to me that this is to ignore that there is a "naissance de l'homme" in the character of Camille, also. In spite of an initial loss of self at the news of young Horace's "triumph," she dies cursing Rome in these terms:

> Que le courroux du ciel allumé par mes voeux
> Fasse pleuvoir sur elle un déluge de feux!
> Puissé-je de mes yeux voir tomber cette foudre,
> Voir ses maisons en cendre, et les lauriers en poudre,
> Voir le dernier Romain à son dernier soupir,
> Moi seule en être cause, et mourir de plaisir! (IV, 5)

And her last word is: "Ah! traître!" Death is an instrument of self-assertion in this "tragic" ingenue. In the first version, the play ended with the following soliloquy by the confidante Julie:

> Camille, ainsi le ciel t'avoit bien avertie
> Des tragiques succès qu'il t'avoit préparés;
> Mais toujours du secret il cache une partie
> Aux esprits les plus nets et les mieux éclairés.
>     Il sembloit nous parler de ton proche hyménéé,
> Il sembloit tout promettre à tes voeux innocents;
> Et nous cachant ainsi ta mort inopinée,
> Sa voix n'est que trop vraie en trompant notre sens:
>     "Albe et Rome aujourd'hui prennent une autre face;
> Tes voeux sont exaucés, elles goûtent la paix;
> Et tu vas être unie avec ton Curiace,
> Sans qu'aucun mauvais sort t'en sépare jamais." (V, 4)

Herland explains its subsequent omission as a way of leaving the spectator's attention fully concentrated on young Horace.[19] But if this is true, in omitting the speech, Corneille is taking back the supposed tragedy of the denouement. As for the possibility that the soliloquy has in fact underscored the *tragic* in Camille's destiny, quite the contrary seems to be the case: in death Camille has realized a happy destiny, as the curtain line emphasizes.

*Horace* is interesting for more than the different challenges it poses to the hero. The problematic dramaturgy conveying these challenges also leads to a consideration of Corneille and his relation to contemporary critics. Given the acute critical sense we have noted in Corneille, parodist of his own work, and given the intense criticism which *Le Cid* had just suffered (1) for a similar dramaturgical fault (the role of l'Infante) and (2) for a similar violation of the *bienséances,* why did Corneille get himself into this difficulty once again? A large part of the answer lies perhaps in his very spirit of *défi.* Corneille is very much his "own man." So much so that even in writing what Croce calls a reworking of *Le Cid* in a Roman setting,[20] Corneille refuses to admit that he is wrong. That is, he will go along with the critics specifically only on all that he feels he can assimilate unto his own spirit without doing harm to that spirit. Thus, he will respect here the unities of place and time—*Horace* is beautifully "classic" in this respect. But these unities were never the crucial matters which the ill-willed, jealous, and equally guilty Scudéry made them in his literal-minded observations on *Le Cid.* As we have seen, much more to the point were the moral matters which lay at the heart of the Académie's remarks. And in these, as usual, Corneille went very much his own way.

The power situation in *Cinna* (1640-41) is less confin-
ing than in *Horace*. Things have not reached the stage of
absolute power—witness the uneasiness of Auguste's power
and his decision to share his regal power with Cinna and
Maxime. *Cinna* is more reminiscent of *Le Cid* in this
respect, in spite of the fact that the kingdom over which
Auguste holds unstable sway is much larger in terms of
the world of the epoch the play conjectures. As he puts
the disposition of his power into the hands of others, we
recognize in this king the weakness of all the Cornelian
king figures to date (with the exception of old Horace
in the first four acts of *Horace*). But there is an important
difference here: this king moves toward, not away from,
the affirmation of his kingship. The change between the
Hamletic figure of the first four acts and the majestic
figure of the fifth act is remarkable. In the very manner
in which he tells Cinna to hold his peace till he, Auguste,
has finished, one senses a different Auguste in this last act.
The impression of firmness is reinforced as he then soberly
recapitulates Cinna's relations to him, repeating the record
of his bounties in a factual, dignified manner, without
reproach and, most importantly, without the note of
excessive self-pity we had become accustomed to hear from
him. He acquires in this long speech the majesty and self-
possession we would expect in the ruler of the world, and
when he reminds Cinna that the latter's position and
power come from him, Auguste, we see at last the proper
and expected relationship between king and subject which
had been missing from the first four acts. There is no
possibility of coequal reign like that between Fernand
and Rodrigue; here the young champion cannot transcend
his king through an identification with Rome. Auguste
is Rome, and in the face of this identification Cinna can

only submit. The pardon by Auguste, for all the "abstractness" of the gesture, constitutes an overt wordly manifestation of his *générosité*, thereby linking him with the "typical *généreux*" of the preceding plays. The paradoxical assertion of kingship through the renunciation of its conventional usage also prepares us for the paradoxical renunciation of *Polyeucte*.

Auguste's clemency robs the play of its tragic potential. I do not mean the possible physical separation of Cinna and Emilie. The unstable characterization of Cinna had already made it difficult to think of him, at any rate, in a truly tragic light. Moreover, even if we accept the Cinna of the third act on as the real Cinna, Emilie's lesson to him in the full implications of *générosité* had already robbed their relationship of tragic potential. Nor do I mean the tragic potential of Maxime. His tragic dilemma has already been untragically resolved in his decision to accuse himself of ignoble behavior: the accusation redeems him, thereby taking back the tragic or irrevocable character of his mistake as much as his shifting of the blame onto Euphorbe. No, the truly tragic potential of the play lies in the character of Auguste himself. Auguste's complexity of character, revealed in his Hamletic debates with himself, is unique in a Cornelian King figure. In his debates with himself, Auguste senses that in the satisfaction of one legitimate desire (and the will to power is legitimate in Corneille) we find the frustration of another which is equally legitimate: the desire for security. Of course, in even finding an antithesis of this nature, the Auguste of *Cinna* is an atypical Cornelian hero. Power and "peace of mind" are no more at odds with one another in Rodrigue than they are in Horace. Nor are they *ultimately* in Auguste. The typical *généreux* has no sense of limitations—which is to say that the hero's view of the universe is essentially nontragic.

Like *Horace* and *Cinna* just before it, *Polyeucte* (1642) involves two sets of relationships among the heroes: one between Pauline and Polyeucte and one between Pauline and Sévère. In *Horace* the plots were successive: Acts I to IV being the conflict between old Horace and the women; Act V being the conflict ostensibly between old Horace and the king but really between young Horace and the king. In *Cinna* the plots were concentric, with the conflict between the conspirators and Auguste being the outer plot and that between the conspirators the inner. In *Cinna* the resolution of the outer plot does not resolve the conflicts of the inner plot, but postpones them. In *Polyeucte* the two plots are interwoven, with now one, now the other coming to the fore and with one of the two coming to explicit resolution (that between Polyeucte and Pauline), the other to an implicit one (between Pauline and Sévère).

The relation between the two plots is close, to be sure. Yet I do not think it is close in the causal way understood by a recent critic, Eugene Falk:

Polyeucte seeks death, for it is his only means of avoiding humiliation in his marriage and of surpassing Severus in heroism and esteem. He renounces life because his sense of honor could not make him endure it, but he is also afraid that, obeying his passion for Pauline, the desire to go on living may rob him of the strength to sacrifice his life. This fear of yielding, of betraying his honor and self-esteem, of stooping to servility, is one of the main causes of his eagerness to die; but there is an even more decisive factor in his headlong rush toward death, and that is his fear of the consequences of self-betrayal, of his weakness and servility, which would rob him of even the dutiful devotion of his wife and would change her devotion to disdain and contempt.[22]

Thus the love between husband and wife is that narcissistic love in which the lover consciously seeks to find his own high self-regard reflected in the beloved. Though we have not seen it pushed to its ultimate consequences in any play yet, I have spelled out the dynamics of this kind of love as it leads to the paradox of total possession in physical disunion.

Now this kind of love is the dominant love motif of the play, but it is found not between Polyeucte and Pauline but rather between Pauline and Sévère. To be sure, Polyeucte loves Pauline:

> Mais vous ne savez pas ce que c'est qu'une femme:
> Ni le juste pouvoir qu'elle prend sur une âme,
> Quand après un long temps qu'elle a su nous charmer,
> Les flambeaux de l'hymen viennent de s'allumer.
> Pauline, sans raison dans la douleur plongée,
> Craint et croit déjà voir ma mort qu'elle a songée;
> Elle oppose ses pleurs au dessein que je fais,
> Et tâche à m'empêcher de sortir du palais.
> Je méprise sa crainte, et je cède à ses larmes;
> Elle me fait pitié sans me donner d'alarmes;
> Et mon coeur, attendri sans être intimidé,
> N'ose déplaire aux yeux dont il est possédé.
> L'occasion, Néarque, est-elle si pressante
> Pour ne rien déférer aux soupirs d'une amante?
> Remettons ce dessein qui l'accable d'ennui;
> Nous le pourrons demain aussi bien qu'aujourd'hui. (I, 1)

Yet, this is hardly the language of love-as-honor. It is more reminiscent of the natural love which conflicted with love-as-honor in *Le Cid,* although it is tinged more with

sentiment than passion. As we consider the haughty creature who like Chimene with Rodrigue, teaches Sévère the
full implications of *générosité,* we may have difficulty
in squaring this with the one we see through Polyeucte's
eyes. But this only serves to remind us that we indeed
have two plots in the play, with the pivotal Pauline
functioning in different ways in each plot. To vary slightly the terms of our analysis of *Le Cid,* for Polyeucte she
is an *objet de jouissance,* while for Sévère she is an *objet
d'estime.*

Yet, the purely *sensual* lure of Pauline does not seriously
conflict with Polyeucte's new-found religion. Rather, his
*feelings* for her do so, and nothing better reveals the
strange brand of Christianity we get in this play than the
fact that tenderness of feeling and human sympathy are
pitted against Christianity in the character of Polyeucte.
Even this conflict is not very real, for like so many of the
emotions and situations of the play, it is only conjectured
—and the conjectural future of the verb is so frequent in
this play that one might say it sets the mode for the entire
play: thus, in I, 1, Néarque speaks somberly of the dire
results of the impending interview with Pauline:

Votre retour pour elle en aura plus de charmes;
Dans une heure au plus tard vous essuierez ses larmes;
Et l'heur de vous revoir lui semblera plus doux,
Plus elle aura pleuré pour un si cher époux.

Polyeucte is also uneasy about the interview—but about
the interview, not its consequences: as we have heard, he
has no doubts about the firmness of his faith. That *exists*
already; it is very definitely in the indicative mood (a fact
we shall have to return to when we consider the doctrinal
aspects of Polyeucte's conversion):

Vous me connoissez mal: la même ardeur me brûle,
Et le desir s'accroît quand l'effet se recule.
Ces pleurs, que je regarde avec un oeil d'époux,
Me laissent dans le coeur aussi chrétien que vous; (I, l)

The first plot (chronologically, that is) has been pre-resolved, then: Polyeucte has been converted to Christianity and he is putting off the overt declaration of the fact out of consideration for his wife who has been upset by a dream in which her former lover stands triumphant over her defeated husband. It is difficult to believe with Falk that Polyeucte's knowledge of his wife's preoccupation with Sévère has driven him to an act of moral superiority, conversion, for we can take the play and the characterizations only in their own terms. The Polyeucte who appears to us in Act I is a self-contained, confident figure, for whom the only worthy antagonist would be God or the devil. This Polyeucte decides his spiritual questions in his own, not God's, good time, while the only one afraid of the devil is Néarque. The hero's "Pour se donner à lui faut-il n'aimer personne" is not a complaint, but a challenge.

A challenge to God. For Falk is right in sensing Polyeucte's preoccupation with honor and glory and self-affirmation—in short, in treating Polyeucte as a *généreux*. This religious hero picks up where Corneille's most recent secular hero, Auguste, left off. In Polyeucte we seem to come to an absolute transcendence of worldly things as means of defining one's integrity. Auguste had denied the traditional uses of kingship in an effort to affirm that kingship at its purest; Polyeucte denies not only the uses of kingship (he is, as Pauline says, "chef de la noblesse") but life itself. Yet in doing so he is not tragically and reluctantly cutting himself off from Pauline as either *objet d'estime* or *de jouissance*. He is fulfilling his entelechy, being himself as fully, as purely and as magnificently as possible. Were he a Christian truly sacrificing himself to the greater glory of God we might describe his "suicide" as a gesture of self-obliteration, an immersion in God of the prideful sense of self. But it is clear that in seeking his own death, Polyeucte is only racing toward a still more exalted conception of himself. The absolute transcendence of the things of this world, the complete disintegration of self-consciousness is not achieved; it is not even being sought. Polyeucte, the "chef de la noblesse," still knows ambition, "mais plus noble et plus belle." And in fulfilling this ambition he continues to use the language of the *généreux,* seeing his God more in the terms of a militant pagan divinity than in those of the merciful, compliant, self-sacrificing Savior:

> Le Dieu de Polyeucte et celui de Néarque
> De la terre et du ciel est l'absolu monarque,
> Seul maître du destin, seul être indépendant,
> Substance qui jamais ne reçoit d'accident.
> C'est ce Dieu des chrétiens qu'il faut qu'on remercie
> Des victoires qu'il donne à l'empereur Décie;
> Lui seul tient en sa main le succès des combats;
> Il le veut élever, il le peut mettre bas;
> Sa bonté, son pouvoir, sa justice est immense;
> C'est lui seul qui punit, lui seul qui récompense.
> Vous adorez en vain des monstres impuissants. (III, 2)

Here there is none of the ultimate abandon of the human will to the divine will we think of as essentially Christian. As Pauline later says of Polyeucte, "Polyeucte est chrétien, parce qu'il l'a voulu" (III, 3).

In Falk's terms one might see Polyeucte's iconoclasm as the desperate gesture provoked by his most recent interview with Pauline (II, 4). Yet here as in the first confrontation Polyeucte gives no sign of jealousy. He indulgently reassures Pauline that he is still alive. This has ever been the point of his concern with her and it reflects not wounded pride, but tenderness. It is Pauline who here uses Sévère in an unsuccessful effort to provoke jealousy in her husband, but Polyeucte is too much in control of himself and too preoccupied with his real concern to take this bait. (Pauline has misconstrued Sévère's character as much as she does Polyeucte's so that the menace she points to is once again conjectural). Quite in keeping with his preceding treament of her, Polyeucte indulgently approves of her interview with Sévère, and when he asks her "Quoi! vous me soupçonnez déjà de quelque ombrage" (II, 4), he is expressing not ill-repressed jealousy or a complicated attempt to show himself as good as Sévère by being above ordinary jealousy—rather he is expressing simple indignation. And when he admires Pauline's *générosité* in II, 4, he is indeed thinking of his own *générosité*—whose object is not Pauline, but God. Ultimately, as I have shown, its object is himself, but the distinction made here is still valid: the vehicle in this case is not Pauline but God.

And, his iconoclasm accomplished and his martyrdom imminent, he just as easily overcomes the danger posed by his last interview with Pauline. Here once again before Pauline's arrival is the potential conflict of human tenderness with heroic purpose. Yet, by the time he completes the *stances* in the following scene (IV, 2) it is clear that he has overcome the temptation which Pauline represents. In these famous *stances* Polyeucte only fleetingly addresses Pauline as the bereaved wife and the object of love he has seen in her up to this time: "C'est vous, ô feu divin que rien ne peut éteindre, . . ." (IV, 2). This, of course, puts Polyeucte's conversion into a somewhat more orthodox light.

If it also suggests more the natural love to which Chimene finally surrendered than the love-as-honor which moves Pauline, we should not see the former love triumphing over the latter. Love-as-honor is primary for Polyeucte —but only in his relations with God. For in the early portions of this celebrated apostrophe, Polyeucte, though moved by divine grace, continues to see his conversion in the willful, militant manner of an heroic chevalier. And his steeling of himself could not have been more appropriate, for when Pauline appears for this third confrontation, she is no longer the bereaved and plaintive wife of the first two, but is the haughty *généreuse* whom we have seen Sévère but not Polyeucte love and admire. It is as if Polyeucte had anticipated that this would be the creature he would now meet, as if he had realized that Pauline's attempt first at tears then at provocation having failed, she would now resort to reproaches to his honor in order to dissuade him from his conversion. But Polyeucte is beyond such arguments:

Je considère plus; je sais mes avantages,
Et l'espoir que sur eux forment les grands courages:
Ils n'aspirent enfin qu'à des biens passagers,
Que troublent les soucis, que suivent les dangers;
La mort nous les ravit, la fortune s'en joue;
Aujourd'hui dans le trône, et demain dans la boue;
Et leur plus haut éclat fait tant de mécontents,
Que peu de vos Césars en ont joui longtemps.
　　J'ai de l'ambition, mais plus noble et plus belle:
Cette grandeur périt, j'en veux une immortelle,

> Un bonheur assuré, sans mesure et sans fin,
> Au-dessus de l'envie, au-dessus du destin. (IV, 3)

Here is the real reason for Polyeucte's aspiration to martyrdom: he wants more permanent expressions or manifestations of his *générosité*. Not a particular human being, but the limited perspective of other human beings is his real antagonist, and he would overcome that perspective in a supreme act of self-affirmation. Since he can so easily overcome that perspective as it is expressed in the final limitation—death itself—the problem of his wife's happiness can be all the more easily settled by his commitment of her into Sévère's hands. Even before his confrontation with Pauline he had sent for Sévère for just this purpose, a fact which defines the purely conjectural nature of the "dangers" in the Polyeucte-Pauline relationship as much as the fact that their confrontations always show Polyeucte in possession of himself and her on the verge of or in an actual state of *emportement*.

> Vivez heureux ensemble, et mourez comme moi;
> C'est le bien qu'à tous deux Polyeucte desire.
> Qu'on me mène à la mort, je n'ai plus rien à dire.
> Allons, gardes, c'est fait. (IV, 4)

And indeed, it is done. These are not his last words, of course. Polyeucte will once more confront Pauline, but just before that occasion there will be no scene conjecturing his possible fall from "grace." By that time Polyeucte will only be a subsidiary character in the play about Pauline and Sévère, a catalyst bringing their relationship to its final resolution. As he utters his final words to Pauline:

PAULINE: Où le conduisez-vous?
>           FELIX: A la mort.
>           POLYEUCTE: A la gloire.
Chère Pauline, adieu: conservez ma mémorie.
PAULINE: Je te suivrai partout et mêmes au trépas.
POLYEUCTE: Sortez de votre erreur, ou ne me suivez pas.
>      (V, 3)

he is not the distraught lover ambiguously looking back upon the wife he must leave, but the martyr teaching his wife a lesson even in his death. He is setting an example—whether the example is Christian we shall determine when we discuss the religious aspects of the play.

The play about Polyeucte and Pauline is over—it has been from the very beginning. The possible conflict between them has always remained merely possible, purely conjectural. The dangers posited in the relationship of husband and wife—that one or both of them derogate from the sense of extreme self-regard or *vertu*—are much more real in the other play to be found in *Polyeucte,* in the Pauline-Sévère conflict.

In this conflict we move back into the concerns of Corneille's previous political plays. Certain of the tensions and themes with which Corneille merely flirted in his earlier plays come very much to the fore in the Sévère-Pauline relationship. Apparently, like Rodrigue, Sévère is to a certain extent, a "self-made man," but, unlike Rodrigue, his social origins are much more obviously inferior. Though the world of the play is still open enough to have allowed Sévère to become like unto a king, if not a king in name, it is still closed enough to have prevented selection from following inclination: because he was ill-born Pauline could not marry Sévère in spite of his obvious merit. That there should be this discrepancy between merit and station suggests that the ambiguously posed question of *Le Cid* has been resolved: in *Le Cid* Rodrigue was not born a king, but he has been born the son of a kinglike figure and he has been set into a world where the actual king is a relatively weak baron, himself only about one generation beyond the sharing of power with other barons. And the world was still big enough and unconquered enough for Rodrigue to accede to a kingship which put him, practically speaking, on an equal with the actual king. Historically, *Le Cid* just moves backwards or creates an irrelevant, pastoral-romantic world in which it never occurs to wonder pointedly about the power relations between the principals. In such a world, station and merit coincide—or appear to (Rodrigue's birth in a noble family and his father's role as a king figure). And in such a world the existential problem of whether a man is what he is born to be or what he makes himself is not too pressing. In *Horace,* the world of the play becomes much more real and, as the power relationships are much more circumscribed, we appear to make an advance over *Le Cid.* But in the separate plots there is an annoying contradiction about the existential problem posed above: in the first four acts the coincidence of station and merit which was somewhat ambiguously implied in *Le Cid* becomes explicit in the absolute power of the king figure of old Horace. But this absoluteness is taken back, so to speak, in the challenge to the actual king by young Horace (through his father). Also, inasmuch as young Horace, unlike young Rodrigue, has not acceded to any actual kingship in the play, merit seems to take precedence over station, as man is what he does. However, we can still recognize that, like Rodrigue, young Horace

has been born of the most renowned house in the kingdom and the significant absence of the actual king coupled
with the majesty of old Horace in the first part of the play
does prepare us psychologically to think of young Horace
as an equal to the king of this play.

In *Cinna* the discrepancy between station and merit is
pushed even further. But strangely enough the discrepancy
is this time in favor of station. Thus, this time, Cinna,
though born of a noble line, compromises his *générosité*
first by his conspiracy and then by his sincere deference
to the king: his merit is not up to his station. And
similarly with Emilie and Maxime, to the extent that the
former participates in the conspiracy and that the latter
both conspires against his king and betrays his friends.
But the most significant example of this unusal discrepancy is in the case of Auguste himself—at least until
he reasserts himself in his magnificent gesture of clemency.
Before that, like the others, he is not up to his station:
born a king, he does not act like one. However, through
his clemency he does put things back into a proper perspective: station and merit do coincide. In fact, they do
so now with a purity and clarity which has not existed
in any of the plays to date.

In *Polyeucte* the coincidence of station and merit at
the purely political level is to be found, not unexpectedly,
in Polyeucte himself. Indeed, it is this absolute coincidence which makes his station basically undramatic and
which forces Corneille, as it were, into the conjectural
mode in which Polyeucte's relationship with Pauline is
cast. The world of this play is relatively unstable, and
yet within it Polyeucte is obviously a born ruler and the
ruler born. Félix, the ostensible "king," is weak and has
frankly cultivated Polyeucte as a means of shoring up

his own power. Polyeucte is not, of course, the king, but a king figure evidently superior to the other king figure of the play. There is a potential conflict between him and Sévère because of this very relationship, but he transcends this rival through his identification with a power more extensive and more enduring than any worldly power. This identification reminds us of Horace's with Rome, by means of which that hero transcended the king's station. And so here with Polyeucte. Significantly, the actual king is absent from the dramatic proceedings, although his existence does have a bearing on the developments of the play—or, once again, on the *conjectured* developments of the play. For Félix' conversion puts him squarely at odds with the Emperor and Sévère's indulgence of both Polyeucte and Félix has the same effect. In fact, then, if not in name, the Emperor is made to appear as weak as any of the previous kings in Corneille's theater, and the real king of the play is Polyeucte. The latter accedes to the kingdom of heaven because there are in reality no more worlds on earth worthy of his heroic efforts; like Auguste, he needs more subtle and surpassing manifestations of his *générosité*.

It is not Polyeucte, then, who raises the existential problems of the previous political plays. In him, station and merit coincide, as they do not in Sévère—or as they once did not. For like Rodrigue, Sévère has acceded to kingship or at least its practical manifestations: in a war with the Persians he had rescued the Emperor, but then, this "rescuer" captured and cherished of his captors, the Emperor bought back Sévère's freedom by releasing his own captive, the Persian king's brother, plus one hundred other "chefs à choisir." But unlike Rodrigue, this savior of kings and equal of princes is definitely of unkingly origin. This champion knows no king figure in the play (like Rodrigue's father or old Horace) who can guarantee his kingship by birth. In fact, Corneille insists on Sévère's lowliness of birth.

> Après l'avoir sauvé des mains des ennemis,
> L'espoir d'un si haut rang lui devenoit permis; (I, 4)

There is no doubt about Sévère's proven *générosité* and about the fact that Sévère has only come into that station which his obvious worth dictated he should occupy. So for the first time in a Cornelian *généreux*, there is an unambiguous discrepancy between the station he was born to and his instrinsic merit.

However,

> Le destin, aux grands coeurs si souvent mal propice,
> Se résout quelquefois à leur faire justice. (I, 4)

says Pauline of Sévère. In spite of this theoretical acknowledgement from within the Cornelian canon of destiny's *frequent* indifference (and perhaps hostility) to the virtuous, one is struck by the fact that in practice the *infrequent* is the rule: only Amarante in *La Suivante*, Sévère in *Polyeucte*, Seleucus in *Rodogune*, the heroes of *Sertorius* and *Oedipe* and *Suréna* would come under "Le destin . . . mal propice." More importantly, one is struck by the fact that such tragic destinies are often found in thematically secondary characters—that is, the character who may be a principal but who does not represent the highest standard of excellence within the world of the play. Still more importantly, the tragic destinies of these secondary characters are somehow nullified—which is to say that the destiny in question is not "truly" destiny. As in the case of Sévère here: "destiny" corrects its own "mistake" by elevating Sévère to the station to which he should have been born.

Or, at least it has partially done so at this point in the action. The true fulfillment of Sévère's entelechy is one of the subjects of the plot between him and Pauline. For if he has fully manifested his *vertu* from a military point of view, he has not yet done so from a moral point of view. Like Rodrigue, he will have to be taught the full implications of *générosité* by a woman, by Pauline. For the Sévère whom we actually see for the first time in the play, (II, 1) seems less fully formed than the Rodrigue of the first confrontation; he seems in the line of the ineffectual suitors of the early comedies (and of Don Sanche in *Le Cid*), even with a *précieux* quality lacking in those insipid characters.

> SÉVERE (having learned that Pauline is married) :
> La constance est ici d'un difficile usage:
> De pareils déplaisirs accablent un grand coeur;
> La vertu la plus mâle en perd toute vigueur;
> Et quand d'un feu si beau les âmes sont éprises,
> La mort les trouble moins que de telles surprises.
> J'ai de la peine encore à croire tes discours.
> Pauline est mariée! (II, 1)

It will require Pauline's reminders before there is as much steel in his soul as in his arm. She tells him:

> C'est cette vertu même, à nos desirs cruelle,
> Que vous louiez alors en blasphémant contre elle:
> Plaignez-vous-en encor; mais louez sa rigueur,
> Qui triomphe à la fois de vous et de mon coeur;

De plus bas sentiments n'auroient pas méritée
Cette parfaite amour que vous m'avez portée. (II, 2)

Here is the lesson which Chimene taught Rodrigue:
should you behave ignobly now—that is, refuse to renounce
me and accept my marriage to Polyeucte—you will have
insulted my very first choice of you, you will give the lie
morally to what you have proved militarily: the justice
of my original inclination for you. Sévère learns well.
The *combats amoureux* are transformed into *combats
généreux* even more quickly here than in *Le Cid*. It is
only for Polyeucte that Pauline will remain in any degree
an *objet de jouissance* and it is only with Polyeucte that
Pauline will cry and entreat and plead and goad and
provoke—in short, "act like a woman." With Sévère she
will offer herself exclusively as an *objet d'estime* and it is
as such that she will henceforth exist for him:

Ah! puisque votre gloire en prononce l'arrêt,
Il faut que ma douleur cède à son intérêt.
D'un coeur comme le mien qu'est-ce qu'elle n'obtienne?
Vous réveillez les soins que je dois à la mienne.
Adieu: je vais chercher au milieu des combats
Cette immortalité que donne un beau trépas,
Et remplir dignement, par une mort pompeuse,
De mes premiers exploits l'attente avantageuse,
Si toutefois, après ce coup mortel du sort,
J'ai de la vie assez pour chercher une mort. (II, 2)

This we remember was Rodrigue's intention as well, one
made academic by subsequent developments. Subsequent
developments in this play will leave Sévère's intention
equally unfulfilled and academic. In fact, as in the
Polyeucte-Pauline relationshp, much in the Sévère-Pauline

relationship is purely conjectural. The very *donnée* of their relationship is the what-never-was-but-might-have-been.

Even the way in which Félix and his daughter regard Sévère reflects the conjectural mode of the play with its projected emotions and theses.

> Que ne permettra-t-il à son ressentiment?
> Et jusques à quel point ne porte sa vengeance
> Une juste colère avec tant de puissance?
> Il nous perdra, ma fille. (I, 4)

says Félix, and Pauline, trying to provoke her husband to jealousy, reminds him that Sévère "... est puissant, il m'aime, et vient pour m'épouser" (II, 3). And Félix once again, weighing the course of action he should take: "Quoiqu'il soit généreux, quoiqu'il soit magnanime, / Il est homme, et sensible, et je l'ai dédaigné" (III, 5). Félix is wrong, of course, and nothing shows his unkingliness more than his inability to see that a *généreux* could not be guilty of the kind of base feelings Félix supposes in him here. We need only remember Sévère's first words on learning of Pauline's choice to see this. Yet Pauline herself in her injunctions to Sévère places the play in a conjectural mode which excites the anxiety of the spectator in a momentary and superficial way. The play almost requires this, of course, and Corneille skillfully injects these emotional *trompe-l'oeil* at just the right moment— for example, at the end of Act IV. At this crucial moment, there is an emotional void, one which must be filled. Sévère appears. He has been summoned by Polyeucte so that the latter can unite these first lovers as he himself goes off to the higher love which he has dedicated himself to. We are on the verge of a happy ending, one in which, Falk's thesis notwithstanding, everybody will be happy. The play, as I have said, could end here—were not Pauline's "defeat" turned into "victory" by her injunction to Sévère to use his wordly influence to save his rival for his beloved. Pauline, like Chimene, tells the man who loves her to perform an act which will only ensure his estrangement from her! From the verge of the "happy ending" we move to the verge of the tragic.

Here, then, are the astringent demands of *générosité* pushed to an inhuman degree—as Sévère fully sees:

> Votre belle âme est haute autant que malheureuse,
> Mais elle est inhumaine autant que généreuse,
> Pauline, et vos douleurs avec trop de rigueur
> D'un amant tout à vous tyrannisent le coeur. (IV, 6)

This is not the playful paradox of *"la belle inhumaine"* inherited from courtly literature and banally restated in the *précieux* poetry of Corneille's day. It is the frightening paradox of *Le Cid*, pushed to an even greater astringency. Here, in the single character of Sévère, Corneille has located the various implications of *généreux* love which he isolated in several characters of *Le Cid*: Rodrigue, Don Sanche, and l'Infante. As with Rodrigue, there is no doubt that the code of *générosité* demands he fulfill the injunction and there is no doubt that he is capable of fulfilling it; as with Sanche, there is no doubt that he must be cut off from the woman he loves but whom he must obey; as with l'Infante, there is no doubt that Sévère will surrender his beloved to another but that he will appear noble in that surrender.

There is a danger in these resemblances. Rodrigue, we

remember, was ever ready to forego love-as-honor for the less demanding natural love to which even Chimene eventually succumbs. But Sévère is a far more apt pupil than Rodrigue—in the present circumstance, he has been not an ignorant, but simply a forgetful *généreux* pupil of Pauline. He accepts her challenge even though he recognizes the inhumanity of it.

La gloire de montrer à cette âme si belle
Que Sévère l'égale, et qu'il est digne d'elle;
Qu'elle m'étoit bien due, et que l'ordre des cieux
En me la refusant m'est trop injurieux. (IV, 6)

In terms of my analysis of *Le Cid*, Sévère sets himself up as a potentially parodistic figure, to be a combination of Sanche and l'Infante not only at this particular moment but also at the end of the play. However, in various ways Corneille counters this interpretation of Sévère's role. For one thing, Sévère's proven *générosité* as well as his new-found station easily allow him to escape the full parallel with Sanche. As for Sévère's potential identification with l'Infante, he is spared this ironic interpretation. Like the Infante-Rodrigue relationship, at least from Sévère's point of view, the Sévère-Pauline relationship never moves off center: he finds himself at the end of the action where we found him at the beginning. Of course, it cannot be denied that his position is exactly the same as l'Infante's at the end of the play. He even assents to a *fait accompli*. But two aspects of this *fait accompli* prevent us from viewing his assent as ironic. For one thing, he does not give away what was never his to give away: unlike l'Infante, he has never had the illusion that Pauline was his. He thought she might be before he learns of her marriage, but once he does learn of it he is ready to confirm his estrangement as originally planned: in death. And, unlike l'Infante, circumstances never allow Sévère to delude himself into thinking things could change. As he himself says of Pauline's injunction to him to save her husband who is determined to die a martyr: "... toujours la fortune, à me nuire obstinée, / Tranche mon espérance aussitôt qu'elle est née" (IV, 6). When Sévère chooses to show himself even more noble than Pauline by accepting her challenge, it might appear that he, at any rate, if not Polyeucte, might be analyzed along the lines of Falk's interpretation of Polyeucte: his sacrifice is intended only to win a moral victory which will establish his personal moral ascendancy over the others with whom he vies in the *combats généreux*. But his decision to do so is not a gambit in a tournament of moral chess; rather, it is an actualization of the potential, an incarnation of the word— *vertu* become *gloire*. Thus, when Pauline takes away from Sévère what she never intended to give him, all the posturing and self-delusion—if any—are on her side.

Even were the conjectural to have become the real, Sévère in fulfilling Pauline's injunction would have only been fulfilling his entelechy as a *généreux*. This does not mean that in circumstances as they do work out, Sévère has *not* realized himself as a *généreux*—at least in his relations with Pauline. When he assents to Pauline's conversion, the *fait accompli* to which he assents is indeed of a different nature from that conjectured (Pauline's reunion with a Polyeucte saved through Sévère's efforts), but in this case as in that, Sévère cannot be accused of suffering from the delusion that he is giving away that which has never been his to give away. Pauline's dramatic relationship with Sévère had come to a close, from his point of view, with her injunction to him to save her husband. Sévère's moment of decision had to come then or never, with the same suddenness as Auguste's gesture of clemency. And so it did. From that moment, Corneille was obliged to introduce an element from the outside in order to keep this heretofore purely internal drama going. This he found in the intemperate behavior of Félix. Félix's execution of Polyeucte provokes Pauline's conversion, which in turn provokes Félix's conversion, which in turn evokes Sévère's sympathy. In the religious fireworks at the end of the play we are likely to be blinded to the fact that Sévère's development as a character had come to an end at the conclusion of Act IV; *his* "conversion" in V is merely implied, only a conjecture. In the "indicative," he has proved himself a *généreux* by his renunciation of Pauline—or better: by his clear, calculating, completely conscious glorification of himself. For, like only one previous *généreux* of Corneille's theater (Auguste), Sévère ultimately seeks no *objet d'estime* in which to find his own reflection; his narcissism is complete; he is truly self-sufficient, although, as we shall see, *relatively* inferior. Where Polyeucte and Pauline require God as an *objet d'estime* in whom they will see the reflection of their own perfection, Sévère is his own *objet d'estime,* finding the reflection of his perfection in his own acts.

Thus, in his personal drama, Sévère triumphs; he proves himself to be the *généreux* Pauline's original inclination for him said he was in spite of his inferior station. But in the political drama, the framework of the play, Sévère's triumph is perhaps more apparent than real. True, by various means Corneille does attempt to repair the tragic discrepancy between Sévère's station and merit which provokes the personal drama betwen him and Pauline.

The relatively unstable political situation does allow him to accede to a kind of kingship. Once the "first best" has gone on to his otherworldly kingdom, the born "second best" naturally takes his place. Again, Sévère's moral and political superiority over the puppet-king, Félix, also serves to exalt him in our eyes. As for his relations with the Emperor Décie, we have already learned how he rescued the Emperor and, in the absence of the latter, Sévère's mission as emissary actually places him in Décie's role. Corneille even carries this relationship to the point where the surrogate becomes more powerful than the Emperor. When Sévère decides to accept Pauline's injunction to save Polyeucte, he leaves himself open to the charge of *lèse majesté,* for he consciously sets about to disobey the Emperor's orders to stamp out the Christian rebels. But, as Sévère "confidentially" points out to his servant, Décie is "injuste" on this score: Décie lacks knowledge about the Christians; he has failed to notice that their sect is no more mysterious than certain Roman mysteries; the Christians have a commendable communal spirit under one God (implying a parallel with the imperium under Décie); the Christians are morally good and even exemplary citizens (that is, submissive). In the first version of the play, Corneille even used the argument that the Roman cults were only an exploitative hierocracy, but he withdrew this potentially embarrassing rationalism in subsequent editions. Sévère's justification of the Christians are made in a spirit of saving the Emperor's face, to be sure, but the implications are nonetheless clear: he, Sévère, thus seems a better man than the Emperor— not only more humane, but politically shrewder. This diminution of the Emperor is not surprising, in view of its echo elsewhere in the play—for example, in the contrast between the "chef de la noblesse," Polyeucte, and Décie's representative in Mélitène, Félix. We may even say that Sévère must be made to appear a better man than the Emperor if his *générosité* is not to be compromised: he must be cast as more than a mere emissary of Décie if his military self-sufficiency and his aspiration to Pauline are to be justified. Corneille obliges him in his relations with the Emperor.

Yet, Corneille postpones, as it were, the real political conflict: that between Sévère and Polyeucte. Such a conflict is imminent in Sévère's accession to kingship, since the very dynamics of *générosité* lead to a coincidence of supreme merit and absolute power and there can ony be one absolute ruler. To a certain extent, we might say that the potential conflict between Polyeucte and Sévère does erupt and is resolved in the Sévère-Pauline relationship, where Pauline functions as Polyeucte might be expected to. But this leads to a consideration of Pauline's character.

Polyeucte's ascension to the highest kingship—heaven's —has been achieved almost from the outset and since it is she who teaches her suitor Sévère the "severities" of *générosité,* we might tear a page from Faguet's analysis of *Le Cid* and say that as that play might easily have been called *"Chimène,"* so this one might have been called *"Pauline, martyre."* She is the most varied of the characters in the play, behaving one way with Polyeucte, another with Sévère. She is beleaguered and bereaved wife to the one and uncompromising, self-possessed *objet d'estime* to the other. The conflict in these two conceptions of her character are not contradictory; they are sequential. Her use of tears and her provocations to jealousy are not hypocritical devices; they are, respectively, attempts to recall Polyeucte to his roles as husband and prince. She is to

Polyeucte as Sévère is to herself: she rises in her relationship with him to the full implications of *générosité* (and, at times not without some ironic overtones: her reproaches to Polyeucte's inhumanity add an ironic point to Sévère's similar reproaches to her). Seen in this light, her conversion is not miraculous, but logical. We might say that she must erase her moral indebtedness to Sévère, she must show herself morally superior to him through an identification with an *objet d'estime* beyond any earthly one. Yet, no more than Polyeucte or Sévère is she deluding herself in this conversion; she is completing herself, fulfilling her entelechy as a *généreuse*. With Pauline's conversion, the paradox is not deflected as in *Le Cid;* it is fully exploited: possession is greater in physical separation than in physical union. Pauline regains Polyeucte through her conversion—that is to say, she finds in God the reflection of her nobility even as he finds his. In doing so, she resolves in her favor the conflict with Sévère which had already been implicity resolved between Polyeucte and Sévère in Polyeucte's favor: in gaining heaven, she accedes to a higher kingship than any Sévère could offer her.

As he was when he first met her, Sévère is behind her, or, to use the political terms appropriate, one rank below her and Polyeucte. Sévère's political ascendancy, including his acumen greater than the Emperor's, cannot gainsay this relationship. Nor can the smoke screen of his indulgence toward the new converts, for at best we can say that his conversion is only implied in this indulgence. It is true that we might regard this implication as practically fulfilled. Sévère's "Et peut-être qu'un jour je les connoitrai mieux" (V, 6) is reminiscent of Don Fernand's "Laisse faire le temps" in *Le Cid.* But to have made this clear would have compromised the characters of both

Polyeucte and Pauline as they were originally conceived. Sévère had been inferior in station to both Pauline and Polyeucte and this is how he finishes. As things work out, station and merit may be said to have proved one, appearance and reality to have coincided, in the case of Sévère as much as in that of Polyeucte and Pauline.

But, it might be objected, Sévère has simply not been touched by God's grace. Yet, as is evident in the numerous quotations referring to the Deity, God has nothing to do with it—at least in this play. And least of all the Christian conception of a humane, tender, merciful, and compassionate Redeemer of mankind. There are no sinners to be saved in this play; only political aspirants seeking "office." It is no accident that ultimately the political and religious coincide in *Polyeucte,* for the religious is assimilated into the political. We have already seen how Pauline's human feelings are, ironically enough, pitted against the demands of her husband's new-found religion. And, at the end of the play, the character who comes closest to Christianity in the tender, compassionate sense we usually associate with the figure of Christ, is Félix. This is ironic from a doctrinal point of view, but consistent dramatically: his essential timidity finds an echo in the submissive form his "conversion" takes, just as Polyeucte and Pauline's essential, vigorous nobility are echoed in the assertive form of their "conversions"—in quotation marks because there really is no conversion. We may say of every character what I have said of Pauline: each follows the logic of his character.

But what of the role of divine Grace in these conversions? On the tension between human will and divine will which plagues theologians, it is clear that Corneille is more Jesuitical than Jansenist: salvation is the result of a cooperative effort between God and man. Polyeucte is a Christian because he wants to be. Undoubtedly, he had to know about Christianity before he could decide to be a Christian and we may say that his learning about it is the work of God. In catechetical terms, God provided the occasion of his conversion. But this is too general for any satisfactory explanation of the conversion—God is responsible for everything—and, more importantly, Corneille does not enter into the doctrinal refinements of which came first, God's grace or man's call for it. Like his nobility by birth, Polyeucte's possession of grace is an assumption in the play, and we can safely say that it can no more be taken away as far as Polyeucte is concerned than can his noble birth. The divine order is thus an analogue of the human, and one to be treated no differently, the play suggests. At best, God seems to be a kind of auxiliary, not a leader in Polyeucte's conversion. When Néarque warns Polyeucte that God's help might be withdrawn without warning, Polyeucte assures him that "Vous me connoissez mal: la même ardeur me brûle, / Et le desir s'accroît quand l'effet se recule" (I, 1). I shall leave the orthodoxy of this position to the theologians, but it is clear here that Polyeucte's theology (and, possibly, Corneille's) leaves God very little to do. Indeed, from a historical point of view, Corneille's treatment of Polyeucte's character could prove as embarrassing as his rationalistic attack on Roman hierocracy. Polyeucte's aggressive Christianity, his headlong rush toward the open declaration of his faith, and his destruction of the pagan idols can only cast the secretive character of early Christianity in a compromised light (certain theologians were said to be openly critical of Polyeucte's destruction of the statues) .[22] As Polyeucte tells the intimidated Néarque, in an effort to steel him for the destruction of the idols:

> Je suis chrétien, Néarque, et le suis tout à fait;
> La foi que j'ai reçue aspire à son effet.
> Qui fuit croit lâchement, et n'a qu'une foi morte. (II, 6)

The tone of Polyeucte's Christianity suggests the most abominable of sins: pride. So much so that perhaps Corneille felt compelled to soften Polyeucte somewhat when he reappears in the fourth act. Yet, as he recites there his famous *stances,* one is struck not by the submissiveness to God but by the tone of regal power with which Polyeucte transcends the charms of this world and glories in those of the other: "Vains appas, vous ne m'êtes rien" (IV, 2). True, Corneille does redress the balance toward the end of these *stances,* and throughout the ensuing confrontation with Pauline does emphasize more the role of grace than of man's own will in his conversion. Yet, when Polyeucte returns in Act V, it is to be the master of his own martyrdom. We might even say that he goads the malleable Félix into ordering his execution, bluntly refusing Félix' offer to cease persecuting the Christians and even to be their protector:

> Non, non, persécutez,
> Et soyez l'instrument de nos félicités:
> Aussi bien un chrétien n'est rien sans les souffrances;
> Les plus cruels tourments nous sont des récompenses.
> Dieu, qui rend le centuple aux bonnes actions,
> Pour comble donne encor les persécutions.
> Mais ces secrets pour vous sont fâcheux à comprendre:
> Ce n'est qu'à ses élus que Dieu les fait entendre. (V, 2)

This reply shows once again Polyeucte's aggressive Christianity. It cannot be argued that Félix is only pretending: as far as Polyeucte can tell at this moment, the governor is making his offer in good faith. But Polyeucte does not take up this offer, with its implied triumph of God's truth on earth, because he is more concerned with his own triumph in heaven. Furthermore, the emphasis upon God's elect at the end of Polyeucte's reply clearly clashes with the "democratic" implications of his earlier reply to Félix that "les rois et les bergers [y] sont d'un même rang" (V, 2). This emphasis upon the elect is not Calvinism; it is aristocracy. Both Polyeucte's aggressiveness and aristocracy may be forgotten, if not redeemed, as Polyeucte is morally put into the right when Félix admits that he was only pretending to offer his protection to the Christians. But nothing can gainsay the improper spirit in which Polyeucte reminds Félix that his faith "est un don du ciel et non de la raison." The orthodoxy of this position is undeniable (although it ill suits Polyeucte's earlier statement in this scene about his suicide that "La raison me l'ordonne, et la loi des chrétiens"—V, 2). Still, he is using this argument to assert his superiority over Félix and to provoke the other into the order for execution which Polyeucte seeks from him. He finally succeeds, but not before one final attack on Félix summarizing his convictions and revealing their worldly basis:

Que tout cet artifice est de mauvaise grâce!
Après avoir deux fois essayé la menace,
Après m'avoir fait voir Néarque dans la mort,
Après avoir tenté l'amour et son effort,
Après m'avoir montré cette soif du baptême,
Pour opposer à Dieu l'intérêt de Dieu même,
Vous vous joignez ensemble! Ah! ruses de l'enfer!
Faut-il tant de fois vaincre avant que triompher?

Vos résolutions usent trop de remise:
Prenez la vôtre enfin, puisque la mienne est prise.
Je n'adore qu'un Dieu, maître de l'univers,
Sous qui tremblent le ciel, la terre, et les enfers,
Un Dieu qui, nous aimant d'une amour infinie,
Voulut mourir pour nous avec ignominie,
Et qui par un excès de cette même amour,
Veut pour nous en victime être offert chaque jour.
Mais j'ai tort d'en parler à qui ne peut m'entendre.
Voyez l'aveugle erreur que vous osez défendre:
Des crimes les plus noirs vous souillez tous vos Dieux;
Vous n'en punissez point qui n'ait son maître aux cieux:
La prostitution, l'adultère, l'inceste,
Le vol, l'assassinat, et tout ce qu'on déteste,
C'est l'exemple qu'à suivre offrent vos immortels.
J'ai profané leur temple, et brisé leurs autels;
Je le ferois encor, si j'avois à le faire,
Même aux yeux de Félix, même aux yeux de Sévère,
Même aux yeux du sénat, aux yeux de l'Empereur. (V, 3)

*Vaincre, triompher, résolution, voulut, veut, je le ferois—*
as this voluntarist vocabulary makes it clear, Polyeucte
is a Pelagian.

And a *généreux*. When Pauline asks where he is going
as he is being led out by Félix's guards, he replies: "A la
gloire." His own, not God's. As renunciation is an improper category in discussing the secular aspects of this
play, so its theological equivalent, abnegation, is equally
improper. Self-sacrifice, self-denial, the *moi haïssable*
which will preoccupy Pascal a generation later—these are
the last terms in which to talk about Corneille's play about
the martyr Polyeucte. Corneille seems to have turned to
a religious framework for much the same reason that he
turned from the pastoral to the mythological and from
the mythological to the political at an earlier period:
experimentally, in a constant search for the new and the

inventive. He has constantly needed different settings in which to exploit his essential themes and, in particular, he has needed new challenges to exalt his *généreux* heroes. As we have seen in *Horace* and *Cinna* he pushed the notion of a superb (*superbe*: proud) self-sufficiency as far as it could go in purely secular or political terms. The very milieu of transcendence—the religious—next lay at hand. Through the use of the religious, Corneille pushes his concepts of worldly honor to their most extreme expression yet. Polyeucte and Pauline make the apparent and the real, the inborn *générosité* and the existence of a kingdom beyond, coincide in the sublime act of conversion. They convert to a religion which is said to reject the things of this world, but it is clear that, like Auguste's act of renunciation in *Cinna,* they use this ascetic concept as a means of defining their worldly worth. They go even further: they do not convert to this asceticism; rather they convert this asceticism into the concept of *générosité,* as is apparent in the military and militant way in which Polyeucte speaks of his God. Only Sévère stands apart from this ascendancy to the kingdom of heaven, a fact which perhaps more than any other defines the purely secular interests of Corneille. Sévère cannot be placed on a par in heaven with Pauline and Polyeucte because he has not been born to it. Heaven in *Polyeucte* is a political realm; conversion a political gesture. In this most Catholic of writers, writing in the heyday of the most absolute of Catholic monarchies, we might read a separation of church and state which would shame even the most democratic of modern republics. Of course, in Sévère's concluding remarks we might read a concordat between Church and state, between secular Rome and Catholic Rome, which clearly says leave unto Caesar the things that are Caesar's and to God the things that are God's. We might see such a concordat—were it not that Corneille very clearly treated everything in the play as Caesar's realm.

With the theme of ascendancy a prominent motif in *Polyeucte,* much of the language is what a German critic has aptly described as "vertical." [23] This we might say is only appropriate in a play which its author designated a "tragédie chrétienne." Yet, the worldly character of this "ascendancy" makes it difficult to accept the "martyr" as Christian—indeed, many a theologian and critic has considered the concept of Christian tragedy a contradiction in terms.* Furthermore, the hero's "illumination" without suffering, his uninhibited realization of his values—whether they are Christian or not—prevents us from considering his destiny as tragic.† Neither the Divine Comedy Polyeucte's presumed "beatitude" seems to make of it, nor the Christian Tragedy Corneille designated it, *Polyeucte* is a heroic comedy.‡

---

*"Christian salvation opposes tragic knowledge. The chance of being saved destroys the tragic sense of being trapped without chance of escape. Therefore no genuinely Christian tragedy can exist." Karl Jaspers, *Tragedy Is Not Enough.* p. 38. Again, aside from the external evidences she cites in her study of the play, Sister Marie Philip Haley properly senses that *Polyeucte* is not Jansenistic. However, Sister Haley's thesis that there is a profound religious feeling in the play seems to me questionable in view of the play's earthbound ethos. See *"Polyeucte* and the *De Imitatione Christi," PMLA,* LXXV, 174-183.

†Comparing Milton's *Samson Agonistes* with *Polyeucte,* D. D. Raphael says that neither gives rise to the pity occasioned by tragedy, since the hero's "death is not presented as a sheer waste of human quality, but is a means to good, so that the reversal of fortune brought about by the poet is from lesser to greater good, or from greater to lesser evil." *The Paradox of Tragedy,* p. 57.

‡There may be a tragedy in *Polyeucte*—what George Steiner (*The Death of Tragedy*) has generalized in Corneille as a "death of the heart." But it would be only Sévère's. And even in his case, his "problem," the conflict of duty and love, is resolved "selon les lois constitutives de l'univers de la pièce," in the triumph rather than the loss of the higher value. For a recent, different interpretation of the play, see Peter Currie, *Corneille: Polyeucte.*

The series of plays which began with *Le Cid* closes with that Q. E. D. of *générosité, La Mort de Pompée* (1642-43). The play is a showpiece and it is its showroom quality which Corneille himself claims he sought, calling attention to the verses of the play years later. One is struck by the number of "set pieces" in this play, as if the character turned not so much to his on-stage vis-à-vis as to the audience, giving the play the air of an elocution contest. To be sure, characters speak very definitely in the "indicative" as they affirm their own worth in these speeches, but the dramatic effect is similar to that created in the conjectural speeches of *Polyeucte*: very little actually does happen. To be sure, the play is full of assassinations, entreaties, revelations, but these incidents do not form part of a progressively developed, integrated plot. They are, rather, occasions for this or that *généreux* to demonstrate his *générosité;* like Cléopâtre's intercession on behalf of her ignoble brother, each incident is an *épreuve*. The dramaturgy of *Pompée* is more deductive than inductive: Corneille demonstrates an aspect or a quality of character—here *générosité*—testing it with various stresses. The quality had been produced and refined in the several "political plays" after *Le Cid*; in *Pompée* it undergoes the final test of quality: control. Like Molière's *Les Femmes savantes* in its kind, *La Mort de Pompée* in its kind is "too perfect." A new kind will not emerge till Corneille turns from "tragedy" to "comedy" once again.

# 3

# Le Menteur to Nicomède

# l'ambitieux

In *Le Menteur* (1643) we find many of the types,
much of the same setting, and many of the themes of the
comedies from *Melite* to *La Veuve:* in Dorante we have
the dexterous *galant;* in Alcippe, the inferior, slightly
ridiculous and ineffectual suitor; in Clarice, the witty but
secondary *galante*; in Lucrèce, the sweet, innocent, if
shallow young thing; in Géronte, the naive, bungling, but
indulgent parent. In setting we leave the heady atmosphere of the early comedies, with an emphasis this time
more upon the bourgeois than the pastoral. Finally, we
explicitly deal once again with the principal theme of
those early plays: the relationship of appearance to reality
in the realm of courtship. Indeed, this theme is explicit
to the point of self-consciousness—so much so that *Le
Menteur* strikes us once again as an *étude* of Cornelian
comedy in the manner of *L'Illusion comique*. But this
time, instead of resuming the dramaturgy of a series of
plays, the playwright projects a new mode of dramaturgy.
    At key points throughout the extremely involved plot
of this play, Corneille has placed whole scenes of sig-

nificant exchanges which comment upon the plot just as those between Pridamant and Alcandre did in *L'Illusion*. This time it is Cliton who is the on-stage spectator and Dorante who is the on-stage playwright and actor. These characters exist in other significant ways in the drama, but in these peripheral scenes they distinguish truth from fiction for us in the involutions of the "play" being acted out in the love-relationships. Thus, in I, 6, Dorante explains to Cliton why he has lied about (1) his "military career," (2) the party on the river, and (3) the length of time he has been back—it's all to make himself a more attractive suitor. And when Cliton warns him that all this lying can only lead to "fâcheux intrigues," he is, like Pridamant in a similar moment of the earlier play, actually voicing the anxiety (and hope!) of the spectator. Or when in III, 4, Cliton warns Dorante that Lucrèce is likely to be as artful in ruse as Dorante himself, he is voicing once again the knowledge which the spectator has gained from a scene which Dorante cannot have witnessed. And Cliton is probably most like a spectator or Dorante like a playwright in the three peripheral scenes of Act IV: in scene 1 Dorante had told Cliton, this "secretary of his heart's secrets," that he and Alcippe are mortal enemies and that he, Dorante, had only just left Alcippe for dead after a savage duel. When the "dying Alcippe" appears in the very next moment to greet Dorante as "cher ami," we indeed recognize that Dorante has been playing around with this "spectator" much as the playwright does—and continues to do so in the following scene with the story of Alcippe's miraculous recovery thanks to a new powder. Finally, in IV, 5, when Cliton smugly warns his master that he has told too many lies to too many people and that the truth is bound to come out between Clarice and

Lucrèce, he is actually voicing the feeling of the spectator.

And, possibly, at this point, the spectator's irritation. Even less than with *L'Illusion* can one afford to put too much weight upon the structure of *Le Menteur*. The plot is built upon a series of plausibilities, any one of which is so tenuous as to make the series implausible: (1) the mistaken identity which starts the whole imbroglio; (2) Géronte's inability to name his choice for his son before his son has finished the lie about a marriage at Poitiers; (3) Dorante's failure to make up a name about a guest at the *fête sur l'eau*; (4) Clarice's curiosity even after she has rejected Dorante, etc. But the improbability of each of these as well as of the even more improbable chain of them is sure to be lost from sight in the fireworks of Dorante's fantastic performance. And it is as a performance that Dorante's "lying" is presented. For as with the two characters from *L'Illusion* whom Corneille has incorporated into Dorante, the playwright Alcandre and the actor Clindor, the frame of judgment must be esthetic rather than ethical. Corneille establishes this frame of reference quite literally in the frame of the play, the first scene. Before the play actually begins with Dorante's query about the two women nearby, he and Cliton discuss in a very general way his penchant for "lying." To his servant's ironic reproaches, he replies:

A ne rien déguiser, Cliton, je te confesse
Qu'à Poitiers j'ai vécu comme vit la jeunesse;
J'étois en ces lieux-là de beaucoup de métiers; (I, 1)

Like Clitandre before he became an actor, Dorante has done many things. And those things, like the things he will do or plan to do in the remainder of the play, are placed in a mode of make-believe: *jeu, songe, rêve, artifice, ruse*—these are the terms used to describe Dorante's lies. And as still another way of removing the ethical sting from his hero's conduct, Corneille deliberately creates an atmosphere in which, at worst, his deeds are made to seem no worse than those of everybody else, and, at best, they may be taken as ingeniously and happily typical of that atmosphere. Dorante justifies his gallantries as satisfying the demands of the ladies of the time for novelistic adventures; Paris itself is described as a setting in which fantasy and metamorphosis prevail:

> DORANTE: Paris semble à mes yeux un pays de romans.
> J'y croyois ce matin voir une île enchantée:
> Je la laissai déserte, et la trouve habitée;
> Quelque Amphion nouveau, sans l'aide des maçons,
> En superbes palais a changé ses buissons.
> GÉRONTE: Paris voit tous les jours de ces métamorphoses:
> Dedans le Pré-aux-Clercs tu verras mêmes choses;
> Et l'univers entier ne peut rien voir d'égal
> A ce que tu verras vers le Palais-Royal.
> Toute une ville entière, avec pompe bâtie,
> Semble d'un vieux fossé par miracle sortie,
> Et nous fait présumer, à ses superbes toits,
> Que tous ses habitants sont des dieux ou des rois.
> Mais changeons de discours. Tu sais combien je t'aime?
>    (II, 5)

Like the first scene of courtship, this exchange serves as a justificatory prologue to one of Dorante's major "lies" (here, the story of his marriage into that family with blatantly literary names, Orphise and Armédon). In such a setting, Dorante's lies are only jokes, told "pour vous faire plaisir."

Is there not a little too sharp an edge to the wit? In particular, are there not certain *victims* of this wit—notably Clarice and Géronte and Alcippe and even, to a certain extent, Lucrèce, in spite of the fact that she does get Dorante at the end? Not really, for each character of the play only gets what he deserves. First of all Clarice. She gets Alcippe and not Dorante because she is not the equal of Dorante. She is a flirt who is as "insincere" as Dorante on the occasion of their first meeting—even more so, inasmuch as she is Alcippe's intended. But even if her behavior were not cast in this dubious light, were she as free as Dorante at this moment, she could not in all conscience expect more than she gives—which is wit and *galanteries.* This is the strongest commitment she shows herself capable of in the play, so it is not without justice that she should get the foolishly irritable, extravagantly jealous, pompous Alcippe. The latter is somewhat of a *capitan fanfaron,* one in whom the sense of caution at one point looks very much like outright cowardice (II, 4). In him, as in the woman he gets at the end, the inner man is very close to the outer man. To be sure, as in the rest of Corneille's universe, appearance and reality coincide, but the appearance is without much substance.

But is this not true of Dorante himself? No. For one thing, Corneille takes great pains to establish this character's fundamental worth. Along with the esthetically oriented student there is in Dorante the true *généreux.* This *générosité* is construed in military terms: witness his interrupted duel with Alcippe, which gives credence to his boast of arms to Clarice. But it is primarily construed in moral terms:

ARGANTE: D'homme de coeur, d'esprit, adroit et résolu;

Il a passé partout pour ce qu'il a voulu.
Tout ce qu'on le blâmoit (mais c'étoient tours d'école),
C'est qu'il faisoit mal sûr de croire à sa parole,
Et qu'il se fioit tant sur sa dextérité,
Qu'il disoit peu souvent deux mots de vérité;
Mais ceux qui le blâmoient excusoient sa jeunesse;
Et comme enfin ce n'est que mauvaise finesse,
Et l'âge, et votre exemple, et vos enseignements,
Lui feront bien quitter ces divertissements.
Faites qu'il s'en corrige avant que l'on le sache:
Ils pourroient à son nom imprimer quelque tache.
Adieu: je vais rêver une heure à mon procès. (V, 1)

It is unthinkable, then, that this worthy hero should not win the most worthy woman of the piece—Lucrèce.

Lucrèce *is* the most worthy woman of the piece. All but Dorante recognized this from the very beginning, for it is she who is the more beautiful of the two whom Dorante meets at the beginning. And in this world where "handsome does as handsome is," if Lucrèce is indisputably the more beautiful she is morally the more worthy. And Dorante should have seen this from the very beginning:

DORANTE: J'ai tantôt vu passer cet objet si charmant:
Sa compagne, ou je meure! a beaucoup d'agrément.
Aujourd'hui que mes yeux l'ont mieux examinée,
De ma première amour j'ai l'âme un peu gênée:
Mon coeur entre les deux est presque partagé,
Et celle-ci l'auroit s'il n'étoit engagé. (V, 4)

The eye is the guarantor and Dorante should have realized (made real) explicitly what had to be implicitly. But then we'd have had no play in which the entire action moves towards the coincidence of the unreal and the actual.

Thus, Dorante's lying leads to fact: he tells Alcippe that he dined with a woman whom the latter can only regard as his mistress, Clarice, and, in fact, Clarice has become the object of Dorante's attention—Dorante is his rival. Thus, he tells a series of lies in order to be able to wed one Lucrèce and the result of these lies is to disenchant the creature he thinks is Lucrèce but who is not truly worthy of him and to give him the creature who is really Lucrèce and whom both his station and his merit dictate should be his.

Does *she* not lie or at any rate intrigue in order to win Dorante? And what of Dorante's "retroactive" justification of his behavior after he learns that Lucrèce and Clarice had switched places, thereby confirming him in his first mistake? The justification is simple and had been given by Dorante to his father:

> Et j'avois ignoré, Monsieur, jusqu'à ce jour
> Que la dextérité fût un crime en amour. (V, 3)

All is not fair in war, as Corneille's military plays had taught us, but all's fair in love as the early comedies had shown us and as *Le Menteur* shows us once again.

But what of Géronte—is he not victimized? Not really. Like the parents of the early comedies or the king figure of the first "*tragédie*," *Médée*, Géronte is a parodistic figure. In a theater where youth is ascendant it is not surprising that he should be "victimized." But that is hardly the term to describe his behavior, for, like Fernand in *Le Cid*, he easily accepts the domination of the younger generation:

> Oui, vous avez raison, belle et sage Clarice:

Ce que vous souhaitez est la même justice;
Et d'ailleurs c'est à nous à subir votre loi (II, 1)

But he accepts this secondary role with such dignity
and passion that for a moment he takes the play out of
its fantastic mode and projects it into the serious mode of
the political plays:

> GÉRONTE: Laisse-moi parler, toi de qui l'imposture
> Souille honteusement ce don de la nature:
> Qui se dit gentilhomme, et ment comme tu fais,
> Il ment quand il le dit, et ne le fut jamais.
> Est-il vice plus lâche, est-il tache plus noire,
> Plus indigne d'un homme élevé pour la gloire?
> Est-il quelque foiblesse, est-il quelque action
> Dont un coeur vraiment noble ait plus d'aversion,
> Puisqu'un seul démenti lui porte une infamie
> Qu'il ne peut effacer s'il n'expose sa vie, (V, 3)

With these reproaches we are suddenly cast back into considerations like those one can entertain about Ptolomée
in *Pompée*: how are we to account for this contradiction
between station and merit? Is Dorante some kind of a
freak, a sport? Hardly, and the father's reproaches are
not really intended to cast doubts on his son's fundamental integrity. Rather, they serve the dramatic value
of bringing the play squarely into reality, of preventing
the tissue of lies from dissolving into the very thin air
of extreme fantasy. The moment of truth is here simply
because the spectator could not go on much further with
the game.

So it is truth which Dorante gives him—even if it is
a truth which is in the very process of changing. But this
change was necessary, and necessary in these serious terms

if the spectator is to give any credence to the doubts which Dorante now expresses about his first love. These doubts are really the preparation for the outcome of the play; they are a step on the way to the reality with which the play ends, in which the name and the thing are one and the same.

*Le Menteur* is very much a comedy, then. But its mood is only ultimately that of the early comedies in which wishes are fulfilled and the dreams of "just pairings" come true. The more prevalent mood is melodramatic. Once the dramaturgy of the "guarantee scene" is established, we are led to *conjecture* that in each of his successive "lies" Dorante might be lying only for a good reason —in order to win the rewards to which his youth and beauty and good intentions "entitle him." And this is true *eventually*. Because it is so "eventually," *Le Menteur* looks forward to the "tragedies" of the forties as much as it looks backward to the early comedies of the thirties. *Le Menteur* looks forward in another important way as well. Before he is justified as a well-meaning soul—a *généreux*—Dorante apparently seeks too much, seeks more than his share of his world. At first, he strikes us as more ambitious than noble. Transpose this conception of character and the appropriate dramaturgy to a "serious" register and we shall have the "tragedies" of Corneille's middle years.

The transposition is not an abrupt one. Like the play from which it derives, *La Suite du Menteur* (1644-45) is strongly reminiscent of the early comedies. The world of the play is not made of very solid stuff and Corneille does not really exploit the exciting possibilities of the dramaturgy of rehabilitation which he introduced with

*Le Menteur. La Suite* even moves backward with its serious fifth act—too serious, as Corneille says, "pour une pièce si enjouée." [1] It is as if the fifth act of *La Suite* were the end of a play in the style of the series which concluded with *Pompée*. The *nouveautés* of a serious hero in the style of Dorante are not exploited till Corneille returns to "tragedy" with *Rodogune*.

In *Rodogune* (1644-45) Corneille gives full vent to his love of invention, manipulation, and theatricality. From the unorthodox exposition to the harrowing *coup de théâtre* with which the play closes, Corneille assaults his spectator with shocking demands, upsetting threats, and surprising revelations.

The exposition was the object of a severe, somewhat just criticism by one of Corneille's most persistent critics, the Abbé d'Aubignac. In his *Pratique du théâtre* the latter censured Corneille for implausibly assuming that Timagéne would not have heard of the purely public events which Corneille has his sister recount at great length in an obvious effort to keep the spectator abreast of the situation. Corneille admits to this weakness, although somewhat cryptically.[2] But attention to this weakness should not obscure the *nouveauté* of Corneille's interruption of the exposition by the beginning of the action proper of the play. In a sliding-panel technique looking forward to the manipulation of time in recent novels (chiefly in the so-called neorealist school, in the work of Alain Robbe-Grillet), Corneille "sandwiches" a moment of the play's present between two moments of its past. Laonice traces the political events of Cleopatre's regency —her supposed widowhood, her marriage to her brother-in-law, the latter's ambition—up to the present moment

when one of her twin sons through Nicanor will be
named by her as the first-born and so receive both the
crown and the queen's former enemy, the Princess
Rodogune. We presumably are about to learn what has
become of both the queen's first husband, Nicanor, and
Antiochus, the brother-in-law she took supposedly in an
effort to protect herself and her sons. But before we can
learn, the exposition is interrupted by the arrival on the
scene of the twin heirs to the throne. Immediately, Corneille surprises us (especially those of us expecting the
typical *généreux*) by having first one and then the other
of the heirs to the throne willingly relinquish it to his
brother for the sake of possessing Rodogune in return.
In a *combat amical* which is a clear parallel to the *combats amoureux* of the earlier plays, the brothers learn that
only in accepting the kingdom can they really acknowledge Rodogune's worth. But with the play thus already
put into motion, with the spectator wondering just how
well they will preserve the friendship they swear in spite
of destiny's choice of one over the other, we return to the
exposition of events and circumstances antedating this
pact. However, we return to it to learn past things which
complicate this present circumstance: that the father of
the twins had not only been living when his wife, assuming his death, had married his brother, but that this same
king had intended to marry Rodogune, the Parthian
princess whom his sons love; that the uncle of the boys
and the queen's second husband had died in battle; that,
presumably acting out of justified concern for her sons,
the queen Cleopatre ambushed her first husband and, it
is conjectured, killed him by her own hand; and that the
Parthian threat to Syria has ended with the Armenian
threat to Parthia. Each of these revelations is given greater

dramatic interest and potentially ironic significance in light of these scenes from the present which interrupted Laonice's exposition of them. Nor is this the end of Corneille's skillfully "delayed exposition": in the first three scenes of Act II Cleopatre reveals the false motives underlying her present accord with both her sons and her former enemy, revealing the purely selfish bases of all the actions described in the interrupted accounts of Laonice in Act I. These scenes thus function like the scenes of guarantee in *Le Menteur* and *La Suite du Menteur,* but here they explain not some new event which has transpired before the spectator's eyes but events reported from the distant to the near past. Scenes 1 to 3 of Act II are thus themselves part of the exposition, but, like Laonice's resumed revelations in Act I, so Cleopatre's revelations here are given greater dramatic interest in that they give concrete shape to the new or present circumstances which had just preceded them: Rodogune's unexplained anxiety, expressed at the end of Act I, that is, presumably at a time when that character had only the best to expect in the light of recent events. A genuinely new event involving Cleopatre does not occur until her harrowing challenge to her sons to purchase the kingdom at the price of their beloved princess' life. Finally, the delayed exposition does not really become complete until Rodogune confirms in III, 3, that Cleopatre had indeed murdered her own husband, a revelation which once again thrusts us into the past only to give greater dramatic significance to some recently transpired event: the exhortation to expediency made by Rodogune's political adviser—"Faites-vous un rempart des fils, contre la mére" (III, 2) .

This sliding-panel use of the present and the past in the exposition also continues once the action of the play moves beyond the near past. In Act IV Corneille resumes the temporal scheme of the two comedies he had just written: Cleopatre apparently forgives her sons, appearing even to confirm this transformation in her character to the "secretary of her heart," Laonice, but in the soliloquy of scene 5 she reveals to the audience only that the transformation has been false. Finally, in Act V, although the audience has been disabused by Cleopatre's soliloquy in scene 1, the pattern of the action is the same: Cleopatre behaves in a conciliatory way toward her enemies and then in a final scene announces that such behavior had been false.

As this temporal scheme suggests, we are far from the open and frank world of most of the earlier political plays. Here we are in an atmosphere of secrecy, suspicion, and expediency—these very terms (*secrets, défiance, art, feinte*) being among the most important key-words of the play. The closest we come to such an atmosphere of suspicion and expediency in *Le Cid* is in Gormas' sarcasm, a form of duplicity which denies itself in its very execution. As for *Horace,* this is the world of *généreux* behavior *par excellence* in which everyone openly voices his ambitions, every one being exactly what he appears to be—including the weak king who avows the expedient bases of his behaviour to the very people who protest it. It is true that in *Polyeucte,* Félix is suspicious and expedient to the point of hypocrisy, but he is a secondary character and he is the exception rather than the rule in the world of that play. Even so, his character is harmonized with that of the principal characters by his conversion. In *Cinna,* where, of the young heroes all guilty of outright political and moral hypocrisy, Emilie comes closest to Cleopatre in this respect, the final events of the play make this compromise of her *générosité* seem purely conjectural. In *Pompée,* with the major characters we return to the fully *généreux* world of *Horace* and, as we have seen even in the case of the compromised *généreux,* Ptolomée, he dies in such a way as to repair the damage to his integrity which his political conspiracy has involved. But Cleopatre is not rehabilitated in this ethical fashion, and we shall want to come back to this fact after we have considered the other characters of this play.

As for the other characters, they can be described as heroic and exemplary in an ethical sense—initially in the case of the twins and ultimately in the case of Rodogune. Antiochus and Seleucus are *généreux* in the tradition of Rodrigue. Or, more precisely, in the tradition of Rodrigue and Chimene, since in the *combat amical* to which I have alluded, Seleucus plays Rodrigue to his more "sophisticated" brother, Antiochus. The latter teaches his brother the full implications of *l'amour généreux:*

> ANTIOCHUS: L'amour, l'amour doit vaincre, et la triste amitié
> Ne doit estre à tous deux qu'un objet de pitié.
> Un grand coeur céde un Trosne, et le céde avec gloire,
> Cét effort de vertu couronne sa mémoire,
> Mais lors qu'un digne objet a pû nous enflamer,
> Qui le céde est un lasche et ne sçait pas aimer. (I, 3)

Given the lesson, Seleucus is an even more apt pupil than Rodrigue. *"Plus royaliste que le roi,"* he urges Antiochus to ever greater heights of paradoxical possession through renunciations. His is a doctrine of self-assertion and willful rejection of fate such as we have not heard anywhere in Corneille, except perhaps in *Cinna* and *Polyeucte.* Such "transcendence" is reminiscent of the later Auguste in

*Cinna* and, still earlier in the action, of the hero in *Polyeucte*. Like the emperor-hero, Seleucus champions an ideal whose concrete expression takes the form of non-action, but, as with the martyr-hero, his gesture involves, at least to the degree of not extending one's present political power, a renunciation of the things of this world. Indeed, Seleucus' idealism is or becomes more Christian in tone than that of Polyeucte, the Christian martyr's. True, it never reaches that full renunciation of self which is the essence of Christian love of the ideal, for Seleucus' idealism has its roots in the "loyalty to the house" which motivated the Cornelian heroes of the older generation of *Le Cid,* Rodrigue himself in large part, and old Horace. But as Seleucus learns first of his mother's and then of his beloved Rodogune's homicidal demands, he turns away from the attempt to pursue the throne:

> J'en ferois comme vous, si mon esprit troublé
> Ne secoüoit le joug dont il est accablé.
> Dans mon ambition, dans l'ardeur de ma flame,
> Je voy ce qu'est un Trosne, et ce qu'est une femme,
> Et jugeant par leur prix de leur possession,
> J'éteins enfin ma flame, et mon ambition;
> Et je vous céderois l'un, et l'autre, avec joye,
> Si, dans la liberté que le Ciel me renvoye,
> La crainte de vous faire un funeste present
> Ne me jettoit dans l'ame un remords trop cuisant.
>     Desrobons-nous, mon frére, à ces ames crüelles,
> Et laissons-les sans nous achever leurs querelles. (III, 5)

and to the ever-hopeful Antiochus who would have the women withdraw their demands by his tears, Seleucus says:

> Pleurez donc à leurs yeux, gémissez, soûpirez,

Et je craindray pour vous ce que vous espérez,
Quoy qu'en vostre faveur vos pleurs obtiennent d'elles,
Il vous faudra parer leurs haines mutüelles,
Sauver l'une de l'autre, et peut-estre leurs coups,
Vous trouvant au milieu, ne perceront que vous.
C'est ce qu'il faut pleurer. Ny Maîtresse, ny mére,
Si je ne pretends plus, n'ont plus de choix à faire,
Je leur oste le droit de vous faire la loy.
Rodogune est à vous, puisque je vous fais Roy.
Epargnez vos soûpirs auprès de l'une et l'autre.
J'ay trouvé mon bon-heur, saisissez-vous du vostre,
Je n'en suis point jaloux, et ma triste amitié
Ne le verra jamais que d'un oeil de pitié. (III, 5)

Seleucus' development thus traces an unusual curve: as
with the typical Cornelian hero to date, its initial movement is upward, but where the latter's upward movement is infinite, with each new challenge being met by
an "upward" gesture surpassing its predecessor, Seleucus
reaches a peak of noble renunciation fairly early in the
play with his pledge of friendship to Antiochus and then
ends his upward movement as he withdraws from the
arena.

Does the curve actually turn downwards, does the character move from outright optimism to downright pessimism, from hope to despair? He certainly rejects the
hopefulness of his brother here and in the invocation of
pity for his brother he shows that sad, reflective dismissal
of the ways of this world which is often the first step
toward religious conversion. In this rejection of the world
of ambition and glory Seleucus actually goes beyond Polyeucte, thus looking forward to another Cornelian hero
who seems to reject the world—Suréna. In *Polyeucte,* we
remember, the hero renounced this world only to seek
a more emphatic arena for his grandiose ambition to

exercise itself. But in Seleucus we have the *généreux* who rejects ambition in this world in terms which cast doubt on the very ideal of worldly ambition. Furthermore, Seleucus apparently looks to "no place beyond" in which the limitations of this world would be truly transcended. In the speeches just quoted as in his final encounter with Cleopatre just before his assassination he no longer attempts to rise above fate by rejecting it in an arbitrary assertion of will; rather, he seems to try to step aside of fate. With great calm and great dignity he shows Cleopatre that he sees through her attempt to pit him against his brother in her "revelation" that he, Seleucus, was the first-born and that in withdrawing from contention he is giving away not only the throne but Rodogune as well:

SELEUCUS: Peut-estre, mais enfin par quel amour de mére
Pressez-vous tellement ma douleur contre un frére?
Prenez-vous intérest à la faire éclater?
CLEOPATRE: J'en prens à la connoistre, et la faire avorter,
J'en prens à conserver malgré toy mon ouvrage
Des jaloux attentats de ta secrette rage.
SEL.: Je le veux croire ainsi, mais quel autre intérest
Nous fait tous deux aisnez, quand, et comme il vous plaist?
Qui des deux vous doit croire, et par quelle justice
Faut-il que sur moy seul tombe tout le supplice,
Et que du mesme amour, dont nous sommes blessez,
Il soit récompensé, quand vous m'en punissez?
CLEO.: Comme Reine, à mon choix je fais justice, ou grace,
Et je m'étonne fort d'où vous vient cette audace,
D'où vient qu'un fils vers moy noircy de trahison,
Ose de mes faveurs me demander raison. (IV, 6)

Here it is Cleopatre who uses the voluntarist language and the real significance of this· encounter lies in the fact that her vis-à-vis, who rejects it, is the character who had earlier been her only potential rival for the title of uncompromising and uncompromised hero in the play. The tearful appeals to the women which Antiochus would use against his mother are honorable enough means but they are hardly the means of a *généreux*. Seleucus rejects those means, but it is not because he considers them weak and undignified—it is because he considers them useless. One wonders if he means that they are as useless as any other means one might choose, including those of forthright and heroic conflict. He appears to be on the verge of uttering this insight, particularly in his "apology" to Cleopatre in the first few lines of his last speech of the play:

> Vous pardonnerez donc ces chaleurs indiscretes.
> Je ne suis point jaloux du bien que vous luy faites,
> Et je voy quel amour vous avez pour tous deux,
> Plus que vous ne pensez, et plus que je ne veux.
> Le respect me défend d'en dire davantage. (IV, 6)

Seleucus is calm and even sad at the realization he hints at. Might not his calm suggest that he has already reached the "tragic illumination" that there is no realm—whether in this world or in another—where man can bend things to his wish? Possibly, although his very last words might be read quite differently:

> Je n'ay, ny faute d'yeux, ny faute de courage.
> Non, Madame, et jamais vous ne verrez en moy
> Qu'amitié pour mon frére, et zèle pour mon Roy.
> Adieu. (IV, 6)

The last two lines, in particular, might be read as a

reaffirmation of the idealism first stated in the *combat amical* of Act I. However, the invocation seems rather listless in this context. The tone of the speech—resignation and acceptance—as well as the context—the mother's rejection of natural love—suggests that the character regards this friendship and loyalty not as the highest but as the only possible virtue in the circumstances. If there is, then, a truly "tragic hero" in the "tragedy" of *Rodogune,* it is Seleucus. But, once again, Corneille has relegated his tragic or potentially tragic character to the secondary.* I shall reconsider Cleopatre's character in light of the analyses of the various other principals, but already it is clear that in spite of a basic resemblance—the *donnée* of self-esteem, which is the essence of *générosité*—Seleucus comes to a different end from his mother: if he has his way it is only in an ironic and incomplete sense.

A similar fate overtakes his brother, but Antiochus' tragic fate is less significant than Seleucus' and may even be described as merely apparent. In the beginning, at least, Antiochus possesses the sureness of temper which his brother achieves only by stages, as it were. It is he who would teach his brother the full implications of *généreux* love, we remember, and it is he who acts constantly as a restraining force on his more tempestuous twin. (In his unrelenting commitment to *générosité* one can already suspect that it is he who is really the first-born. Also, according to the *généreux* ethos whereby "class tells," in Rodogune's instinctive love of Antiochus, one

---

* J. Hubert has properly caught this tragic aspect of Seleucus' character, although as Amarante of *La Suivante* has shown us, it is less new as a "discordant note" in Corneille than Hubert believes. As for the degree to which Hubert generalizes Seleucus' tragic significance, see my subsequent analysis. See "The Conflict between Chance and Morality in *Rodogune,*" *Modern Language Notes,* LXXIV, 234-239.

might see still another sign of his primogeniture—
although, it must be said, we hardly expect Cleopatre to
reveal the truth of this matter.) More importantly, he
remains the most consistently "Cornelian" hero in his
unremitting hopefulness. However, the particular form
of his hope makes for a relatively impure *généreux*: he
relies on entreaty and tears. This behavior reminds us (in
its very nature, first of all, then in its results) of that of
the ineffectual suitors of Corneille's early comedies. Com-
pared with the vigorous, hardheaded, and, at least in the
case of one of them, unscrupulous behavior of both his
mistress and his mother and considered in the light of
the fierce dedication to glory of both of these women,
Antiochus' stratagem of tears is sentimental. Further, inasmuch as it does not have its desired results, it proves
to be worse than sentimental: ridiculously unrealistic.
Antiochus maintains that upward movement which is the
essential direction of the *généreux,* but, morally, he ends
up by seeming the naive twin while his brother, who is
more naive that he at the beginning, ends up seeming
the more truly perceptive and sophisticated. Antiochus'
last words to his mother show him ever clinging to hope:
"Ah, vivez pour changer cette haine en amour." (V, 4) ,
and his last speech still shows him unchanged in his basic
hopefulness:

> Oronte, je ne sçay dans son funeste sort
> Qui m'afflige le plus, ou sa vie, ou sa mort,
> L'une et l'autre a pour moy des malheurs sans éxemple,
> Plaignez mon infortune. Et vous, allez au Temple
> Y changer l'allegresse en un dueil sans pareil,
> La pompe Nuptiale en funébre appareil,
> Et nous verrons après, par d'autres sacrifices,
> Si les Dieux voudront estre à nos voeux plus propices. (V, 4)

In the directions to Oronte to change the wedding plans into funeral plans he reveals not an insight into the funereal aspect underlying all human behavior, but simply bewilderment at his mother's behavior. Though it is he who is really "eccentric" in the world of the play— a world of suspicion and intrigue and unruly ambition, as Rodogune and Cleopatre know from the beginning and as Seleucus learns—Antiochus treats Cleopatre as if she were the exception, not the rule. Finally, in his very last two lines he looks forward to more propitious days from the gods. His brother knew better than to expect such things from the gods (usually called fate by him). Antiochus is tragic then only in that relative sense that newspaper reports so describe the unhappy destiny of some world figure. He lacks that awareness that would put him on a par with tragic heroes like Oedipus or Phèdre: of an irreconcilable conflict between man's hope and destiny's dicta.

But what of Rodogune, the character who gives her name to this play which Corneille called "*tragédie*?" When we first meet her she is a noble character filled with disquiet and foreboding, the potential tragic victim *par excellence*. If she soon forsakes this posture for the familiar one of the aggressive, heroic stance we have long associated with Corneille's *jeunes premières*, it is not with the loss of tragic *potential*. In her we find in its purest expression the conflict between love and duty which has been taken as the very essense of the Cornelian conflict:

> RODOGUNE: Ne croy pas en tirer le secret de mon ame.
> Quelque époux que le Ciel me vueille destiner,
> C'est à luy pleinement que je me veux donner.
> Et si du malheureux je deviens le partage.
> Je sçauray l'accepter, avec mesme visage,

L'Hymen me le rendra précieux à son tour,
Et le devoir fera ce qu'auroit fait l'amour,
Sans crainte qu'on reproche à mon humeur forcée
Qu'un autre qu'un mary régne dans ma pensée.
LAONICE: Vous craignez que ma foy vous l'ose reprocher!
    (I, 5)

This appears to be the paradoxical doctrine of possession through renunciation; rather, it is the deliberate sacrifice of one value to another. Physical or natural love had preceded the call of duty in this case:

RODOGUNE: Il est des noeuds secrets, il est des sympathies,
Dont par le doux rapport les ames assorties
S'attachent l'une à l'autre, et se laissent piquer
Par ces je ne sçay quoy, qu'on ne peut expliquer.
Cest par là que l'un d'eux obtient la préférence, (I, 5)

Corneille is "Racinian" a quarter of a century before the great dramatist of love. And the Racinian or genuinely tragic potential of this irrational love is underscored by the fact that, in theory at least, this love could go to an object whom fate has not placed in a high station. It is this case which Rodogune conjectures in the long speech from which I have just quoted, declaring that she would sacrifice natural love to duty. Indeed, she is more vigorous in this obligation to duty than even Chimene. Like the latter, she claims to be defending a dead hero and, in fact, her relationship to the dead Nicanor is more that of daughter to father than that of mistress to beloved: Corneille takes great pains to stress the filial nature of Rodogune's devotion to Nicanor. The honor she thus defends is apparently the feudal honor of the "house" or the "gens."

But at times Rodogune sounds as ambitious for the

crown, that public testimony of supreme worth in the
play's universe, as Cleopatre. Rodogune herself acknowledges:

> L'orgueil de ma naissance enfle encor mon courage,
> Et quelque grand pouvoir que l'amour ait sur moy,
> Je n'oublîray jamais que je me dois un Roy.
> Ouy, malgré mon amour, j'attendray d'une mére
> Que le Trosne me donne, ou vous, ou vostre frére.
> Attendant son secret, vous aurez mes desirs,
> Et s'il le fait régner, vous aurez mes soûpirs;
> C'est tout ce qu'à mes feux ma gloire peut permettre,
> Et tout ce qu'à vos feux les miens osent promettre. (IV, 1)

However, the last speech occurs after she has withdrawn
her harrowing matricidal demand of the twins and before
we can consider the speech's full implications we shall
have to consider the demand at some length. Pragmatical-
ly, it is perfectly justifiable: in the fierce world of which
Cleopatre is the ruler, such a weapon is to be taken for
granted. Moreover, Corneille elaborately gives greater
pragmatic justification to Rodogune's demand than to
Cleopatre's. At worst, Rodogune stole Nicanor's heart
from Cleopatre, but Cleopatre stole his life, and the justice
of the son vengefully slaying the mother who has murdered the father has an ancient and respected dramatic
example. That it should be at the insistence of a beloved
mistress is a piece of *schadenfreude* which Corneille
evidently considered one of his happier "inventions" in
the manipulation of the sources. But given the idealistic
character of those upon whom the demand is made and
considering the idealism which both their love for her
and her own behavior to this point have shown, Rodogune's demand at this point can only be shocking. Indeed,

she seems at first prepared to refuse such a course of action as it has just been presented to her by Oronte. We feel a sense of relief as the character rejects a devious course of action for an open one. But Rodogune does not reject action of any kind:

> Sentimens étouffez de vangeance et de haine,
> Rallumez vos flambeaux à celles de la Reine,
> Et d'un oubly contraint rompez la dure loy,
> Pour rendre enfin justice aux Manes d'un grand Roy.
> Rapportez à mes yeux son image sanglante,
> D'amour et de fureur encor étincelante,
> Telle que je le vy, quand tout percé de coups,
> Il me cria *vengeance. Adieu, je meurs pour vous.*
> Chére Ombre, hélas! bien loin de l'avoir poursuivie,
> J'allois baiser la main qui t'arracha la vie,
> Rendre un respect de fille à qui versa ton sang;
> Mais, pardonne aux devoirs que m'impose mon rang.
> Plus la haute naissance approche des Couronnes,
> Plus cette grandeur mesme asservit nos personnes,
> Nous n'avons point de coeur pour aimer, ny haïr,
> Toutes nos passions ne sçavent qu'obéïr. (III, 3)

This is a call to arms, but, reassured by the first part of the speech, we still have no reason to believe that she is going to call upon Cleopatre's sons as the instruments of her revenge on their mother. This part of the speech is disturbing for another reason: the implication that she, Rodogune, will take revenge on the queen. This, of course, must negatively affect the love she feels for one of the sons. The speech also leaves us with the anxiety of this peril and possibly some doubt as to the true nature of Rodogune's relationship with Nicanor (the speech might be taken as that of a vindictive mistress).

Nevertheless, the speech specifically reassures us that Rodogune will not take the course of action proposed by her counselor in the preceding scene—which is precisely what she does in the scene after this reassuring speech!

> Vostre gloire le veut, l'Amour vous le prescrit;
> Qui peut contr'elle et luy soulever vostre esprit?
> Si vous leur préférez une mére crüelle,
> Soyez crüels, ingrats, parricides comme elle.
> Vous devez la punir si vous la condamnez,
> Vous devez l'imiter si vous la soûtenez.
> Quoy, cette ardeur s'éteint! l'un et l'autre soûpire!
> J'avois sçeu le prévoir, j'avois sçeu le prédire . . . (III, 4)

Later on Rodogune will take this demand back, claiming that she was only "testing" her lovers, a fact which Corneille will recall to the critics of this astonishing demand by Rodogune. The last two lines above might even be read as a clue to this interpretation of her behavior and her final injunction to the twins is sufficiently ambiguous to allow for a similar defense:

> Il n'est plus temps, le mot en est lasché,
> Quand j'ay voulu me taire, en vain je l'ay tasché.
> Appelez ce devoir haine, rigueur, colére,
> Pour gagner Rodogune, il faut venger un pére,
> Je me donne à ce prix. Osez me mériter,
> Et voyez qui de vous daignera m'accepter. (III, 4)

The "prix" is quite simply the vengeance for a father—not necessarily the murder of a mother. Rodogune is as wily as Cleopatre, but she is not really immoral. As with Emilie in *Cinna*, her perfidy is purely conjectural, with an even greater measure of rehabilitation being hers in that she herself and not circumstances prevents the un-*généreux* deed she projects from being realized. But the occasion for her rehabilitation robs her of tragic potential, or more precisely, it shows that these bases for tragedy in her case were purely theoretical. In demanding of the twins that they kill their mother, Rodogune seems to be acknowledging that circumstances force us to the choice of a nonvalue over a value—in short, to a compromise of principles. This remains purely theoretical and con-jectural in the case of Rodogune.

But in rehabilitating her as a consistent *généreuse*, Cor-neille reopens the possibility of tragedy in still another sense: the sacrifice of love to duty:

> Je n'oublîray jamais que je me dois un Roy.
> Ouy, malgré mon amour j'attendray d'une mére
> Que le Trosne me donne, ou vous, ou vostre frére. (IV, 1)

Corneille leaves no doubt as to which is the lesser value in Rodogune's eyes—natural love or the throne!

> Et moy, si mon destin entre ses mains me livre,
> Si pour d'autres que vous il m'ordonne de vivre,
> Mon amour . . . mais Adieu, mon esprit se confond, (IV, 1)

Rodogune momentarily casts doubt on the worth of the throne at the sacrifice of Antiochus, but she immediately makes a typically *généreux* expression of hope in the in-junction to her beloved to return with the crown. Cir-cumstances will not disappoint this hope. Once again, the tragic remains purely potential.

> Prince, si vostre flame à la mienne répond,

Si vous n'étes ingrat à ce coeur qui vous aime,
Ne me revoyez point, qu'avec le Diadème. (IV, 1)

Neither Antiochus nor Rodogune is tragic; Seleucus
is only secondarily tragic. Is there no tragic figure in this
*tragédie*? Perhaps in the figure of the queen mother to
whom, after all, Corneille wanted to give the title of
the play? Hardly. Her behavior right up to the very
moment of her death is not only untragic, but it may be
described as an outright despisal of the tragic. Never once
does Cleopatre express doubts over the validity of *any*
technique to maintain power. She forcefully states the
value of those tactics explicitly or implicitly rejected by
the others as nonvalues. She is unique in this respect not
only in this play but in all of Corneille's theater thus far.

If we wish to find a close parallel in Corneille's early
career for Cleopatre—in the wicked *généreux* or the vil-
lainous heroine— we must go first to the character he
himself evokes in discussing Cleopatre: Médée. But even
Médée, for all her ferocity and awesome self-esteem, did
not resort to the wiles and lies of Cleopatre. For this
conception of character we must look not to Corneille's
"tragic practice" but to his "comic practice": to *Le
Menteur* and *La Suite du Menteur*. The analysis of the
dramaturgy of the play has already suggested such a relationship—the sequence of what might be called presenta-
tional-scenes followed by explanatory guarantee-scenes.
Only now the milieu in which this *donnée* is to be worked
out is to be changed—from the amorous to the political,
or in somewhat more familiar critical terms, from the
fantastic to the realistic. Corneille had already made a
similar transposition earlier in his career, when he shifted
from *La Place Royale* to *Médée* and, in fact, that early

comedy is transitional in much the same way that *La Suite du Menteur* is transitional. The relation of serious to non-serious is ambiguous in both comedies and the "hero" of each comedy, Alidor and Dorante, is ambivalent, half-villain and half-hero.

But it would be unfair to assume from this parallel development in Corneille's canon that this *"seconde Médée,"* as he himself calls Cleopatre,[3] is only a re-edition of the first. Far from it: we have had no character so thoroughly, so frankly, so marvelously, so complexly "inhuman." Her speech opening Act II is one of those *coups de théâtre* with which Corneille loved to assault his audience at the beginning of acts. The terrifying and paradoxical language of the speech shatters the relatively calm surface of the play, giving unexpectedly vigorous justification to Rodogune's generalized suspicion of Cleopatre at the end of Act I. But because the speech also expresses release from anxiety the effect is to satisfy the spectator, to cast the speaker, Cleopatre, not in a negative but in a curiously positive light. True, in Act I, Cleopatre has been reported for the most part in the favorable light of the beleaguered widow queen and the outraged wife. Nevertheless, there have been intimations of devious behavior (the relatively sudden remarriage, a rather quick concern with the use of power, the ambush of her first husband, the fierce enmity toward Rodogune, the strangely prolonged "exile" of her sons) and these, coupled with Rodogune's suspicion of Cleopatre, have the effect of wearing down the generous construction of her behavior which the spectator might be tempted to give in light of her high station and the provocation of circumstance. The residue of ambiguity with which Act I concludes is dispelled, then, by this shattering and honest speech with which Act II begins. Corneille has thus maneuvered the spectator into the curious position of approving a character for the admission of wrongdoing. The approval is at first purely psychological, of course, like a sigh of relief: at last and at least, says the spectator, I know where I am. However, Corneille also presents certain, more solid justifications of Cleopatre's wrongdoing. For one thing, we are made to rejoice with an obviously highborn character in the release from constraint which is by definition intolerable to the highborn. Note that in the first thirteen verses of Cleopatre's speech we can point to nothing specifically wrong: she has been forced to behave falsely, but this is no indication that she will do something even more "ungenerous." It is possible that she is now going to confront Rodogune in an honest, open clash similar to that between César and Cornélie in *Pompée*. Again, though the ambiguity is resolved, the bases for it are still present in the spectator's mind. One of these we remember was that Cleopatre was more sinned against than sinning (Cleopatre quickly reminds the spectator of this: "que m'imposa la force et qu'accepta ma crainte"); again she apparently condemns "reasons of state" ("vains fantosmes d'état"). Cleopatre does justify as noble, kingly behavior the art of concealment and disguise, but the traditional *généreux* ideal of open and aboveboard behavior is acknowledged with vigour: "Eclatez, il est temps, et voicy nostre jour." In the familiar Cornelian metaphor of brilliant and extravagant gesture, Cleopatre *bursts* into an honesty which is rendered temporally and atmospherically: day and light—meaning that the time has come and it is now possible to show things "honestly," that is, openly.

Neverthless, it cannot be gainsaid that, ethically, for the

first time, we have a Cornelian "hero" who justifies the use of dishonesty and expediency. And Cleopatre definitely is the hero in the purely technical sense of the central character (Corneille himself acknowledged as much).[4] But we need only consider the major roles of the play to verify as much. Corneille has, of course, long been tempted by the figures of exemplary and heroic women—Médée, Chimene, and Pauline are the most obvious examples—so much so that, in the case of the last two, the plays in which they figure might easily have born their names. As for *Rodogune,* it bears that name only because Corneille wished to avoid a confusion of his Cleopatre with a more famous bearer of that name. Certainly, Corneille's Cleopatre lives up to the implications of her name. Thus Cleopatre's suicide is perhaps more emphatic and self-congratulatory than that of the original Cleopatre. In a play abounding in verbal and dramatic paradoxes the suicide is the most astonishing of the paradoxes; it expresses not despair, but supreme hope; not an inability to cope with circumstances but the absolute control over circumstance. As with Polyeucte, death is Cleopatre's instrument of self-assertion and demonstration of worth.

Not that she uses it to achieve some timeless realm of supreme power. Cleopatre is the most concrete of Corneille's kings and queens in her self-esteem: she requires the full panoply of royal power and prerogative to achieve her full sense of self. She is the most self-reliant of Corneille's heroes to date, as her refusal to keep even Laonice in her confidence indicates, and she is also the most self-possessed, as the shifting developments of the last act reveal. As the news of Seleucus' death comes she immediately accuses Timagéne, and when his account makes it clear that the dying twin had accused one of the women, she as readily accuses Rodogune. Finally, at Rodogune's warning to Antiochus not to take the wine proffered by the queen mother, she seizes the cup with these words:

> Je le feray moi-mesme. Et bien, redoutez-vous
> Quelque sinistre effet encor de mon couroux?
> J'ay souffert cet outrage avecque patience. (V, 4)

And when the naive Antiochus persists in helping her, she brushes him aside with these words:

> Va, tu me veux en vain rappeler à la vie,
> Ma haine est trop fidelle, et m'a trop bien servie,
> Elle a paru trop tost pour te perdre avec moy,
> C'est le seul déplaisir qu'en mourant je reçoy; (V, 4)

Cleopatre is a poor example of the Aristotelian tragic hero: she is *all* flaw. She is certainly not sacrificing a lesser value to a higher: all which does not contribute to her self-esteem is a nonvalue and so may be sacrificed—including certain natural "laws." Unlike Seleucus she would overcome contingency in all its manifestations, including the biological. In terms of one of the persistent metaphors of the play, she is an undoer of *noeuds naturels* as much as she is a weaver of *noeuds secrets*. Whether convention or instinct, mother love is useless in her eyes unless it serves her ambition, so that when she slaps Seleucus it is with perfect consistency and without compunction: he is no longer her son, but her enemy. Nor is Cleopatre tragic in existentialist terms: her horrifying acts are not, like those of Camus' Caligula, the plausible expression of a philosophy of the absurd. For Caligula there are no values, and a "good deed"—that is, one which does no physical harm to another—is no better than a "bad deed," one which does do harm. For Cleopatre there is a value—herself—and, as we have seen, when all other means fail, she uses death to affirm that value. Needless to say, she succeeds. She dies unilluminated because, in the universe of the play, there are no higher powers than those of Cleopatre. Necessity does not drive Cleopatre to suicide; her freedom leads her to it. The gods themselves may be said to fear her: "Je maudirois les Dieux s'ils me rendoient le jour" (V, 4). Cleopatre is not tragic.

But to say this is to pose one of the greatest problems of the play. It may be variously stated: why is this immoral character triumphant; why does she come to the same "happy ending" (according to her own lights) as the moral hero (Rodogune and Antiochus according to their lights, for example)? In his *Discours de la tragédie* Corneille speaks of her suicide as dictated by despair [5] and he might well have offered *à propos* of Cleopatre his remarks (presumably provoked by the Médée to whom he has earlier alluded) from his "Epitre" to *La Suite de Menteur,* the play which appeared just prior to *Rodogune*:

> Et comme le portrait d'une laide femme ne laisse pas d'être beau, et qu'il n'est pas besoin d'avertir que l'original n'en est pas aimable pour empêcher qu'on l'aime, il en est de même dans notre peinture parlante; quand le crime est bien peint de ses couleurs, quand les imperfections sont bien figurés, il n'est point besoin d'en faire voir un mauvais succès à la fin pour avertir qu'il ne les faut pas imiter.[6]

Yet, we may suspect from Corneille's critical practice elsewhere that this is *post-facto* reasoning in answer to the ascendant moralistic criticism of his time. Not that he wished to be diabolical. Anything but. His esthetic was morally neutral, as is implied in the first portion of the quote from the dedicatory letter to *La Suite,* and he was compelled to go beyond this neutralism (as in the second half of the quotation) only when provoked by unfavorable criticism. Cleopatre is not *necessarily* to be emulated according to such an esthetic. She and many another Cornelian hero or heroine assault the spirit, intrigue the mind, shock us, frighten us, appall us, seduce us, excite us, repel us, awe us—and this is all that is intended. Corneille sees himself as an artist and an artificer, not a moralist or a teacher. A clue to this intention (if we seek intentions and not that expression of them which is the play itself) lies in his justification of Rodogune's conjectured immorality in his "Examen" of the play. Corneille first specifically points to the interpretation of this gesture which I have elaborated in these pages:

Elle avoue elle-même à Antiochus qu'elle les haïroit, s'ils [the twins] lui avaient obéi; que comme elle a fait ce qu'elle a dû par cette demande, ils font ce qu'ils doivent par leur refus; qu'elle aime trop la vertu pour vouloir être le prix d'un crime, et que la justice [the death of their mother] qu'elle demande de la mort de leur père seroit un parricide, si elle la recevait de leurs mains.[7]

This is an essentially moral justification, as in the second part of the quotation from the "Epître" given above. But Corneille goes on to say:

Je dirai plus: quand cette proposition serait tout à fait condamnable en sa bouche, elle mériteroit quelque grâce et pour l'éclat que la nouveauté de l'invention a fait au théâtre, et pour l'embarras surprenant où elle jette les princes, et pour l'effet qu'elle produit dans le reste de la pièce, qu'elle conduit à l'action historique.[8]

Corneille's esthetic premises here should serve as a caution to those who see in him a precursor of Nietzsche. He is not Nietzsche, though, undoubtedly, Nietzsche found in Corneille much to appropriate for his own special attack on the culture of his time, which he regarded as destroying individualism and exalting mediocrity.* But Corneille does not preach; he depends on certain moral values in order to create certain dramatic effects. He allows Cleopatre to work out the purely political implications of *générosité* to a pleasingly appalling degree. Her response to the rapid series of challenges in the last act is representative. She is absolutely unfazed by revelations which might easily become the occasion for an avowal of guilt, and turns each of them to her own ends. When Timagéne reports the secret murder of Seleucus, she immediately accuses the bearer of the news of the crime since only the perpetrator could know the secret; but when the bearer of the news reports the dying twin's last words, she seizes on their ambiguous reference to "une main . . . chére" to accuse Rodogune; finally when Rodogune warns Antiochus against drinking from a cup prepared by his mother, the latter seizes the cup and drains it. We, of course, have known from the first scene of the act that Cleopatre has killed Seleucus and that she has put poison in the cup. Now such foreknowledge might suggest that her accusations of Timagéne and Rodogune as well as her draining of the cup are gestures of desperation. Far from it. They show rather her unconquerable spirit, her supreme confidence in herself, her readiness to use any instrument in order to remain mistress of circumstance—including death

---

*I do not mean to imply that there is no real possibility of a Nietzchean *use* of Corneille. In his article, "Nietzsche and Corneille," R. Virtanen has culled "points where they meet, or at least approach each other." *Symposium*, XI, 225.

itself. When Cleopatre goes off, she does so with disdainful pride, unreconciled to defeat, her very last words being the language of ascendancy and aspiration which the German critic, Merian-Genast, sees as a key semantic complex in all of Corneille:

> Je maudirois les Dieux s'ils me rendoient le jour.
> Qu'on m'emporte d'icy. Je me meurs, Laonice,
> Si tu veux m'obliger par un dernier service,
> Après les vains efforts de mes inimitiez,
> Sauve-moy de *l'affront de tomber à leurs pieds.* (V, 4;
>   my italics)

This is the language and the manner of Rodrigue, of Horace, of Auguste, of Polyeucte—the language and the manner of the *généreux.* As Rodogune is restored to the first injunction of *générosité* by her retraction of the demand on the twins, so Cleopatre is rehabilitated according to that injunction: to be oneself, to make the apparent coincide with the real. Gone is the deceit, gone the treachery as Cleopatre shows herself for what she is, as she realizes her entelechy. Though negatively, the *ambitieuse* has become a *généreuse.**

The critic Corneille may "justify" his heroine—through an esthetic neutralism or an ambiguous *post-facto* condemnation in which he appears to join other critics. And we may note a formal similarity between Cleopatre and the other *généreuse* of the play. Nevertheless, the play does give us a world where, "for no reason clear to the ethical understanding,"[9] the best happens to the worst!

---

*In this moment more than in any other she possesses those qualities which Tastevin regards as the chief qualities of the Cornelian heroine: energy and lucidity. *Les Héroïnes de Corneille,* passim.

But the best also happens to the best. The ambassador Oronte tells Antiochus:

> Encor dans les rigueurs d'un sort si déplorable,
> Seigneur, le juste Ciel vous est bien favorable.
> Il vous a préservé, sur le point de périr
> Du danger le plus grand que vous pûssiez courir,
> Et par un digne effet de ses faveurs puissantes
> La coupable est punie, et vos mains innocentes.     (V, 4)

We might read this speech as "proving" Corneille's contention that the wicked are punished—for reasons clear to the ethical understanding. But this would be to ignore Cleopatre's self-vindication. Rather, Oronte's final line smacks of the "conditional" happy ending of what we have heard Henry James call "romance" ("La coupable est punie et vos mains innocentes"). At most the speech tells us that counterbalancing the evidence that "the universe is *not* run according to moral principles" is evidence that the universe *is* run according to moral principles, principles of *généreux* behavior which are better represented by Rodogune than by the Antiochus in whose name Oronte offers this evidence. Rodogune in her final *indications* takes back the *conjectures* which bid to make her still another piece of evidence of cosmic evil. She thus stands against Cleopatre as well as the "tragic" Seleucus in this ending (we remember that it is her sense of caution which forces Cleopatre finally to declare herself). The universe of the play is, then, half tragic and half comic. Like Molière's *Le Misanthrope* it ends in a moral stalemate. The tragic "lesson" is one falling short of the full force of the tragic: the worst happens to the second-best, to Seleucus.

In *Rodogune*, Corneille seems to have writen a "problem play" in spite of himself. That is, when we compare it with the rest of his canon, we see that it leads to the tragic (at least partially) because Corneille follows that temptation to place esthetic values over ethical values which has been obvious ever since the early plays. The world of the play gives a negative proof of the tragic (the best happens to the worst) precisely because Corneille is concerned with Cleopatre's energy and *éclat*. Cleopatre —and not Attila, as in the opinion of some critics—represents the uncontrolled, the ethically irresponsible explosion of "Cornelian energy." In her case, *un*handsome does as *un*handsome is. Now, though this concept is not projected in the play as the evidence of an all-pervasive cosmic evil, like Seleucus' fate, it does strike a "discordant note," not only in the play but in the Cornelian canon —a note more significant in any consideration of Corneille than Amarante's fate in *La Suivante*. Because of it, the play strikes me as inadvertent in the Cornelian canon.* In this respect, it resembles Racine's *Iphigénie*. The dramaturgy of *Iphigénie* anticipates that of *Phèdre* in that the tragic figure takes a number of "human" measures to frustrate fate: exclusion, flight, seclusion, etc. They all fail, as they were bound to, and bring him progressively closer to the tragic illumination that man's resources and values are limited and insufficient in an unknowable, if not hostile, universe. But with the revelation of Eriphile as the Iphigénie destined for sacrifice, Agamemnon is spared that act which will complete his growing awareness

---

* "Cléopâtre alone comes close to taking its [*hasard*] place, and becoming, if only for a moment, as absolute as destiny itself." Hubert, "The Conflict between Chance and Morality in *Rodogune*," *Modern Language Notes*, LXXIV, 235. But there is also Rodogune's moral destiny: to assume the throne morally unsullied and thus worthy of the king, Antiochus.

of human limitation. The 'tragic lesson" is deflected in *Iphigénie* even as the opposite lesson is deflected in *Rodogune*.†

*Rodogune* may be described as a mystery story in which the question of identity is paramount. The most obvious question of identity concerns the order of birth of the twins, but there is a more profound problem of identity: can we recognize as heroic the women of the play? In the plays after *Rodogune* Corneille continues to write "mystery stories": *Théodore* (1645-46) is full of indirections, suppositions, suspicions, threats, and calculations. Théodore herself mysteriously conceals her identity as a Christian for a very long time, while her rescue from the ignominy of prostitution comes through the surprising conversion or change of identity of her suitor, Didyme. *Héraclius* (1646) is much more obviously a "mystery story," one squarely based on the question of "who is who?" The mere recounting of its plot indicates the direction Cornelian dramaturgy takes at this time:

Phocas, Emperor of the East, is uneasy on the throne, having come to it through revolt rather than through natural heritage. His uneasiness is increased by the report that the legitimate heir Héraclius, son of the Emperor Maurice, lives, not having been slain as a child by his governess, Léontine, at

---

†It might have shocked Corneille, a churchwarden and the translator of religious works (*Stabat Mater, De Imitatione Christi*), to be told that his Cleopatre represented "cosmic evil" or that this play answered to Borgerhoff's apt statement of the requirements of tragedy: "some sense of something unexplained, unfinished, cosmically disquieting even if ultimately believed to be just ... some intuition of evil which at times carries up into the source of good and renders imperfect a nonetheless deeply felt relationship between the metaphysical and the ethical world." *The Freedom of French Classicism*, p. 74. Borgerhoff properly notes in this same context the absence of such a "sense" in Corneille.

the father's behest. Rather, Léontine had substituted her own child, Léonce, for the Prince. The question to be solved is who is the real Héraclius: he who goes under the name of Martian and is believed to be Phocas' son, or he who goes under the name Léonce and believed to be Léontine's son. Léontine could reveal the whole truth, but she prefers to reveal it in parts so that Léonce, who is really Martian, son of Phocas, will slay the latter, thinking that he is acting as Héraclius, son of the usurped Maurice. Léontine will thereby be avenged for the slaying of her own son as an infant in order to preserve the line of legitimacy, Maurice-Héraclius. This piecemeal revelation plus other "evidence" leads to Léonce's hoped-for mistake and, thereby, to his supposedly incestuous relationship to Pulchérie, his beloved before the "identification," as well as to his arrest by Phocas. The real Héraclius makes a vain effort to identify himself and thereby spare his friend's life (which would be taken, however inadvertently, by his real father). Phocas cannot believe him and the matter is not cleared up until Exupère, a patrician of Constantinople, secretly harboring a desire for revenge on Phocas for his tyrannies and still loyal to Maurice, slays Phocas. The latter dead, Léontine produces a letter from the Empress proving "Martian" to be Héraclius and, implicity, "Léonce" to be Martian, so that Héraclius can wed Eudoxe, Léontine's daughter, and Martian can wed Pulchérie, Héraclius's sister.

In Phocas' and Martian's persistent inability to know themselves and in the real Héraclius' doubts following his early and assured knowledge of himself as the legitimate heir, Clifton Cherpack finds Corneille using the *cri du sang* as "a *'murmure imparfait'*" which pushes characters struggling for self-knowledge deeper into a morass of inner uncertainty where Will and Reason cannot help them, .... [Corneille thus makes] a significant psychological

motif of what is usually an expedient trick."* Cherpack
does well to show that Corneille's heroes are more than
mechanical monsters of will and reason, but we may
question whether the inner uncertainty is as pronounced
in one hero as in the other. Even before the "external
validation" of Héraclius as the legitimate heir, it is, as
Cherpack acknowledges, Martian who admits to being
finally uncertain as to his real identity. As so often before,
and as we shall see in subsequent Cornelian "mystery
stories," the hierarchy of *générosité* manifests itself in that
the highest born (or first born) is so recognized precisely
in the degree that he behaves as such a hero would. This
does not mean that he blindly follows destiny—as Cherpack notes, the *"murmure"* is *"imparfait."* However, the
action of the play is the *per*-fection or *real*-ization of the
*cri du sang*, of this derived sense of self. So it is in the
"machine play," *Andromède* (1649-50), in which the
identity of the heroic-appearing, wandering stranger is

---

* *The Call of Blood in French Classical Tragedy*, p. 53. In showing us
a more subtle psychologist than recent criticism would seem to allow in
Corneille, Cherpack's close reading of the plays is particularly useful.
However, Cherpack himself skims perhaps a little too quickly over lines
which might seem mere clichés of Corneille's period but which have a
profound bearing on just how "irrational" the *cri du sang* is in Corneille.
The *cri* is so often described as heaven-sent that one is puzzled by Cher-
pack's failure to comment on the connection. In three of the five quota-
tions Cherpack cites as evidence of instinctual love in Corneille, this
connection is made explicit: "Le coup en vient du ciel" (*Comédie des
Tuileries*, III, 2) ; "Souvent je ne sais quoi que le ciel nous inspire"
(*L'Illusion comique*, III, 1); and, the most telling for my own thesis of
"supernatural selection":
Et ce don fut l'effet d'une force imprévue,
De cet ordre du ciel que verse en nos esprits
Les principes secrets de prendre et d'être pris.
(Domitian in *Tite et Bérénice*, II, 2)
As for the role of "l'aveugle sympathie" which seems to make a mockery
of this "divine rightness of things" in the lovers of *Agésilas*, see my
analysis of the play below, pp. 231-238.

not revealed until he has rescued Andromède from the monster: he is the divinely derived Persée. Naturally—for this world—his feat leads to the further identification of Andromède herself as one destined to a heavenly marriage.

In *Don Sanche* (1650), too, the central theme is identity. However, the way in which the theme is developed differs from that used in preceding "mystery stories." Ever ready to renew himself, Corneille does not here ask "what is a hero?" as in *Le Menteur* through *Théodore,* nor "who is the hero?" as in *Héraclius* and *Andromède.* Rather, he now asks "whence the hero?" To ask this question calls the very bases of the most recent Cornelian world into question more fundamentally than does: who is the hero? It is to return us to some of the perplexities and ambiguities of those plays based on: what is a hero? Through Alvar, Manrique, and Lope in this play, Corneille reminds us of the assumption of the great political plays that only the nobly born can do noble deeds, that handsome does as handsome is. But their formulation of this concept rings hollow against the fomulation of the opposite concept by the character whom they themselves admit to be of greater prowess:

> CARLOS: Se pare qui voudra des noms de ses aïeux:
> Moi, je ne veux porter que moi-même en tous lieux;
> Je ne veux rien devoir à ceux qui m'ont fait naître,
> Et suis assez connu sans les faire connoître.
> Mais pour en quelque sorte obéir à vos lois,
> Seigneur, pour mes parents je nomme mes exploits:
> Ma valeur est ma race, et mon bras est mon père. (I, 3)

Like Rodrigue, Carlos is a law unto himself. He is the self-made man before whom even kings might tremble ... at least kings of the stamp of the Don Fernand of *Le Cid.*

Carlos proves to be Don Sanche of Aragon, however, so that here as in every play of this period the threat to the conventions of the canon to date is only seeming, a conjecture. The last-minute identification of Carlos as Sanche justifies his earlier assertions: only a king could talk as he did, only a king could lay down challenges to the Manriques, the Lopes, and the Alvars of this world. What was ambition on the lips of Carlos is *générosité* on the lips of Sanche. The identification clears up ambiguity and explains many a hesitation. Isabelle's mysterious confidence that heaven ("Le ciel") prompted her refusal of her well-born vassals is justified, and so is her mysterious ("secret") hesitation to carry out the vengeance of a queen upon hearing Carlos declare for Elvire. Alvar's deference to Carlos throughout now is seen for what it really is: not the cowardice of a rival suitor (for Elvire, in this case) but the adumbration of the respect Sanche's inherent worth demands. Finally, though it is not specifically justified in these or any other terms, Carlos' penchant for Elvire appears not as an unnatural but as a natural attraction of brother to sister—a characterization skillfully prepared for both by Carlos' hesitation between Elvire and Isabelle and by Elvire's otherwise mysterious penchant for Alvar. Ultimately, everyone behaves and is seen to have behaved as his origins say he should behave. Class tells, birth shows, nature vindicates fortune, destiny becomes manifest, handsome does as handsome is.

The world of the play is ultimately the stable world of the great political plays. Indeed, it is even more stable, for, with Carlos's identification as Sanche, the rigidity of the concept of *générosité* as it is applied to the setting in which the lovers work out their destiny exends to the relations between the lovers themselves and between the lovers and the world. And the character, Sanche, is not the self-made man he was as Carlos. In assuming kingship, Sanche no longer sounds those notes of pure self-assertion which distinguished Carlos, even though such notes might be described as the ultimate expression of kingship. The king has no need to *do;* like a poem, in the opinion of some critics, he has only to be.

In *Nicomède* (1651) we know what a hero is, who fills the role, and we know where he comes from: a hero is a man who conquers three kingdoms and stands up calmly and courageously to the growing power of Rome and the intrigues of a scheming stepmother. The man who behaves in this way is Nicomède, the true son of a true king and the legitimate heir to the throne of the kingdom in which the action of this play is situated. We are obviously back to the hero as he is identified in the great Roman plays.

Yet, *Nicomède* is the least "Roman" of the plays in which Rome figures prominently. The relation between the hero and Rome in this play is just the opposite of that of *Horace;* Nicomède is a hero not because he sees himself as Rome but precisely because he sees himself against Rome. Politically, the Empire functions in this play more like the baronial backdrop of *Le Cid:* it is a confederation of powers in which each member loses part of his sovereignty. But this time the confederation is much stronger, and Prusias is a weak king who has preferred to give in to the "warring barons" rather than to lean on the Rodrigue-like Nicomède. The world of this play, that is, is far more stable, giving far less room to the hero to move in than the world of *Le Cid* gave to Rodrigue. Nor is there, as there was for the Polyeucte who was similarly hemmed in, another realm to which the hero can turn in order to fulfill himself. Like Don Sanche, the hero can turn only to himself, turn the steel of his being against the steel of Rome.

And against the stealth of Arsinoé, the second queen of Prusias and so Nicomède's stepmother. It is the character of the queen that links this play with all those plays whose essential theme was one of identity—from *Le Menteur* to *Don Sanche*. Arsinoé is a Cleopatre: when Cléone reproaches her mistress for concealing from Attale her conspiracy with Rome to displace Nicomède in favor of Attale, Arsinoé replies:

> Je crains qu'en l'apprenant son coeur ne s'effarouche;
> Je crains qu'à la vertu par les Romains instruit
> De ce que je prépare il ne m'ôte le fruit,
> Et ne connoisse mal qu'il n'est fourbe ni crime
> Qu'un trône acquis par là ne rende légitime. (I, 5)

But there is no question of this Cleopatre-like mother being the heroine of the play. There is not that ambiguity about her motives from the very beginning found in the case of the queen-mother in *Rodogune*: Nicomède clearly indicates his knowledge of her intrigues in the first scene, as he tells Laodice about the false emissaries who, like Guildenstern and Rosencrantz in *Hamlet,* have been sent to spy on him. And when the queen-mother is surprised by Nicomède's announcement that he has brought one of her agents back with him, it is not to puzzle us about her real motives; quite the opposite, the enmity between the two is made overt as the queen's condemnation of her agent actually verifies for the spectator Nicomède's earlier characterization of her. Of course, we learn in the following scene that Métrobate's "betrayal" of the queen was arranged by the queen precisely to bring Nicomède back to the kingdom in order for her to implicate him still further with his father. Yet, this follow-up scene does not act like the "guarantee' scenes of the plays from *Le Menteur* through *Théodore*. Rather than "take back" a previous scene, the follow-up underscores the shrewdness of Arsinoé. The dramaturgy is much more direct in *Nicomède*. The heroes and the "villains" give themselves as such to their adversaries even as they do, for example, in *Cinna*.

This openness of motives, if not of devices, provides a measure of the hero's courage.

> NICOMÉDE: Prince, faites-moi voir un plus digne rival.
> Si vous aviez dessein d'attaquer cette place,
> Ne vous départez point d'une si noble audace;
> Mais comme à son secours je n'amène que moi,
> Ne la menacez plus de Rome ni du Roi:
> Je la défendrai seul, attaquez-la de même,
> Avec tous les respects qu'on doit au diadème.
> Je veux bien mettre à part, avec le nom d'aîné,
> Le rang de votre maître où je suis destiné;
> Et nous verrons ainsi qui fait mieux un brave homme,
> Des leçons d'Annibal, ou de celles de Rome.
> Adieu: pensez-y bien, je vous laisse y rêver. (I, 3)

Nicomède tells Attale (and Arsinoé, thereby) as he takes leave of his enemies after their first encounter. Nor is Nicomède without a certain shrewdness of his own. When his father threatens to place Attale on the throne to please his wife and in defiance of traditional rules of succession, Nicomède tells him:

> Me voyez-vous pour l'autre y renoncer moi-même?

Que cédé-je à mon frère en cédant vos Etats?
Ai-je droit d'y prétendre avant votre trépas?
Pardonnez-moi ce mot, il est fâcheux à dire,
Mais un monarque enfin comme un autre homme expire;
Et vos peuples alors, ayant besoin d'un roi,
Voudront choisir peut-être entre ce prince et moi.
   Seigneur, nous n'avons pas si grande ressemblance,
Qu'il faille de yeux pour y voir différence;
Et ce vieux droit d'aînesse est souvent si puissant,
Que pour remplir un trône il rappelle un absent.
Que si leurs sentiments se règlent sur les vôtres,
Sous le joug de vos lois j'en ai bien rangé d'autres;
Et dussent vos Romains en être encor jaloux,
Je ferai bien pour moi ce que j'ai fait pour vous. (IV, 3)

Thus Nicomède to his father, the king. Yet, it would be a mistake to see in the son's pronouncements a challenge to the *king,* an attack upon the concept of kingship like that implied in Carlos' "existentialist" self-sufficiency in *Don Sanche.* Nicomède provides the most memorable defense of kingship in the entire theater of Corneille. When Prusias tells Nicomède that the nomination of Attale as his successor will enable him to reconcile both love and nature, to be both a father and husband thereby, Nicomède tells him:

Seigneur, voulez-vous bien vous en fier à moi?
Ne soyez l'un ni l'autre.
Prusias: Et que dois-je être?
Nicoméde: Roi. (IV, 3)

The isolation of this single syllable is as poetically effective as old Horace's famous: "Qu'il mourût."

In saying that love and nature are separated and so must be reconciled through naming Attale, Prusias is once again testifying to the split between the private and the public, between natural love and love-as-honor, which we have frequently encountered in Corneille's plays, but which has not issued in the triumph of natural love since *Le Cid*. Yet, the split has never been very profound in the principal characters, in fact, since the hero and heroine of *Le Cid*: hero and heroine have chosen one another because it was only one another that their innate heroism could lead them to choose, and through the peripetia of the action each challenge only forced each lover to deepen his understanding of his inevitable choice of the other.* And so it is with Nicomède and Laodice. They are meant for each other and nothing can change their destiny. They do not, of course, have to read lessons to each other in the meaning of love-as-honor. Arsinoé's intrigues on behalf of Attale only drive them physically and spiritually closer together, if that were possible. For these lovers possess each other at the beginning of the action to an extent unique in the theater of Corneille thus far, so that this firm love is one of the components of the unshakable determination with which Nicomède confronts his enemies.

Who turn out not really to be his enemies. For as with all the characters of dubious reputation thus far—principal and secondary alike—and with the single exception of Cleopatre in *Rodogune,* this play too ends with the moral

---

*This necessary coincidence of love and honor is so persistent in the canon that Bénichou seems to be giving more his own than the Cornelian view of the relation when he writes: "tout ce qu'on écrit à son [Corneille] sujet sur l'amour d'estime n'empêche pas que l'élection amoureuse ne doive résulter de l'instinct." *Morales,* p. 41, n. 1. But Bénichou says earlier in the body of his book: "Il serait facile de montrer que Corneille lui aussi confond l'honneur et le coeur plus profondément qu'il ne les oppose, et que tout le mouvement du drame va, chez lui, de la division passagère de l'âme à la conscience retrouvée de son unité" (p. 38).

rehabilitation of those whose *générosité* has been compromised. The mode of the play is once again conjectural: the machinations of Arsinoé, the weakness of Prusias, the ambition of Attale fail to issue in the downfall of Nicomède. The Cornelian hero replies to the gravest threat yet to his sense of self not in the realm of private awareness of his superiority but in the public domain of manifest destiny. His enemies "knuckle under." Nicomède shows himself a king to others as well as to himself. In praising his hero in his own comments on the play ("Au lecteur" and the later "Examen") Corneille calls attention to the "grandeur de courage" which makes the hero look upon his misfortunes "d'un oeil si dédaigneux qu'il n'en sauroit arracher une plainte."[10] But the appearance must coincide with the reality, and Nicomède's moral triumph must be matched by a physical triumph.

At the same time it must remain moral—consistently *généreux*—and this means that the hero must win out over Arsinoé without resorting to her wiles. In the world of Arsinoé this very purity bids to defeat him. The wiles of Arsinoé being so very great, it must be by wile that she is bested; the resolution must come not from within Nicomède, for he has no such "inner dimension," so to speak (this does not mean he is without complexity—he is simply without duplicity). The solution must come from without, from another who is capable of such duplicity. And so it does: from Attale. Attale is the ineffectual suitor rendered effective—at the loss of some of his own *générosité*. But not an implausible loss according to the laws or values of the play: he is the *second* son of Prusias, born of an alliance with Arsinoé. His blood line, that is, allows of such "duplicity," though it is a duplicity, we must hasten to add, which is justified by the end he seeks: the restoration of the rights of his older brother. There is, of course, some danger in allowing such an important role to Attale, since his practical-mindedness in the world of the very practical-minded Arsinoé tends to cast his strait-laced brother in the role of the ineffectual principal, recalling the relationship between *damoiseau* and *confidant* in Corneille's early comedy. But once he has "betrayed" his mother and so enabled Nicomède to appear before the people (whose power gives him his real bargaining leverage with Arsinoé and Prusias in the final encounter), Nicomède must somehow regain the *"généreux* initiative." This he does by the gesture through which Auguste regained the initiative from the rebellious Emilie in *Cinna*: an act of pardon and a distribution of honors. And in this act of pardon we might even read what might be called a retroactive legitimation of Cleopatre: Arsinoé's machinations are justified as the legitimate ambitions of a mother for a son and are seen at worst as only misguided. Nicomède thus satisfies the mother even as he justifies her by awarding to Attale one of the many kingdoms which wait for Nicomède's conquering hand (there is, of course, no doubt that he will conquer them). In becoming a king Attale thus puts aside the "Romanism" which his education at Rome has understandably fostered. Indeed, the Romans themselves put aside their "Romanism," or, more precisely, can do nothing but put aside their "Romanistic" attempt to check the threat to the Empire represented by Nicomède's growing power. Nicomède's offer of friendship to Rome actually constitutes a reproach to the Empire, and Flaminius' reply places the Empire at worst in the role of dependent power in the "compact" of equals. At best, it reminds one of the Pascalian division of orders between the Christians and Sévère at the end of *Polyeucte*: it renders unto Nicomède the things that are Nicomède's and unto Caesar the things that are Caesar's. However, considering that Caesar wanted the things that were Nicomède's, this division of "orders" can itself only represent a defeat for Rome.

Or, to retain the mood of the play, a triumph for Nicomède. In this respect, the play reverses the relationship which obtained in *Rodogune* where, until the crucial moment of retraction in Rodogune's case and defiance in Cleopatre's, behavior was unemphatic and unkingly, while the emphatic behavior was found at best in the "secondary" twins. In *Nicomède,* the relationship is reminiscent of that of *Horace*: the hero is always hero and the final peripety of the play only provides the hero with the greatest occasion to show what he is made of. But there is not, as there was in *Horace*, a complete shift of dramatic interest (from young Horace to old Horace), a surrogate relationship between two characters. What little there is of this in the Nicomède-Attale relationship is quickly superseded by Nicomède's magnanimous clemency. And as for the displacement which old Horace's challenge to the king represented, that is neatly accounted for in this play by the fact that Nicomède is the son of a king, his legitimate heir. Finally, Prusias properly enough has the last word: an appropriately conventional deference to the gods as the sovereigns of all. The stable conceptions on which the play is based issue in a stable denouement.

Corneille tells us that he had conceived another denouement, one which we might characterize as less conventional: with Prusias and Flaminius not returning from their flight. However, says the playwright, the conventions of our theater demanded that all the principal characters appear on stage at the end of the action, and he followed this convention in spite of the fact that it falsified history (which reports that Nicomède had his father slain).[11] One feels in Corneille's justification of this treatment his ironic thrust at those who would hold him quite literally to historical truth: the theater has its own truth and this is just one more occasion for him to remind his literal-minded critics of this fact. But the denouement as it appears also serves other internal needs: it emphasizes the embarrassment of Rome, a fact which Corneille records as if apologizing for it. It also enables Prusias to rehabilitate himself in our eyes and so eliminate any doubt about his paternity of Nicomède. His return shows us the return of his courage and that he is not a "freak" in the world of kings. The father is worthy of the son and the integrity of the world of the play is ultimately more important that the integrity of historical fact. Not that Corneille might contentiously say with Valéry: "tout ce que l'histoire peut observer est insignifiant." [12] Corneille is falsifying history in this denouement as well as in the circumstances surrounding Annibal's death as reported in the play for dramatic purposes: in the denouement to preserve the integrity of the moral code of the world of the play and in the Annibal-Flaminius-Arsinoé relationship (1) metaphorically to link his hero with the renowned Annibal and (2) to measure the strength of the forces against which his hero tests himself.

There is nothing new in *Nicomède*. For once in praising a play Corneille does not take credit for *"nouveauté"* and *"invention."* He does, it is true, pridefully call attention to the fact that this is his twenty-first play and that after putting forty thousand verses "on the stage," it is rather difficult to be original—implying, one might reasonably assume, that he has nevertheless been original once again.[13] But to describe that originality in another of his favorite words, he characterizes certain aspects as *"extra-ordinaire."* And, as with *Don Sanche,* he calls attention less to the structure than to the texture of the play. His verse has not been so emphatic since the great political plays, and the elegiac note which carried the passional love themes of recent plays—a note which some describe as *précieux*—is largely absent.

Elegiac, introspective verse is relatively rare in the first version. It is present, to some extent, but Corneille only a few years later (1656, and again 1660) pruned the language in the direction of greater sobriety, directness, and stateliness. The lovers are more concerned with their public selves—or, since the dichotomy implied by that description does not really exist in this play, with the self which cannot conceive of any but a public recognition of its worth. Once again there is frequent use of language of ascendancy in Corneille: Nicomède and Laodice often reject various forms of *"bassesse,"* they refuse to be *reduced* in status (I, 1; II, 3). This concern with "ascend-ancy" is expressed negatively in the play, as in these scenes, but this is understandable in that, even more than Polyeucte, Nicomède is hemmed in by his enemies. Yet, the hero is in no way anxious and constrained in his behavior. This characterization belongs to his enemies. Where Nicomède confidently evokes the many realms he has already conquered and will conquer, his adversaries (the Roman emissaries) constantly try to hold the line or direct their attention to stabilizing their hold on a small kingdom. Where his tendency is outward, theirs is inward; where his language suggests firmness (the image of his strong arm—*bras*—is frequent), theirs suggests weakness and instability. This, of course, reflects their moral positions as well: Arsinoé and her cohorts work under cover, they break the "ordinary" laws of above-board behavior (I, 1); and they are fearful of ascendant motions (II, 1). Arsinoé, Prusias, and even Attale are often without self-possession:

> NICOMÉDE: Instruisez mieux le Prince votre fils,
> Madame, et dites-lui, de grâce, qui je suis:
> Faute de me connoître, il s'emporte, il s'égare;
> Et ce désordre est mal dans une âme si rare:
> J'en ai pitié. (I, 3)

The always self-possessed Nicomède and Laodice are thus unique in this world. Nicomède is an uncompromised hero in that neither his own deeds nor circumstances lead us to question his status as a *généreux*. Although the *structure* of events is melodramatic, melodramatic *characterization* is found more in the hero's adversaries than in himself. It is they who are *ambitieux* in this world. Nicomède is closer to Polyeucte than he is to Héraclius or Rodogune. As Ramon Fernandez has said, "il échappe à la tragédie par en haut."[14]

# 4

## Pertharite to Psyché

## l'amoureux

The questioning of the hero's heroism which began with *Le Menteur* reaches its most drastic stage in *Pertharite* (1652). Yet, the nature of the doubts cast on the identity of the hero are so different as to portend a new development in the canon; the doubts are no longer "external"—matters of circumstance; they are internal—matters of quality. The identity of the hero is doubted almost exclusively in deed. Identified as "roi des Lombards" in the *dramatis personae* and so treated by his wife in the opening scenes, Pertharite's deeds before the play begins have compromised him: he has been defeated by an inferior who has thereby usurped his throne. And when he returns to the scene, his "deeds" compromise him still further: he gives himself over without a struggle to his conqueror in order to plead for the return of his wife. Furthermore, as he does return to the scene, his identity is put into question quite literally: doubt is cast upon his claim to be the missing king,

Pertharite. But most importantly, the very *données* of his claim, like the situation of so many others in the play, show that as the play begins and, indeed, until its very last moments, the "laws of the world" of the previous plays are almost completely in abeyance.

For Pertharite's claim to the throne is only relatively superior to that of the usurper, Grimoald. Pertharite is the second son of the dead king Aripert and, as such, he acceded to the throne of Lombardy only after the death of his brother Gundebert. But this situation arose only after the brothers had fought over the kingdom their father had divided between them. Of course, the father had done this by way of acknowledging Pertharite's apparent worth:

> Il vit en Pertharite une âme trop royale
> Pour ne lui pas laisser une fortune égale;
> Et vit en Gundebert un coeur assez abjet
> Pour ne mériter pas son frère pour sujet. (I, 1)

This description of things shows the extreme slackness of this world, in such stark contrast to the world of, say, *Don Sanche,* in which action was arrested precisely because the code of *générosité* prevented a count from dueling with a fish-peddler's son. Here a king makes the mistake of dividing his kingdom among his sons, a mistake which the counselor not to a king but to a usurper (!) recognizes as unkingly:

> Ce mauvais politique avoit dû reconnoître
> Que le plus grand État ne peut souffrir qu'un maître,
> Que les rois n'ont qu'un trône et qu'une majesté,
> Que leurs enfants entre eux n'ont point d'égalité,
> Et qu'enfin la naissance a son ordre infaillible,
> Qui fait de leur couronne un point indivisible. (I, 1)

But this mistake only compounds destiny's mistake in having made the more worthy son the second born. Destiny has made other mistakes: it has located the soul of a supreme *généreux* in the person of a relatively low-born man. The most obvious evidence of this lies in Grimoald's military prowess, but lest, like the returned Pertharite, we attribute this to chance rather than destiny, Grimoald also shows himself to be *généreux* in the more important ways familiar to us ever since the *combats amoureux* of *Le Cid*: in his respect for himself and the corollary respect of the beloved *généreuse*. There is some question as to just who his beloved is, and as we shall see, this ambiguity compromises his *générosité* just as Pertharite's origins and behavior in another domain compromise his *générosité*. But even in his defection from Edüige for the sake of the widowed queen, we are shown signs of the usurper's curious preoccupation with a code of honor: "Ce n'est pas que longtemps il n'ait tâché d'éteindre / Un feu dont vos vertus avoient lieu de se plaindre" (I, 1). And when he does propose to Rodelinde he does so only because her husband is presumed dead. Such a personage wins the respect even of his enemies (I, 2) and, in what is perhaps the greatest testimoney to Grimoald's *générosité,* Rodelinde reminds us that her hate is objective, the kind of hate Cornélie pays the César of *Pompée*.

As for Grimoald's fickleness in love, it is real enough. For a long while he pursues the disdainful Edüige, but as soon as he becomes king he disdains her and pursues the queen Rodelinde. Yet, he holds off proposing to the queen until her husband is reported dead and, as for his rejection of Edüige, the fault lies more in his stars and in Edüige than in himself. He is worthy of her in every way but in birth, and in this fact he reads the motive for her disdain of him before he was king. There is perhaps some misunderstanding here; it is quite possible that Edüige really did refuse to marry him because of her*"amitié"* for the brother whom her lover pursued with enmity even as he pursued her with love. Like Rodelinde, Edüige is a *généreuse* such as those we have known in the previous plays, so that she could not subscribe easily to the division of the self which Grimoald's retort here implies. That she *understands* such a division (as Pauline or Emilie would not) is implied in her very love for a lesser-born creature; but her tergiversation over two years suggests some efforts to reconcile private felings (the penchant for Grimoald) with public duty (the *amitié* to her beleaguered brother, Pertharite). Of course, but for Grimoald's infidelity, circumstances have resolved this conflict. Pertharite is apparently dead, so that Edüige's private feelings could have coincided with her public responsibilities: she would then only be following her brother's orders.

Grimoald's motives are more to the point here. As indicated, there is in him that clear-cut split between the public and the private world, between natural love and political ambition which Edüige apparently tries to patch. At first, in his interview with Edüige, it appears that he is motivated solely by the private motives. He aided Gundebert and became a king, he tells her (as Unulphe earlier reported for us), as a means of winning Edüige. And even as he rejects her we might read in his disdain for Edüige here a demeaning vindictiveness, indeed, a petulance manifesting hurt pride. Yet, as his courtship of Rodelinde shows, the relationship between private and public self is somewhat more complicated. He would satisfy public ambition, but he would use love as the means of elevating himself. Speaking from that *généreux*

concept of love in which the private and the public self
are fused and according to which the heart goes only to
the noble, Rodelinde warns Grimoald that virtue alone
should dictate his behavior, that people will say he was
virtuous only because he loved a woman. He replies:

> Donnez-moi cette honte, et je la tiens à gloire:
> Faites de vos mépris ma dernière victoire,
> Et souffrez qu'on impute à ce bras trop heureux
> Que votre seul amour l'a rendu généreux. (II, 5)

Thus, not his love for Rodelinde, but her love for him
would make him a true *généreux*: it would repair destiny's
mistake. Love will do for him what birth did for other
kings. It is because he has become a king, and this
due to his *deeds,* that Grimoald feels he has the *right* to
demand Rodelinde. Such a reparation is incomprehensible
to Rodelinde. In stressing his status as a self-made king,
Grimoald only reminds Rodelinde (and us) that he cannot
coerce destiny to reverse itself: he is not a king born and
so he can make no claims on Rodelinde. Up to this point,
the means he would use to force Rodelinde's (and
destiny's) hand are honorable, a fact which only stresses
the pathos of his situation. But now he decides to use less
honorable means: he allows Garibalde to threaten the life
of Rodelinde's son. The fact that he does not do it directly
himself, that he proposes it chiefly as a device and that
ultimately circumstances prevent its actual carrying out,
does, of course, mitigate to a certain extent the compromise of Grimoald's honor.

The decision to use such a threat is itself demeaning,
a way of showing the "king's" character. It also stresses the
role of Rodelinde, giving her one of the great moments

of Corneille's theater. In this character a tendency (perhaps an important clue for those reading with a view to the author's psychology) of Corneille's theater evident from the earliest comedies is realized: the location of pure heroism or *générosité* in the principal female character. If *Le Cid* might, as Faguet suggested, have been properly called *"Chimène,"* this play might have been called *"Rodelinde."* Of course, Corneille had given in to this tendency before (notably in *Médée* and *Rodogune*), but in those two plays the heroine was not consistently *généreuse*: her self-sufficiency was without honor. But in Rodelinde we have a *généreuse avant la lettre*. Even what seems the most flagrant derogation from *générosité*, her own proposal to kill her son, provides the proof of her sense of honor: she will only be anticipating, she says, his ultimate fate, and better it be by her hand than by the hand of less worthy people. Here is a projected transcendence of material condition which not even Polyeucte achieves (heaven, we remember, was to him just another kingdom, more visible than invisible). And the material conditions in which Rodelinde finds herself are the most inhibiting which any Corneille character has had to confront to date. With Théodore, Rodelinde shares the distinction of being the only principal character who is a physical prisoner that Corneille has thus far put on the stage. (Cornélie in *Pompée* was a "prisoner"—but one almost immediately released by her captor.) As Voltaire noted, Rodelinde's status as prisoner anticipates that of Racine's *Andromaque*:[1] she finds herself obliged to forego loyalty to her dead husband Pertharite (Hector) for the sake of her captor Grimoald (Pyrrhus) at the risk of losing her infant son. But the characterization is no more Racinian than it was in the "pre—Racinian" situation of

the lovers of *Nicomède*. But it is hard to speak of "les
larmes de Rodelinde" as one does of "les larmes d'Andromaque." The gravity of her situation simply provides an
occasion for measuring the heroism of Rodelinde:

> Puisqu'il faut qu'il périsse, il vaut mieux tôt que tard;
> Que sa mort soit un crime, et non pas un hasard;
> Que cette ombre innocente à toute heure m'anime,
> Me demande à toute heure une grande victime;
> Que ce jeune monarque, immolé de ta main,
> Te rende abominable à tout le genre humain;
> Qu'il t'excite partout des haines immortelles;
> Que de tous tes sujets il fasse des rebelles.
> Je t'épouserai lors, et m'y viens d'obliger,
> Pour mieux servir ma haine, et pour mieux me venger,
> Pour moins perdre de voeux contre ta barbarie,
> Pour être à tous moments maîtresse de ta vie,
> Pour avoir l'accès libre à pousser ma fureur,
> Et mieux choisir la place à te percer le coeur. (III, 3)

Spirit, as Lionel Trilling has said in another connection,
would free itself completely from the contingent.[2]

Rodelinde's uncompromising *générosité* makes her
unique among the principals of the play thus far. Pertharite's return at this very moment in no way imperils this
uniqueness. Indeed, measured not only against his wife as
the guarantor of value in the play but literally *by* his wife
in that role, he is the least *généreux* of the principals, with
the exception of the scheming Garibalde.

Or at least he is so judged according to the first version
—a fact which is obvious in the following:

> Je cède à leurs [the subjects] désirs, garde mon diadème,
> Comme digne rançon de cette autre moi-même;

Laisse-moi racheter Rodelinde à ce prix,
Et je vivrai content malgré tant de mépris.
Tu sais qu'elle n'est pas du droit de ta conquête;
Qu'il faut, pour être à toi, qu'il m'en coûte la tête:
Garde donc de mêler la fureur des tyrans
Aux brillantes vertus des plus grands conquérants;
Fais voir que ce grand bruit n'est point un artifice,
Que ce n'est point à faux qu'on vante ta justice,
Et donne-moi sujet de ne plus m'indigner
Que mon peuple en ma place aime à te voir régner. (III, 4)

In political terms, the original version presents the most "compromised" *généreux* Corneille has ever put on the stage—and one compromised *in fact* by his own estimate of his situation, a situation which is itself a reality and not merely, as so often before, a conjecture. His very motive for return in this original version betrays that thoroughgoing split between the private self and the public self which we have heretofore found real in secondary characters or only as a finally unrealized possibility in principal characters. Here is a Corneille "hero" for whom love is all—and not love in the same sense we have just examined in the Grimoald-Rodelinde relationship: a means of acquiring (or here reacquiring) the values usually conferred by birth in the Cornelian universe. Rather, this hero bargains away his throne—or since he is not really in a position to bargain, he does what is worse: he argues that the throne has no value once it is lost and that he wishes only to salvage his love. He even recognizes the influence of the people, rejecting the usual characterization of them as at best a mob ("une foule importune"). His only appeal to the concepts of *générosité*—that Grimoald act nobly rather than as a tyrant—is invoked not as an end in itself but as a piece of moral blackmail in order that Pertharite might have the woman

for whom he has returned. This, of course, is precisely
the misunderstanding of his station which Rodelinde saw
in Grimoald's plea for her love. Is it any wonder, then,
that in the first version she replied:

> Non, c'est un imposteur,
> Il en a tous les traits, et n'en a pas le coeur;
> . . . . . . . . . . . . . . . . . .
> Ses discours à son rang font une perfidie . . . (III, 4)

As a confrontation with the final version shows, Corneille attempted as much as possible to save face for his
compromised hero when he returned to the play after
1656. The revision of Pertharite's first long reply to
Grimoald shifts the emphasis from the pathos of the
defeated and pleading Pertharite to the virtues of the
acting king, Grimoald. (This might also implicitly stress
Pertharite's own virtue inasmuch as it shows a continuing
preoccupation with such values.) Furthermore, the revision denies the irrevocability of Pertharite's defeat which
is so apparent both in the explicit statements and in the
tone of the original. In the revision, his defeat is a matter
of fortune: "Peut-être un autre temps me rendra des
amis. / Use mieux cependant de la faveur céleste" (III, 4);
and his failure to find a single ally to succor him is not
mentioned (the very mention of this dependence in the
original compromised the hero and stood in embarrassing
contrast to Rodelinde's solitary defiance of the forces
which crowded in upon her). Finally, in the revision, the
hero lays down a direct personal challenge to the acting
king, thereby putting himself in the position assumed
earlier by Rodelinde in her quarrel with Grimoald: he
shifts the burden of defense to his opponent.

For the play to continue, of course, the question of the

newcomer's identity must be left open in the revision, as it was in the original. In the original it is credible that there be some doubt as to the identity. Not in the spectator's mind, of course: Rodelinde's recognition of the physical resemblance is proof enough. But, on the other hand, in the terms in which he has been presented, Grimoald's suspicion of her motives is equally convincing. He is incapable of understanding the unity between appearance and reality whose lack she deplores. Furthermore, in implying that she would use the newcomer whatever his identity, he betrays his misunderstanding of the code of *générosité* as it applies not only to the newcomer's behavior but to her own. In the revision, the strengthening of Pertharite's character precisely in the direction sought by the indignant Rodelinde (of the first version) dictated changes in her own reply to Grimoald's demand that she identify him. Corneille might have had her identify her husband directly, but this would have had the disadvantage of calling the spectator''s attention to the husband, and no amount of "beefing up" of his character could hide the fact that he is in the hands of his conqueror. That is, Pertharite's physical dependency would have been emphasized. Of course, as with Rodelinde, this very dependency might have been the occasion for a rehabilitation of Pertharite's character at this point—instead of in the concluding moments of the play as originally written.

This is to say that Corneille would have had to rewrite the play completely. But, because of the very conception of Grimoald's character in the original, so drastic a revision was not necessary. Corneille simply expanded the suspiciousness of his character, used it as a way of carrying the attack back to him, an attack which shifts much of the moral onus of the situation from the captive Pertharite to his captor. The latter's very suspiciousness contrasts with the openness of the behavior of Pertharite (in the revised version). This suspiciousness does not of itself necessarily demean him. Indeed, following consistently from the original characterization, it simply remains a neutral basis of contrast to the (revised) emphatic character of Pertharite. If Grimoald continues to derogate from the ideal *généreux* behavior it is not in his understandable suspicions; it is rather in the action he takes on the basis of those suspicions—for example, his bargaining with Edüige where he implies that he will return her love once again if she will name the impostor.

Corneille can shift the onus of un-*généreux* behavior only so far onto Grimoald and his scheming lieutenant, Garibalde. The *donnée* of the play remains there to haunt him in his revisions: Pertharite is a defeated *généreux* and returns to the scene of defeat only as a lover to recover his mistress, not as a king his throne; the husband his wife, not the king his queen. No amount of defiant challenge can obscure this fact—indeed, the challenge to a personal duel is aimed only at winning the hand of the beloved. Corneille can omit further reminders of the *précieux,* lachrymose Pertharite of the original version, as in his omission of Grimoald's puzzled reflections about the return (beginning of Act IV). But the confrontation of Rodelinde and Pertharite cannot be avoided and during it somehow the fundamental relation between the public and the private self must be resolved in one of three ways: in favor of the public self (the choice of Grimoald); in favor of the private self (the choice of Pertharite of the original version); or in the paradoxical fusion of the two (the position of Rodelinde).

The events leading to this key confrontation are essentially the same in both versions: Pertharite defies Grimoald. Consistent with previously discussed revisions, Pertharite's accents are more emphatic in these antecedent versions, but the really significant revisions do not occur until husband and wife are left alone. As noted earlier, Rodelinde's specific recognition of her husband ("Je connois mon époux . . .") can only lead to Grimoald's impugning of her motives, but, more important from a dramatic and moral point of view, it only underscores the discrepancy which exists between the basic positions of husband and wife. In both versions, Pertharite's famous "Il est temps de tourner du côté du bonheur" makes a mockery of his defiance of Grimoald in the immediately preceding scene. The revision attempts to attenuate this effect in two important respects. The first of these is in the by now familiar strengthening of Pertharite's character. He is given the first speech in the new Act V, and its import is to stress his return as an exceptionally courageous act performed in the face of great hazards. The second means by which Corneille attempts to rehabilitate Pertharite is by softening the character of Rodelinde. At the beginning of her new first reply the tone of exhortation and affirmation gives way to one of elaborate regret (lines 1399-1404) and almost mincing self-satisfaction. This inevitably dilutes the accents of affirmation and exhortation when Corneille does finally return to them in her speech: "mon amour généreux" becomes "l'amour que j'ai pour vous," and where in the original the emphasis was completely upon her responsibility to herself, in the revision she speaks of Pertharite's "malheurs" rather than her own "douleur." In short, she sounds much more like a woman with a female psychology than like the paradox she herself stressed in the original version: a woman in whose "coeur de femme" an *amour généreux* . . . "a su s'affermir." This shift shows itself again in Rodelinde's:

Est-ce là donc, Seigneur, la digne récompense
De ce que pour votre ombre on m'a vu de constance? (IV, 5)

Where in the original Rodelinde immediately reminded her husband of her "résistance," the revised Rodelinde speaks more the language of courtship: "récompense." The shift in tone which this semantic aspect of the verse reveals is further revealed in the very rhythm of the verse. Where the original verse showed an uninterrupted rhythm and a logical, emphatic, and argumentative tone ("donc"), the revision is interrupted by the longer pause as the character turns from her concern with herself and her inner logic to caress the lover whom she "reproaches" with a deferential "Seigneur." The revision tends to make of the *combat désamoureux* much more of a *combat amoureux* like those of Rodrigue and Chimene, of Sévère and Pauline, albeit here a somewhat sweeter one. Of course, Corneille retains the essential fact of the original: Pertharite's proposal that Rodelinde give herself to Grimoald. In each version there is the projected sacrifice of Pertharite's life, but in the original we are reminded still again of Rodelinde's ideal *générosité*: her identification of kingship and heroism, of public behavior and private motive—the familiar conception that she loves a king not *because* he is a king but *in that* he is a king.

In the original it is precisely this view of their relationship which Pertharite rejects. As he tells his wife that he would have given up an even higher throne, he sounds patronizing toward the old conception. He seems to be advising her to marry Grimoald simply because she cannot rise to this new conception of love as something superior to the throne. Of course, in saying that love is superior to the throne, Pertharite is not repeating Grimoald's desire to raise himself to a higher station in life; love in this instance is not replacing birth but surpassing it. Nor, in the manner of Rodrigue and Chimene is love the domain in which their innate *générosité* manifests itself. Love is not the same as duty, love is not overcoming duty—love is beyond duty. We have thus a reversal of the value relations as they are usually thought of in Cornelian criticism. In the terms of that criticism, love is now the higher value and duty the lesser value.

Whether the new higher value would have actually triumphed in its conflict with the lesser value as represented in Rodelinde's refusal to accept her husband's suicide and its concomitant "surrender" of her to Grimoald—all this remains unsettled as the play works out, with Grimoald renouncing his claims both upon Pertharite's kingdom and Pertharite's wife. But certainly since this denouement holds in both the original and the revised versions, the presentation of private love as a higher value remains a bothersome feature of the play if we take as the rule the paradox of love-as-honor in the political tetralogy. In such a context, it remains an aspect of the action which cannot be retroactively justified by the outcome of events as so many bothersome features of previous plays are (for example, the behavior of the real Héraclius until the moment of firm identification). But love-as-honor is precisely one of the "commitments" which are suspended in the play.

The revisions of the play, do, of course, square better with previous denouements. In the present instance, for example, the revised verses do rehabilitate Pertharite as a *généreux* in precisely the terms desired by his wife. There is no more talk about the superiority of love over the throne; rather, the throne is evoked as the *only* value in question and his death as the means to reacquire it for his wife. The fact that he does not resolve to regain the throne himself cannot be gainsaid, but at least he does show an ideal respect for the throne and there is even the implication that his death will represent not a loss or a defeat, but a supreme triumph, inasmuch as his own glory will be "transmigrated" to his wife. Indeed, according to verse 1449 during the years 1660-64,* the transmigration would be to Grimoald himself, but this revision suggests a contradiction of the sense of the other revisions: a pure, noble soul of a born *généreux* could be transferred to his legitimate spouse, but could not be transferred to the low-born soul which had usurped its own physical "owner."

Whether transferred to herself or to Grimoald, Rodelinde will have none of such a proposal: to marry Grimoald under such circumstances would be a betrayal of her honor. This is to be expected of Rodelinde. If the play is to retain any of its moral consistency and thereby its source of conflict, Corneille cannot revise her character in any significant way; indeed, his radical revisions of Pertharite's character depend precisely on the fundamental consistency of her *généreux* position. But in the face of such adamancy, he must continue to "adjust" the character of Pertharite and so, where this confrontation ended in the first version with Rodelinde's refusal to listen to such a proposition, in the revision Pertharite is allowed to argue:

---

*"Pour briller avec gloire, il lui faut mon trépas."

Non, Madame,
Il ne faut point souffrir se scrupule en votre âme.
Quand ces devoirs communs ont d'importunes lois,
La majesté du trône en dispense les rois:
Leur gloire est au-dessus des règles ordinaires,
Et cet honneur n'est beau que pour les coeurs vulgaires.
Sitôt qu'un roi vaincu tombe aux mains du vainqueur,
Il a trop mérité la dernière rigueur.
Ma mort pour Grimoald ne peut avoir de crime:
Le soin de s'affermir lui rend tout légitime.
Quand j'aurai dans ses fers cessé de respirer,
Donnez-lui votre main, sans rien considérer:
Epargnez les efforts d'une impuissante haine,
Et permettez au ciel de vous faire encor reine. (IV, 5)

Rodelinde might easily pick her husband up on these doctrines for derogating from the concept of *génė-rosité,* this time in the opposite direction. The proposition that kings are laws unto themselves even to the point of denying obligations towards other noble-born persons has been held by very few other Cornelian kings—so far, in fact, only by Médée and Cleopatre—and in those two cases at least it was "first-born kings" who were defending the proposition *as it applied to themselves.* Here, true enough, it is a proposition being defended by a king born, but applied to a king born a second son, "out of line" that is.

Yet the possibility of this development remains as un-realized in the revised play as the possibility of private love's exclusive triumph in the original play. The denoue-ment avoids the issue (or issues) of the play. The final confrontation between Pertharite and Grimoald after the former's escape from Garibalde is the occasion of one final extensive revision by Corneille. Extensive as this revision is, it does not involve the major shifts in conception of the earlier. In the original, Pertharite is still somewhat subservient to the acting king, but his actual escape puts him in a far different position than in his earlier confrontations with that character. The revision makes his own self-definition as a king more explicit and less abstract than the *account* of his escape in the original. Matching Pertharite's *générosité* in deed (original version) and in word and deed (revised version) is Grimoald's abdication of his illegally obtained throne precisely because it is illegally obtained:

> Mais c'est trop retenir ma vertu prisonnière:
> Je lui dois comme à toi liberté toute entière;
> Et mon ambition a beau s'en indigner,
> Cette vertu triomphe, et tu t'en vas régner.
>   Milan, revois ton prince, et reprends ton vrai maître,
> Qu'en vain pour t'aveugler j'ai voulu méconnoître;
> Et vous que d'imposteur à regret j'ai traité . . . (V, 5)

In such a gesture the world of this play is moved towards its "proper" bases: Pertharite's loss of his throne is treated as a matter of fortune and not of destiny. This admission by the usurper, coupled with Pertharite's courageous escape from Garibalde, suggests that retroactively the identity of the newcomer was validly put in question by Rodelinde as well as by Grimoald, albeit on different grounds in each case. Indeed, Grimoald's grounds were in part those of Rodelinde, for he could not see any better than she how a hero-king could behave as the newcomer did upon his return.

However, the universe is still not completely restored to the ethos of the earlier plays in which each man knows his place, where handsome does as handsome is, where high-born "instinctively" falls in love with high-born. Even as he recognizes the *générosité* of this adbication, Pertharite refuses to follow suit:

> Ah!, c'est porter trop loin la générosité.
> Rendez-moi Rodelinde, et gardez ma couronne,
> Que pour sa liberté sans regret j'abandonne:
> Avec ce cher objet tout destin m'est trop doux. (V, 5)

Not that he refuses to be *généreux*. Rather he reasserts the superiority of private love over public status, and there is something patronizing in this refusal of Grimoald's offer even as there was in his earlier proposal to give Rodelinde to Grimoald as a way of satisfying not *his* private feelings and *his* public duty, but *his* private feelings and *her* public duty. Viewed in the perspective of the political tetralogy, the basic issue of the play is, then, still in doubt here. Of course, the proposal made by Pertharite would spare Grimoald from a tragic destiny. But in abdicating the kingdom Grimoald reminds us that destiny has located great virtue in a low station and, time being what it is, the fact of order is irrevocable. In earlier plays, Grimoald would turn out to be the son of a neighboring king, or in a still better solution, he would be able to conquer a kingdom "on his own." But kingship has been posed chiefly in metaphysical, not practical terms throughout this play and so the evocation of other worlds to conquer —though suggestive of the real ending—would be too "outside" a possibility. The concept of *générosité* as finally defended by Grimoald and as constantly defended by Rodelinde throughout the play remains imperiled from two sources: from Pertharite's assertion of the primacy of private love and in Grimoald's proposal itself, indicating as it does the tragic discrepancy between his worth and his birth.

However, the challenges to the ideal of *générosité* which these developments point up are simply sidestepped as both Pertharite and Grimoald become kings, the former of Milan, the latter of Pavie. Whether of Milan or of all of Lombardie, as king, Pertharite is once again worthy of Rodelinde's love—which is to say, her love-as-honor, the only kind she knows. As for his own private love, this *can* coincide with his occupancy of the throne. As for Grimoald, destiny has perhaps not been so cruel after all. The "outside possibility" which the very *données* of the play suggested becomes a reality. There were two thrones, so that he can accede to the throne of Pavie, left vacant by Pertharite's brother. Indeed, he is apparently a more worthy occupant than that absent character was, and there is even a legitimation of his ascendancy in that he is following the order of a king in marrying the person whom that king named the legal heir to the throne, Edüige. This commitment takes precedence over the commitment which obtained in the serious plays to date, whether in a persistent or in an ultimate way. Doubts about Pertharite's patronizing attitude toward the purely political connotations of *générosité,* the cleavage between himself and Rodelinde which this attitude suggests, Grimoald's self-made character, the ups and downs of Edüige's fate—all these doubts are disengaged in the neat pairings of the lovers and the double ascension to kingship with which the play romantically concludes.

Corneille has played around with his usual concepts in a new and, apparently for his contemporaries, annoying way. The play failed—right upon the heels of the resound-

ing success of *Nicomède*. Perhaps the nearness of that play
had much to do with the failure, for it stressed the stable
values of the world of all his previous plays and, in this
artist desirous to please his audience, the values of the
spectators. This interpretation, I am aware, is counter to
that of a leading school of Corneille commentators: that
*Pertharite* presented a reaffirmation of the "ethos of the
hero and glory" at a time when these values had been
seriously compromised by the developments of the
Fronde.[3] It would be difficult to state the precise relationship between the play and the circumstances surrounding it, but an examination of the play itself hardly
suggests a reaffirmation of the ethos of the hero and glory.
Not that the theme is absent from the play. In fact, in the
person of Rodelinde, it is the measuring rod, the guarantor of values within the world of the play, as I have
said. But as such it serves as a theme to be varied, not as
some ethical dictum according to which the public was
to behave before the events of the Fronde. And inasmuch
as the variations on the theme wound up almost completely diluting the theme, it might be suggested that the play
failed not because it reaffirmed the ethos of glory and
heroism but precisely because it appeared to vitiate it.*

*Oedipe* (1659) is at once a continuation and a break
with the Cornelian canon to date. As in the tetralogy,
one of the central themes of the play is political *générosité*, the demands of a code of honor as they are *demon-
strated* in a hero. As in the plays just before Corneille's

---

*And so perhaps represented too radical a departure for a public
which Corneille had led to expect something very different. It is because
it is such a departure that I do not follow the practice of locating
*Pertharite* in a chronological grouping based on Corneille's great "silences,"
or on the relation of the play to its historical sources. See, for example,
Lawrence Melville Riddle, *The Genesis of and Sources of Pierre Corneille's Tragedies from "Médée" to "Pertharite."*

long "silence," another key theme is that of identity—
which means that to a certain extent the play is based on
a *testing* of a hero, or, of necessity, of two or more characters vying for the name of hero. Now, heretofore these
two antithetical means of defining the hero have theoretically implied two different modes of dramaturgy: a
deductive (the hero is a certain essence, he can only
show forth this essence), or an inductive (the hero makes
himself, the actions prove the man). As we have seen, the
second of these dramaturgies was always conjectural: in
the denouement, whenever there was a question of a
hero's identity, he was shown to have acted heroically only
because he had in fact been born a hero (or king). Essence
really did precede existence. The real, the underlying
premise of plays like *Le Menteur* or *Héraclius* was the
same as that of the great political plays. In *Oedipe* the two
modes are still present, but one does not so much overlay
the other as follow it. Corneille once again treats the
theme of identity as if he were answering the purely
external question: *who* (or *which one*) is the hero?
But ultimately he must answer the questions which
Sophocles posed in first treating the subject of Oedipus:
what is the meaning of his destiny?

Corneille obviously continues the inquiries of *Héraclius* and *Don Sanche* and *Pertharite*. But his answers carry
out certain directions of those previous inquiries in such
a way as to mark the different direction in his thought I
first traced in *Pertharite*. In Thésée's first words we can
note that split between the private self and the public
self, between love and honor which has become increas-
ingly pronounced in the later plays:

La gloire d'obéir n'a rien qui me soit doux,
Lorsque vous m'ordonnez de m'éloigner de vous.

> Quelque ravage affreux qu'étale ici la peste,
> L'absence aux vrais amants est encor plus funeste; (I, 1)

By itself the first verse, for example, might be said to be the very expression of *générosité* as it was worked out by Horace or by Polyeucte, but here it is only one part, the subordinate part, of an elaborate conceit placing the public image at the service of the private emotion. Such accents have been sustained by other *généreux* as I have noted—but not by other *généreuses*. In spite of the dangers to her blood relatives,

> [Et] mon cœur toutefois ne tremble que pour vous,
> Tant de cette frayeur les profondes atteintes
> Repoussent fortement toutes les autres craintes! (I, 1)

Dircé tells her beloved Thésée after the latter refuses her exhortation to escape. Heroes who place love above all *and* heroines who urge their lovers to flee danger—the combination is new. As Thésée tells Oedipe (when the latter would have the prince marry one of his daughters):

> Si vous avez aimé, vous avez su connoître
> Que l'amour de son choix veut être le seul maître;
> Que s'il ne choisit pas toujours le plus parfait,
> Il attache du moins les cœurs au choix qu'il fait;
> Et qu'entre cent beautés dignes de notre hommage,
> Celle qu'il nous choisit plaît toujours davantage. (I, 2)

The old syntheses no longer hold: it is now conceivable that destiny mismatch lovers, that a high-born fall in love with a lesser born and that all virtue (including its manifest sign, physical beauty) not be located in a single character. Combinations are possible among the three ingredients which were heretofore inseparable and indistinguishable: station, behavior, and physical appearance.

It is true that the old paradoxes of love-as-honor are heard in the play, especially on the lips of the heroine (as far back as Rodrigue, the hero has followed the example of the heroine). Thus, when Oedipe demands as king that his "stepdaughter" obey him and marry Aemon, Dircé warns this king she regards as a usurper:

> Mais si vous attentez jusqu'à me commander,
> Jusqu'à prendre sur moi quelque pouvoir de maître,
> Je me souviendrai lors de ce que je dois être;
> Et si je ne le suis pour vous faire la loi,
> Je le serai du moins pour me choisir un roi.
> Après cela, Seigneur, je n'ai rien à vous dire:
> J'ai fait choix de Thésée, et ce mot doit suffire. (II, 1)

Such a formulation of her relationship with Thésée suggests that her choice of that hero simply follows automatically from her station. But when she is confronted by her lover, neither she nor he can respond to the stern demands of *générosité*, whether those involve the paradox of supreme spiritual possession in physical separation or the rejection of the paradox, a split into its components, with higher value residing in the sense of honor. Thus, before the end of the first scene from which I have quoted above, Thésée tells his mistress: 'J'aurois en ma faveur le courage bien bas, / Si je fuyois des maux que vous ne fuyez pas" (I, 1), and he promises to die by his own hand should she not survive the plague. As in the *combats amoureux* of earlier plays this is interpreted as an insult to her own sense of honor, and she reads a lesson in *générosité* to her lover:

> It faut qu'en vos pareils les belles passions
> Ne soient que l'ornement des grandes actions.
> Ces hauts emportements qu'un beau feu leur inspire
> Doivent les élever, et non pas les détruire;
> Et quelque désespoir que leur cause un trépas,
> Leur vertu seule a droit de faire agir leurs bras. (I, 1)

Yet, as Thésée retorts and Dircé does not deny: "Ah! Madame, vos yeux combattent vox maximes: / Si j'en crois leur pouvoir, vos conseils sont des crimes" (I, 1).

This first confrontation of the lovers sets the pattern, in fact, for all subsequent confrontations: the stern implications of *générosité* are invoked only finally to be denied. Thus, at the end of Act II, Dircé confronts Thésée once again with the need for her death as the designated victim of the oracle. She then invokes his own heroic deeds as the pattern of that which she seeks in her self-sacrifice, arguing that such a death will make her "digne du grand Thésée," urging him to follow her example by living for the public even as she dies for it. He carries his plea for private values even further than the Pertharite of the original version:

> Périsse l'univers, pourvu que Dircé vive!
> Périsse le jour même avant qu'elle s'en prive!
> Que m'importe la perte ou le salut de tous?
> Ai-je rien à sauver, rien à perdre que vous?
> Si votre amour, Madame, étoit encor le même, (II, 4)

Duty is no longer a lesser value; it is a nonvalue and, to the extent that it imperils the value of love, an antivalue. Such stern denials of public value force the beloved of this *combat amoureux* not to a higher stage of *générosité* but to the actual refutation of that ideal. Reminding her lover of the ravages of the plague, Dircé begs of him:

Laissez-moi me flatter de cette triste joie
Que si je ne mourois vous en seriez la proie,
Et que ce sang aimé que répandront mes mains,
Sera versé pour vous plus que pour les Thébains. (II, 4)

The public motive is only the guise for satisfying the personal. This revelation appears to shock Thésée precisely as a *généreux,* but in the context of his previous condemnation of public duty, the dynamics of *générosité* have now been turned completely inward and there is even good reason to believe that this appeal to the demands of the code is designed precisely as a stratagem to prevent Dircé from sacrificing herself. Thésée's further appeal in this very scene suggests this strong sentimental (as well as a muted sensual) basis:

La gloire de ma mort n'en deviendra pas moindre;
Si ce n'est vous sauver, ce sera vous rejoindre:
Séparer deux amants, c'est tous deux les punir;
Et dans le tombeau même il est doux de s'unir. (II, 4)

It is undoubtedly this kind of language which contemporary critics of Corneille reproached as *"précieux,"* but what strikes one in the perspective of Corneille's long career is the persistence of a sensual strain. Rather than representing a departure from a "Cornelian" style of grandeur and sobriety, such a strain here represents a return to an earlier lyrical and elegiac style.* Of course,

---

* Crétin contends that "dès qu'il [Corneille] songe à un objet, son esprit intervient pour en éliminer toutes les qualitès sensibles, à l'exception du mouvement. Cette élimination se fait sans effort: less couleurs et les formes restant chez lui à l'arrière-plan de la conscience, il lui est facile de les oublier." *Les Images dans l'oeuvre de Corneille,* p. 324. This is generally true, especially of the final versions of the plays. But there are significant exceptions. Morover, Crétin tends to ignore the dramatic context of this "abstract, emblematic" language: for example, the "bedroom scene" of *Clitandre* or Rodrigue before Chimene with the sword which has slain her father.

such a style here has none of the concreteness and spice of the original versions of love scenes in *Clitandre* or even *Le Cid*. Be that as it may, Thésée's appeal, however muted its sensual bases be, does strip away the last vestige of "love-as-honor" in Dircé and she tells him to flee because

> La gloire de ma mort est trop douteuse ici;
> Et je hasarde trop une si noble envie
> A voir l'unique object pour qui j'aime la vie. (II, 4)

and therefore ". . . il est temps de fuir quand on se défend mal." And that Thésée also drops the implications of *générosité* becomes clear in his speech closing the interview and the act:

> Le véritable amour ne prend loi de personne;
> Et si ce fier honneur s'obstine à nous trahir,
> Je renonce, Madame, à vous plus obéir. (II, 4)

Act III opens with *stance*s by Dircé reminiscent of Rodrigue's "debate with himself" at the end of the first act of *Le Cid*. Like Rodrigue, Dircé resolves the conflict between love and duty in favor of duty, but with far less conviction than Rodrigue. We recall that he had begun with the vision of his beloved as *promesse de jouissance* and had concluded with *himself* as *objet d'estime*. Dircé begins with the demands of her sense of honor and so soon moves toward Thésée as a *promesse de jouissance* that almost the entire speech of fifty verses may be really said to "conclude" in favor of love over duty, to be, as she says at the end of the first *stance*: "un soupir à l'amour." But if in the privacy of her soul as in her private debates with her lover, Dircé hesitantly heeds the

call of honor, in her confrontation with all others she is
more than equal to the demands of honor. Her mother
demands that she live rather than die as the supposed
sacrificial victim designated by the oracle. Jocaste even
indulgently approves of her daughter's love for Thésée:

Le Roi n'y prend pas garde, et je ferme les yeux.
C'est vous en dire assez: l'amour est un doux maître;
Et quand son choix est beau, son ardeur peut paroître.

(III, 2)

But to the implied derogation from the code of honor,
Dircé replies haughtily:

Que pour avoir reçu la vie en votre flanc,
J'y dois avoir sucé fort peu de votre sang.
Celui du grand Laïus, dont je m'y suis formée,
Trouve bien qu'il est doux d'aimer et d'être aimée;
Mais il ne peut trouver qu'on soit digne du jour
Quand aux soins de sa gloire on préfère l'amour. (III, 2)

And so it goes in her subsequent discussion with Oedipe
when the latter arrives on the scene.

Still, confrontations with her *lover* break down this
haughty exterior. When circumstances would seem to
relieve her of the need for self-immolation for the sake of
preserving the lives of her people, but especially her
lover's, her commitment to love rather than honor only
becomes the more obvious. For when it is "revealed" that
Thésée is the missing son, Dircé laments the bitter possibility of life without him. This revelation paves the way
for some of the most interesting scenes of the play. The
lovers' continued love-making in the face of this presumed
consanguinity is perhaps shocking. But in light of

Thésée's further revelation that this claim was only a stratagem, the love-making is more titillating than shocking. Eventually, Thésée does reveal that his nomination of himself as the missing son is only his own plan to prevent his beloved's self-sacrifice. Still, though this retroactively "justifies" the love-making (Corneille has, after all, titillated us with conjectures of incest before), its graver implications cannot be gainsaid by the "happy ending." Thésée's stratagem is a lie—or it is potentially one in his own view. It is conceivable that he would have turned out to be what he said he was; in this case, he would simply have assumed a role prematurely. This is the kind of justification we might expect from Corneille's earlier practice. But this is not what happens, and so we have the first case of a hero deceiving his mistress and others. Still further in the direction of compromising the code of *générosité* is the fact that the mistress does not reproach him for his behavior. This goes much further than Pertharite's forthright rejection of the demands of duty, of behavior based on a public image of himself. And it cannot be judged on the same basis as Dorante's in *Le Menteur*: this stratagem is presented as exceptional and desperate, not as part of a pattern of "stratagems" conceived all in fun. Nor is there any justification of the means through the ends: the stratagem does momentarily prevent Dircé from taking her life as she intended, but it does not force that revelation of the true facts which makes Dircé's self-sacrifice meaningless. That revelation comes from without. In doing so, it leaves the lovers finally compromised in their *générosité*. It leaves them treating love as a superior value without in any way justifying their compromise of the value of honor.

With Thésée's revelation that he has merely assumed

the identity of the missing son, the play about *"which one or who is the hero?"* may be said to come to an end and the play about Oedipe himself to begin. Of course, from the point of view of the spectator, dramatic interest in Thésée does not lag with this revelation. For some it will shift attention to Oedipe, the only other candidate in the world of the play for the identity in question. But for others—especially those familiar with Corneille—there is always the possibility that Thésée will, as I have suggested, in fact turn out to be the missing heir. On the face of it, such a possibility seems impossible in the very facts of the legend. But if Corneille has, in a relatively rare instance, taken an extremely well-known subject, he has not been any the more inhibited in manipulating it than he has been with other, less known subjects. In addition to the Oedipe and Jocaste whom we find in Sophocles's *Oedipus Rex,* Corneille uses Thésée, whom Sophocles used in *Oedipus at Colonnus,* and the herdsman is called Phorbas, as in Seneca's version of the legend. Corneille also introduces for the first time dramatically the character of Dircé. Finally, there are significant omissions: neither Tiresias nor Creon appears in Corneille's version.*

In his comments on the play, Corneille does not hesitate to point to his manipulations. He makes rare deference to the *vraisemblable,* priding himself with having been more credible than Sophocles. He also claims to have omitted the "eloquent and curious descriptions" of Oedipus's self-blinding which occupies both of the endings of his classical models, but which would have been especially offensive to the ladies; and he finally justifies the inclusion of an extended love interest as still another

---

* "Tirésie" is alluded to but does not appear.

concession to the taste of his times (particularly among
the ladies). These comments reflect the dramatist's continuing awareness of the public, yet what shows through
even more is the desire to be independent of his predecessors:

> Ces changements m'ont fait perdre l'avantage que je m'étois
> promis, de n'être souvent que le traducteur de ces grands
> génies qui m'ont précédé. La différente route que j'ai prise
> m'a empêché de me rencontrer avec eux, et de me parer avec
> leur travail; mais, en récompense, j'ai eu le bonheur de faire
> avouer qu'il n'est point sorti de pièce de ma main où il se
> trouve tant d'art qu'en celle-ci.[4]

And there undoubtedly is great skill in the way that Corneille prevents the full meaning of the successive revelations of the plot from gradually revealing to Oedipe his
identity as the slayer of his father and the hero guilty
of an incestuous relationship. The oracle makes its prediction in sufficiently vague terms for Dircé to feel that it
could be the blood of Laïus in her veins which will save
the city. Again, the reported designation of the princely
slayer of Laïus as an inhabitant of the city could apply
to Thésée. As for the incident at the crossroads, Phorbas'
report that his king was slain by brigands clearly indicates
to Oedipe the same three brigands whom he had slain
at that place. There is, of course, the matter of incest as
part of the identification. But Corneille splits the identification. First, the oracle and Tiresias identify the parricide and, secondly, Jocaste evokes vaguely, almost in
passing, the matter of the incest:

> Eh bien! soyez mon fils, puisque vous voulez l'être;
> Mais donnez-moi la marque où je le dois connoître.

Vous n'êtes point ce fils, si vous n'êtes méchant:
Le ciel sur sa naissance imprima ce penchant;
J'en vois quelque partie et ce desir inceste;
Mais pour ne plus douter, vous chargez-vous du reste?
Etes-vous l'assassin et d'un père et d'un roi? (III, 5)

So, with Thésée's assumption of Oedipe's identity, the solving of the second half of the identification—the charge of incest—plausibly omits the acting king from possible nomination: Thésée's love for Dircé, the daughter of Laïus, appears as an incestuous brother-sister love.

Thus, if Corneille concludes with the same revelation as his predecessors, these variations change the significance of the revelation. I do not merely mean that the revelation has a greater dramatic impact than in the classical versions. The impact is not in and for itself; it is a symptom rather than a cause. That Corneille's Oedipe has no inkling that he could be the guilty heir is not due merely to the lack of convincing evidence. Rather, the very possibility of such an identification could not occur to him. As previous heroes of Corneille have believed, so too Oedipe: if destiny is inexorable, it is benevolent as well.

It may seem, then, as though Corneille has chosen the most tragic legend of antiquity simply to pose another of his magnificent paradoxes (like Polyeucte's ascension to heaven not as servant of the Lord, but as coequal and possibly as replacement) :

Oedipe: Hélas! qu'il est bien vrai qu'en vain on s'imagine
Dérober notre vie à ce qu'il nous destine!
Les soins de l'éviter font courir au-devant,
Et l'adresse à le fuir y plonge plus avant.
Mais si les Dieux m'ont fait la vie abominable,
Ils m'en font par pitié la sortie honorable,

Puisqu'enfin leur faveur mêlée à leur courroux
Me condamne à mourir pour le salut de tous,
Et qu'en ce même temps qu'il faudroit que ma vie
Des crimes qu'ils m'ont faits traînât l'ignominie,
L'éclat de ces vertus que je ne tiens pas d'eux
Reçoit pour récompense un trépas glorieux. (V, 5)

But the play does not end with this dubious face-saving interpretation of destiny. Before he takes leave of Dircé, Oedipe poses a very different relationship between himself and his destiny. When Dircé proposes that she offer herself in his stead as the expiation for the slain Laïus, he retorts:

Vous voulez que le ciel, pour montrer à la terre
Qu'on peut innocemment mériter le tonnerre,
Me laisse de sa haine étaler en ces lieux
L'exemple le plus noir et le plus odieux!
Non, non: vous le verrez demain au sacrifice
Par le choix que j'attends couvrir son injustice,
Et par la peine due à son propre forfait,
Désavouer ma main de tout ce qu'elle a fait. (V, 5)

And the last words we hear directly from his lips are not the plaints of Sophocles's Oedipus but the language of firmness and self-possession we have heard in the "Cornelian hero" ever since Médée:

Adieu: laissez-moi seul en consoler la Reine;
Et ne m'enviez pas un secret entretien,
Pour affermir son coeur sur l'exemple du mien. (V, 6)

Oedipe is the first Cornelian principal character to know a tragic destiny. Fate is not on his side in the final moments of the play. There is no avoidance of his tragic

destiny through the announcement that some other
Oedipe is meant by the oracle (such an interpretation
avoids the tragic in Racine's *Iphigénie*). The hero is shown
pitted against an irreversible series of events; his relationship to outer reality is flawed. However, the flaw is
not in his makeup. In evoking this concept, I do not mean
to subscribe to such an explanation of the tragedy of
Sophocles's *Oedipus*. Whether the motive which led
Sophocles's Oedipus to slay the stranger at the crossroads
was anger, or if anger, whether unjustified, are debatable
propositions. But Corneille has completely exculpated his
Oedipe from the charge of such an "internal flaw" in his
play: Oedipe slew men whom he took to be brigands; his
action was in self-defense at worst, and, in its better light,
was a positive act ridding society of criminals. And both
in his behavior and, as finally revealed, his origins, he has
been a king: handsome does as handsome is. He is a *fully*
virtuous man and so his fate is utterly unjust.*

---

*Cherpack contends that Oedipe's "double failure to recognize Laius as
a king and a father, and thus as a person inviolably protected from
attack, is probably Oedipus' tragic flaw in Corneille's eyes." *The Call of
Blood*, p. 42. It should be noted, however, that the failure, if there is one,
is only single: Oedipe does recognize the majesty of the second man he
slays at the crossroads, even if he does not recognize in him his father.
Indeed, as Cherpack himself notes, Oedipe even feels a strong emotional
reaction towards this majestic figure whom he slays, so that the failure to
recognize his father is only partial. But, in any case, to regard either
"failure" or both as a tragic "flaw" seems to contradict the understanding
of the legend which Corneille gives both discursively in his *Discours de
la tragédie* and dramatically in the play itself. Oedipe, says Corneille in
the *Discours*, "me semble ne faire aucune faute, bien qu'il tue son père,
parce qu'il ne le connoît pas, et qu'il ne fait que disputer le chemin en
homme de coeur *contre un inconnu qui l'attaque avec avantage*." M-L,
*I*, 56-57 (my italics). Cherpack quotes this passage as if it contradicted
what Corneille "says" in the play. It may contradict what THÉSÉE says
in the play (quoted by Cherpack): that kings are recognizable no matter
how they conceal their majesty and so are inviolable and that the slayer
of Laius is worthy of death. But to this argument OEDIPE in the play
repeats the argument of the Corneille of the *Discours* "Mais ce furent
brigands, dont le bras . . . etc." (IV, 5).

What is Oedipe's reaction to his tragic destiny? The question may seem odd, for nearly two millenia of critical discussion of tragedy have practically conditioned us to assume that there is only one possible "reaction" to tragedy: the acceptance of it. Yet, Corneille's Oedipe rejects the classical notion of illumination. He also rejects the notion of a radical separation between man and his world, whether the world be viewed in Manichean terms as overtly hostile or in existentialist terms as merely "there." In such a view of man's relation to his destiny, Oedipe's protest would be hollow and self-delusory, a metaphysical whistling in the dark. His self-blinding in such a relationship would be merely an attempt at identification with the world as either nonvalue or antivalue by the obliteration of himself-as-value. Rather, as Nadal has brilliantly observed, his self-blinding is aimed at forcing heaven to justify itself.[5] Oedipe thus remains consistently heroic or *généreux;* the play remains open-ended as we wait for heaven's reply to Oedipe. From Oedipe's point of view, heaven's behavior here cannot be taken as definitive, and Corneille leaves the door open for just such an interpretation:

> Dircé: Un autre ordre demain peut nous être donné.
> Allons voir cependant ce prince infortuné,
> Pleurer auprès de lui notre destin funeste,
> Et remettons aux Dieux à disposer du reste. (V, 9)

It is left in the hands of the gods; this is based on the "acceptance" of the possibility for change. In such a context, Oedipe's blindness is a sign that, though he is the intended victim, heaven might very well have no more to ask of him than his blindness. The significance of Creon's absence in this play is now obvious. Coupled

with the fact that neither the oracle nor Oedipe himself
has demanded the expiatory exile of the offender, Oedipe
remains in possession of his kingdom.

Even as Oedipus, then, the most famous tragic hero of
antiquity, the Cornelian hero remains atop the situation
confronting him. This does not mean that in Oedipe we
have at last an existentialist self-made man—one who, as
it were, becomes more than a king, who becomes a man.
The thinking is still "essentialistic." The unrealized but
realizable promise at the end of the play remains the
promise realized at the end of previous plays: the fulfillment of a benevolent destiny. The dramaturgy of realization or demonstration thus puts the play squarely in the
mode of the great political plays. But this dramaturgy
"out of the past" characterizes only two of the five acts
of this very long play. With his emphatic self-affirmations
in the fifth act, Oedipe seems as out of place in the world
of Thésée and Dircé as Médée was in the world of Jason,
or as Sophonisbe will be in the world of her lover, Massinisse. Corneille's *Oedipe* is more romance than tragedy
or even, to use one of Corneille's rubrics for similar plays,
heroic comedy. We are closer to the world in which heroes
are *also* lovers—the world of Pertharite and the world of
Jason of *La Toison d'or*.

Oedipe's unitary personality harks back to the personality of heroes in the great political plays, particularly
the heroes (young *and* old Horace) of *Horace* and Auguste
of *Cinna*. The struggle of these heroes is with external
reality as it manifests itself in political or social circumstances. The demands of natural love have no meaning
for them—and indeed, for Oedipe as for Auguste, do not
really exist in the play. To this extent, *Oedipe* is excep-

tional among the plays since *Le Menteur* and it especially
deviates from the concerns of the plays immediately surrounding it. On the surface, this might suggest that Corneille intended to mark his return to the theater by a
return to the conceptions of his great political plays. Yet,
both the dramaturgy of the play as well as the circumstances of its composition suggest otherwise. The play was
written "on command" and Corneille, for all his independence, could not very well have written of an Oedipe
beset by love and renouncing his destiny in the same way
that Pertharite did (or might have done). Still more significantly, the "Oedipus subject" in *Oedipe* really functions
independently of another subject of the play: the conflict
of love and honor as it is worked out in the relationship
between Thésée and Dircé. As we have seen, this relationship carries even further the premises and the conclusions
of such a conflict as it had been developed in a "conjectural mode" in the great identity plays before Corneille's long departure from the theater. Thésée, like
many a hero before him, showed himself ready to place
love first: Dircé is the first among the gallery of "strong
women" Corneille has created to show herself ready to do
likewise.

The heroes and heroines of Corneille's second *pièce à
machines, La Toison d'or* (1600-61), go still further in this
direction than Thésée and Dirce. Médée, Absyrte, and
Hypsipyle are all prepared to place the demands of the
private self over the demands of the public self and Jason,
though he "privately" differs from them in this respect,
does voice at great length the greater validity of the
demands of love or of the private self. Love rules all and,
in the case of Médée, ruins all. Or will ruin all for her,
as we are advised by Jupiter in the denouement of the

play. Thus, "beyond" the play, the fate of Médée appears tragic. Again, as in *Oedipe*, tragic potential is found in the principal character rather than in the secondary character. The destiny Médée will meet will involve the revelation of the uselessness of that force in which she put her faith: love. She has already been a victim of illusoriness of love as a permanent value, as is evident in her relationship to the gods in the play: she has been deceived by Junon, who has taken the appearance of her sister as a means of goading her on to love. But the fully tragic consequences of this illusion are not brought out in the play. Not that Corneille allowed this Médée, as he had allowed the first Médée and the more recent Oedipe, to challenge destiny. This time his "refusal" of the tragic is indirect: for one thing, the tragic relationship of Jason and Médée is only reported, not shown; for another the unhappiness of Médée is obscured by the happy ending of Absyrte and Hypsipyle (expressed especially in the more spectacular aspects of the play—for example, the descent of the gods in the machines). But dissipating the tragic potential still more is the destiny of Médée herself. Her ultimate destiny appears not to lie with Jason, but with that unnamed being who will father through her the son who will found the Medes. As Jupiter says, there is but "un peu de temps fatal"—not all of time. In the fulfillment of time, one of the conditions of the romance of *Le Cid,* we remember, lies the fulfillment of the very conditions of the character of Médée as these are given to us by legend. As in *Oedipe*, the final connotation of *générosité* as it applies to the principal character is political. True, an unhappy love is one of the conditions through which this connotation must arise; Médée is unfulfilled as an *amoureuse* before she is fulfilled as a *généreuse*. Yet, at

the same time we find we have the secondary lovers fulfilled as both *amoureux* and *généreux,* so that we may say
that *La Toison* leans far more in the direction of James's
romance than in the direction of heroic comedy. This is
appropriate in a *pièce à machines,* in which the "vulgar
commitments" not only of the real world but of ordinary
staging are disengaged. A more perplexing return to those
"vulgar commitments" awaits us in Corneille's next play.

In the world of *Sertorius* (1662) we no longer have a
self-sufficient hero different from an entourage of *galants*
and *précieux* (Oedipe vis-à-vis Thésée and Dircé) nor a
hero exclusively dedicated to an external entity which
demands the use of gallantry and *préciosité* as strategies to
fulfill a higher purpose (Jason vis-à-vis Médée and Hypsipyle). The closest we have come to the peculiar relationships of Sertorius to his world has been in *Pertharite,*
where the hero found himself surrounded by split types
and was himself a split type.
A return to the values of duty—albeit of an ambitious
kind—over those of love is heard from the very first lines
of the play:

> PERPENNA: En vain l'ambition qui presse mon courage,
> D'un faux brillant d'honneur pare son noir ouvrage;
> En vain pour me soumettre à ses lâches efforts,
> Mon âme a secoué le joug de cent remords:
> Cette âme, d'avec soi tout à coup divisée,
> Reprend de ces remords la chaîne mal brisée;
> Et de Sertorius le surprenant bonheur
> Arrête une main prête à lui percer le coeur. (I, 1)

Perpenna will, of course, abandon these noble principles,
but what is significant in terms of Corneille's more recent

dramatic practice is that we have here a return to a perfidy aimed at securing political power, not winning the
personal love of a mistress.

However, the return to an idealistic sense of duty rather
than to personal love is also found, especially in the
women. Not for the pressed, proud Viriate, Dircé's ultimate outburst of "all for love"; not for the rejected,
indignant Aristie, the rejected Médée's readiness to forgive
"all for love." Aristie is prepared to forgive Pompée, to
restore her love to him, it is true:

> L'ingrat, par son divorce en faveur d'Emilie,
> M'a livrée aux mépris de toute l'Italie.
> Vous savez à quel point mon courage est blessé;
> Mais s'il se dédisoit d'un outrage forcé,
> S'il chassoit Emilie et me rendoit ma place,
> J'aurois peine, Seigneur, à lui refuser grâce;
> Et tant que je serai maîtresse de ma foi,
> Je me dois toute à lui, s'il revient tout à moi. (I, 3)

But it is not a split which Aristie wishes to repair within
the self—between the public image of the self as it centers
around the concept of *gloire* and the private, "accidental"
desire as it centers around the concept of love-as-love. We
have returned rather to the paradoxes of love-as-honor.
Still more importantly, the concept is not "defended" but
"affirmed." The tone is positive, without the vindictiveness or anxiety which characterized similar defenses of
honor in recent plays.

Viriate is equally affirmative in her call to honor.
True, when she first speaks of her love for Sertorius, she
strikes the elegiac note which is familiar to us in recent
*généreuses* and might disturb us as much as it does her

*suivante,* Thamire. She quickly corrects this impression
for both Thamire and us:

> Ce ne sont pas les sens que mon amour consulte:
> Il hait des passions l'impétueux tumulte;
> Et son feu, que j'attache aux soins de ma grandeur,
> Dédaigne tout mélange avec leur folle ardeur.
> J'aime en Sertorius ce grand art de la guerre
> Qui soutient un banni contre toute la terre;
> J'aime en lui ces cheveux tous couverts de lauriers,
> Ce front qui fait trembler les plus braves guerriers,
> Ce bras qui semble avoir la victoire en partage.
> L'amour de la vertu n'a jamais d'yeux pour l'âge:
> Le mérite a toujours des charmes éclatants;
> Et quiconque peut tout est aimable en tout temps. (II, 1)

*Eclatants* is one of the key words of this play. In light of
the return to the paradoxes of love-as-honor, it is not surprising that it be used oxymoronically:

> VIRIATE: Seigneur, vous faire grâce, est-ce m'en éloigner?
> SERTORIUS: Ah! Madame, est-il temps que cette *grâce éclate?*
> VIR.: C'est cet *éclat,* Seigneur, que cherche Viriate.
>
> (IV, 2; my italics)

Viriate, more than any other character in the play, rises
above those "tendresses d'amour . . . emportements de
passion . . . narrations pathétiques" which Corneille
claimed were absent from the play[6] but which, as we shall
see, were to be found ironically enough in the hero alone.
Viriate reads lessons in *générosité* to Sertorius. Nor do
these lessons terminate, as in the case of recent *combats
amoureux,* with the abdication of honor for the sake of
love. Viriate, like Aristie, remains true to the code of
*générosité.* Its paradoxes sound and resound in their pro-

nouncements from one end of the play to the other.

As they do not in the pronouncements of the male principals. That they could not in the case of Pompée is not surprising in view of Corneille's previous practices. The hero's rival had often been unequal to the full demands of the code. In the case of Pompée as in the case of Perpenna in this play, tergiversations and derogations from the code are made out of ambition, in the name of the public image of the self and not for the sake of private desire. Love is secondary; political prudence is all:

> POMPÉE: Et quand Sylla prépare un si doux changement,
> Pouvez-vous m'ordonner de me bannir de Rome,
> Pour la remettre au joug sous les lois d'un autre homme;
> Moi qui ne suis jaloux de mon autorité
> Que pour lui rendre un jour toute sa liberté?
> Non, non: si vous m'aimez comme j'aime à le croire,
> Vous saurez accorder votre amour et ma gloire,
> Céder avec prudence au temps prêt à changer,
> Et ne me perdre pas au lieu de vous venger. (III, 2)

This is not, of course, the outlook of the ideal *généreux*, for whom appearance and reality had always to coincide, for whom every act had to manifest the very bottom of his heart, for whom such duplicity was meaningless because there existed no difference between ends and means. There is such a difference for Pompée and it manifests itself most clearly in the relationship between love and duty, where duty does not so much triumph over love as merely take precedence over it. Where Aristie and Viriate would restore the unity between love and honor in a single act (or, with each act testify to its reality), Pompée makes an appeal to "realism" which is unusual among recent Cornelian *amoureux*. In so doing he returns us to the

concerns of the great political plays. Were he to be pitted
in such a world only against Viriate or Aristie, we might
expect a complete return to that world. But his real rival
in that part of the action where he is involved is not
either of these women, but Sertorius. Nor is the basis of
the conflict amorous, a love rivalry between the two. It
is rather the conception of kingship: Pompée's unprin-
cipled ambition versus Sertorius' sense of honor. Sertorius
reproaches Pompée for refusing to respect the liberty of
others, of subjugating them in his own name. The effect
of these reproaches is not so much to compromise Pompée
(his politics of prudence in the love conflict of the play
have already done this in Aristie's reports of his infidelity).
Rather, the effect is to elevate Sertorius as a true *généreux*.

Yet there is a great deal of dramatic *trompe-l'oeil*:
Sertorius sounds like the Horaces as he tells the ambitious,
scheming Pompée:

> Le séjour [Rome] de votre potentat,
> Qui n'a que ses fureurs pour maximes d'Etat?
> Je n'appelle plus Rome un enclos de murailles
> Que ses proscriptions comblent de funérailles:
> Ces murs, dont le destin fut autrefois si beau,
> N'en sont que la prison, ou plutôt le tombeau;
> Mais pour revivre ailleurs dans sa plus vive force,
> Avec les faux Romains elle a fait plein divorce;
> Et comme autour de moi j'ai tous ses vrais appuis,
> Rome n'est plus dans Rome, elle est toute où je suis. (III, 1)

Yet, the conception of Rome which he defends is less
reminiscent of the imperial narcissism by which Horace
identified Rome with himself than the anonymous republicanism which Jason defended in evoking Greece.

Sertorius rejects the dynamics of kingship which Pompée represents, however unscrupulously. To the Pompée who refuses his proposal to serve as a lieutenant on the grounds that such a role is demeaning, Sertorius replies "Du droit de commander je ne suis point jaloux" (III, 1). Sertorius' defense of the simple virtues is peculiarly unimpassioned, "uncommitted" as we might now say. If his defense of these virtues rehabilitates him, it does so in a disturbing, strange way which suggests that he is not so much above them as beyond them. For one thing, the challenges of *générosité* which are under discussion are relatively uncomplicated matters of military conduct and public policy which do not create the moral dilemmas and painful challenges of *généreux* love. For all the brilliance and vigor of its conflict, then, this long scene functions somewhat irrelevantly in the economy of the action. We might at best say that it rehabilitates Sertorius to some extent, after his tendencies to give "all to love."

Even were we to give the scene more value in the economy of the play, seeing it as a crucial moment of what might be called the subsidiary conflict among Sertorius, Pompée, and Aristie, we are obliged to note that the values which Sertorius defends in this scene are ultimately not exactly defended nor defeated. Sertorius' point of view does not win out, Pompée's does. Though not precisely in the way he predicted, Sylla does lose power. Prudence, not *générosité,* triumphs. Sertorius, of course, is not around to testify to this truth. He is dead and that his virtue is testified to by Pompée, his adversary, no more rehabilitates him or spares us from seeing his fate as tragic than the fact that he dies at the hands of the treacherous Perpenna. If anything, the latter fact in particular points up the truly tragic nature of this *généreux*'s destiny: he is the victim of duplicity; the world is no longer the stable world where all is justified and integrated, where the treacherous cannot ultimately triumph over the virtuous. The political universe, if not the political hero of the play, is flawed.

In the other "world" of the play, the hero Sertorius is flawed—or *perhaps* he is. Sertorius is a peculiar Cornelian hero in that he is not fully committed to either of the values which are central in the other conflict of the play, the struggle between himself and Viriate. Here, as with Pompée, he is more passionately dedicated to the code of honor, but the passion is in the name of something else: he defends honor not for its own sake or for himself as the embodiment of it, but rather for Viriate's sake. Sertorius is thus beyond honor, somewhat patronizingly and indulgently so, like Pertharite with Rodelinde. That he does truly love her in terms of the split between public and private selves comes in his famous reply to Thamire's emphatic defense of public values:

> SERTORIUS: Ah! pour être Romain, je n'en suis pas moins
> homme:
> J'aime, et peut-être plus qu'on n'a jamais aimé; (IV, 1)

But unlike recent *généreux* who testified to this split in their selves, Sertorius does not assert the superiority of love. Nor does he attempt to use love as Grimoald had: as a means to correct destiny's act of making him to the manner but not the manor born. Rather, Sertorius is unique among Cornelian heroes in this position, in that he *accepts* this destiny.

And it remains his destiny. There is no sudden news at the end of the play that happily rehabilitates as a born king this maverick *généreux*. Rather, Sertorius acts to formalize his destiny, to realize it: "Non, je vous l'ai cédée, et vous tiendrai parole. / Je l'aime, et vous la donne encor malgré mon feu" (IV, 3). And he is one of the few Cornelian heroes to go off-stage uttering words of defeat and sorrow:

> Je partage les maux dont je la vois comblée.
> Adieu: j'entre un moment pour calmer son chagrin,
> Et me rendrai chez vous à l'heure du festin. (IV, 3)

Nor do the fireworks of the happy ending easily obscure the hero's peculiar defeat and resignation to defeat, as they did, for example, for Phinée in *Andromède* and for Médée in *La Toison*. If Sertorius is a hero in trouble in the military-political conflict of the play, he is that even rarer figure in the Cornelian world to date: the troubled hero.

He is in trouble thanks to his destiny and troubled thanks to the mysterious force of a natural love which disregards the old equations and injunctions of *générosité*. He loves a woman beyond him in station and too far below him in age. Sertorius is indeed a misfit in the world of the play in which the old equations and injunctions are respected by all others (even Pompée, eventually). So, Sertorius is removed from this world—without protest. His "punishment" does not, like that of Corneille's Oedipe, constitute a judgment upon his destiny, a defiance of it. It represents rather a fulfillment of that destiny: the ill-born (a relative concept, of course) cannot expect to occupy the highest place in a world integrated around the concept of *générosité*. The denouement makes this explicit. For a brief moment, in the exclusively political-military aspect of the action, the old equations and injunctions of *générosité* seem in force: Sertorius is a better man than Pompée and shows it. But he is a better man according to a political theory which makes a mockery of the dynamics of *générosité*: republicanism. The happiest construction of the relationship between Sertorius and Pompée is not that Sertorius is a better man, but that Pompée is a lesser man. But not even this construction conceals the fact that Sertorius' prowess cannot lead to kingship. Were Pompée as good a Roman as Sertorius, the two would be equals, with the only difference between them being not the qualitative one conferred by birth but the quantitative one conferred by age.

Corneille has eviscerated the concept of *générosité* in the politics of the play. Moreover, if he has seemed to restore it fully in the politico-amorous tie-in, it is only once again to embarrass his hero. Here, Sertorius can do no more than regret his republicanism—or, more significantly, the fact that he has not been born the political equal of the woman he loves. That he loves her at all points to a grave imbalance in the world of the play. He is removed, we might say, because he must be removed if the world is to be restored to its "natural balance." One is thus reminded of Kitto's explanation of the mood of reintegration at the close of *Oedipus Rex*: the cause of the imbalance having been removed, the universe is restored to its delicate metaphysical and moral balance.[7] So it is with *Sertorius* which, like all other Cornelian plays to date, concludes with a note of integration and harmony, with a "happy ending." But Sertorius *has* existed in this world: he is the best it *has offered* and the best has not been done unto him. Like Médée in the play by that name, Sertorius thus stands out as an unintegrated element in the world of his play. But the difference in their separate destinies measures the more problematic character of Sertorius. Metaphysically, Médée's destiny was "comic": an affirmation of her moral superiority over the others in the play, an affirmation of her limitless self-sufficiency. Sertorius' destiny is tragic: a demonstration of his moral inferiority according to the values of the play (not our evaluation of its values, by the way), a proof of his limitations.*

For once we have a Cornelian hero who cannot do everything and for whom destiny has not created the conditions in which he can do everything. The dramaturgy of realization has for once given us the entelechy of a tragic figure, but one whose relation to the tragic still does not allow us to speak of an ultimate tragic sense of life in the play. The worst has not happened to the best: Sertorius is not, by his own admission the best the universe *can* or *has* to offer. This accounts for the relatively unheroic terms in which he posits his relationship to his beloved. There, he is, so to speak, pretragic. Never protesting his destiny, the very opposite of the emphatic Oedipe, he is resigned from the very first to failure in his love. Resigned because his own position in the hierarchy of *généreux* dictated his failure. Only second-best, then, it is impossible to view Sertorius' destiny as the supreme demonstration of the tragic in Corneille. The "romantic" denouement, with its usual pairings and projected marriage, might be justly described as not truly disengaged. But even this interpretation does not return us to a fully tragic universe. *Sertorius* remains still another example of Corneille's "untragic awareness"—but only by default.

---

*For one school of thought, the character of Sertorius is autobiographical. See Couton, *La Vieillesse de Corneille*, p. 73, and, for a more tentative statement of the idea, J. Streicher, *Sertorius*, "Introduction."

As I have indicated, Corneille's *Sophonisbe* (1663) resembles his *Oedipe*: the emphatic *généreux* (*généreuse* here) stands in sharp contrast to the *amoureux* who surround her. If Massinisse would die for love, she will let him, but she will die for nobler reasons. The final limitation on human possibility becomes her instrument of self-affirmation. In saying that "une telle fierté devoit naître romaine" Lélius attempts to assimilate *générosité* into the concept of Rome, but the very fact he points to (that Sophonisbe was not born a Roman) betrays his wish, and Rome is at best cast in an equal light. One is reminded of Sévère's deference to Christian heroism at the end of *Polyeucte*. It should also be noted that in this play Rome is a very different ideal from that of *Sertorius*. The politics are the same—a "republican" fear of any one state growing too big—but the spirit is closer to the imperial expression of *Horace*'s identification of Rome with a hero (see, for example, Lélius' reproach to Massinisse for ceasing to be a *généreux* in order to become an *amoureux*). But whether we look to the imperial spirit or the republican letter of Lelius' Romanism, it is clear that Sophonisbe "toute à Carthage, digne sang d'un tel père," is, in her received sense of self, beyond Rome, beyond love and beyond tragedy.

*Othon* (1664) and *Agésilas* (1666) repeat the romantic disengagement of *Pertharite*. Indeed, the hero of the former play seems not so much beyond the cares of state as actually bothered by them; he is a comic-pastoral type trying to escape the world of the *généreux*. Even the unhappy character, Camille, reminds one not so much of the unhappy characters of the "serious" plays (Seleucus of *Rodogune* or Sertorius) as of Amarante of *La Suivante*. Georges May has, in fact, noted the strong resemblance between many of the "later tragedies" and the "early comedies."*

The return to the premises and practices of the early comedies is most pronounced in *Agésilas* (1666). Indeed, the ingenious combinations and mathematical solution of conflicts in "values" as well as the indulgent, *galant* tone suggest an almost complete restoration of the outlook of the early comedies. Nevertheless, it should be noted that this restoration is artificial, that it takes place within the framework of a key relationship in which the principal character is more concerned with honor than with love. The paradox of love-as-honor is split into its components, but the final relationship between the terms is more reminiscent of that of *Oedipe* and to a lesser extent *Pertharite* than that of *Sophonisbe*: love and honor triumph separately, with honor being "honored" in the principal character and love being "honored" in the lesser characters.

As frequently in the plays which began with *Pertharite,* the play functions on two levels, one *amoureux* and the other *généreux,* one private and the other public. And as with *Othon* and *Oedipe,* the "secondary" characters bid to take over the whole of the action. The dramaturgy is, as it were, defocused, shifting from the presumed hero—presumed, at any rate, from the title—to his cohorts or rivals. This pattern is familiar to us from earlier plays, but there the shift was to a single dominant character (Cleopatre in *Rodogune,* Martian in *Héraclius*). Here there is a more or less equalized shift to Spitridate and

---

*"Des pièces comme *Othon, Agésilas, Attila, Tite et Bérénice, Pulchérie, Suréna,* ressemblent étrangement à des comédies, surtout à celles de Corneille." *Tragédie cornélienne,* p. 92. I would agree less about the last two plays. See my discussion below, pp. 244-258.

Cotys and Lysandre among the men, while among the women, there is now an excessive emphasis upon Aglatide, the woman whom Agésilas presumably loves, now upon Mandane, the woman whom he finally admits to be his true love, but whom he rejects. And as the play places emphasis on the "secondary" characters from its very beginning, one is tempted to believe that it is indeed going to function exclusively at the level of private feeling; that the conflict between "love" and "duty" which is raised by various characters is, after all, not very profound, and is in fact "preresolved" in favor of love; that all that is necessary is the solution —in mathematical terms, in fact— of the relations among the six characters. With Agésilas' first entry in the third act, one fully expects him to be introduced less in the political light in which he is evoked by his political rival, Lysandre, the father of ill-assorted mistresses, than in an amorous light. This king promises to be just another "factor" designed to complicate the "problem" which Corneille has first posed in the criss-cross of station and dramatic function in his paired lovers.

Yet, the very solutions which "love" demands among the secondary characters depend on the conception of Agésilas as a *généreux* rather than an *amoureux*—or, more exactly, as an *amoureux* who renounces love in the name of *générosité*. For the play is built on a principle of complication in which, theoretically, there is no solution to the complications unless one of the characters committed to love breaks with love. Appropriately enough, it is the king figure of the play who does so. But as he does so, he is not bereft of love, for there remains at hand a female character, Aglatide, who herself had been beyond love from the very beginning, or at least had denied love except as it might be located in a king figure.

There is, as it were, a built-in solution to the dilemmas which *Agésilas* poses, so that there is no good cause to attempt to resolve the place of the paradox of love-as-honor in the play. The ultimate argument which Mandane uses shows that she actually testifies to the split in the self between a public and private part, one in which the public part *may* be at variance with the private part, one in which appearance and reality do not coincide. This is the position which she presents to Agésilas—without the tears and without the threat of suicide implicit earlier (IV, 5). It may be that she is simply using this split strategically, a fact which suggests that she is more given to love than she is to duty. Yet there is no reason to believe that, should the stratagem fail, she would not carry out her public role as queen while at the same time loving Cotys (sentimentally, of course). Her use of this split, then, fits the moral pattern of the rest of the resolutions in the play: it is an honorable act of self-interest. It in no sense diminishes her stature as *généreuse* nor imperils her position as Cotys' beloved. Cotys can only recognize that she followed her brother's "orders" (expressed really as desires in this play in which the injunctions of the code have been softened). Politically speaking, then, both in her external situation at the end of the action as well as in her motivation, Mandane does not derogate from the familiar position of the *généreuse*: she does receive a king figure, Cotys, so that her essentially *"généreuse"* outlook is not frustrated "selon les lois constitutives de l'univers de la pièce." As far as her not receiving the supreme king figure, we must remember that her compulsion to majesty was not as great as that of Aglatide, who does receive the supreme king figure, Agésilas.

And the fact that Agésilas does turn to Aglatide is the

final and most conclusive proof that at heart the conflict between love and duty, between person and station, is indeed only seeming. In renouncing Mandane, he is, of course, following the dialectic of challenge and counter-challenge so familiar to us in previous heroes, notably those of the great political plays. But not for this hero the subtleties of the paradox of love-as-honor as we first heard it stated by Chimene (only to be rejected by her, we remember). For him courage and love are not two sides of the same coin; they are separate coins, each existing in two different "value systems." Agésilas chooses for the value system in which Mandane is seen not as a *promesse de jouissance* but an *objet d'estime* and (in still a further distinction from earlier formulations) as an *objet d'estime* not to be equalled but surpassed. In rejecting Mandane, Agésilas confirms his right to kingship. But that relegitimation is not complete: he must also restore his purely political relations with Lysandre to a firm *généreux* basis. Until this moment they have been on a prudential basis. Like many a recent Corneille king or king figure Agésilas has behaved more like a "party boss" than an absolute king (including the Oedipe who pitted his daughter against Dircé as a means of checking Thésée's nascent power). He now must conquer both his own political prudence and the hate of Lysandre it has led him to, even as he has just conquered love. He does so:

> Un roi né pour l'éclat des grandes actions
> >  Dompte jusqu'à ses passions,
> Et ne se croit point roi, s'il ne fait sur lui-même
> Le plus illustre essai de son pouvoir suprême. (V, 6)

The magnanimity is reminiscent of Auguste's behavior toward Cinna, and the restoration of supreme *générosité* is even more firm in that Agésilas openly admits to have derogated from its imperatives to openness, honesty, fairness. In rejecting his own sense of caution and its political expression as prudence, Agésilas reminds us that the *généreux* is free of anxiety. Possessing an unshakeable confidence in the rightness of his own behavior, he need not suffer the anxities which prudential behavior reflects. This gesture restores the universe even to the extent of not merely rejecting Agésilas' "fated passion" but in *sealing* the secondary place which such passion must take to the "reasoned passion" of a love between *généreux*: Agésilas takes Aglatide, for

> J'aime à voir cet orgueil que mon choix autorise
> A dédaigner les voeux de tout autre qu'un roi:
> J'aime cette hauteur en un jeune courage;
> Et vous n'aurez point lieu de vous plaindre de moi,
> Si votre heureux destin dépend de mon suffrage. (V, 8)

Yet, like Mandane's *générosité* before Cotys, so Agésilas' functions here within the framework of a limiting "republicanism." His remarks do not fully restore the world of the great political plays, but more the balanced world of the early comedies. This is not really love-as-honor with all its dialectical complexities: Aglatide and Agésilas seem to get each other as a sort of consolation prize or to satisfy a need to "round out" the symmetry. We might even state the plot mathematically: let $A$, $B$, and $C$ be the principal women of the play and let $A'$ $B'$ and $C'$ be the men whom they love, (or, in the case of Aglatide and Agésilas, the kind of mate they desire). The problem is to "match" each letter with its prime in face of the initial mismatches. Thus, the plot runs:

$A$ pledged to $B'$

$B$ pledged to $C'$

$B$ and $B'$ are linked by Lysandre's indulgence: this leaves

$A$ pledged to $C'$

$C$ pledged to $A'$

and when $A'$ "rejects" $C$, $C$ and $C'$ "cancel out" and this leaves no place for $A'$ to go but to $A$.

Q. E. D.

Corneille did not have to 'round things out" this nicely; he had not done so even in his early comedies (think of *La Suivante*) and not even as recently as the preceding play. Yet round them out he does and in terms which justify the union of Aglatide and Agésilas in a positive rather than in a negative way: not only does the most ambitious and duty-bound female of the play get the most ambitious and duty-bound hero, but she gets him *back*. For if the king had been the "victim" of his own eyes as they gazed upon Mandane and of her eyes as they gazed upon him, even before that the eyes of Aglatide "s'étoient fait un empire" in the heart of the king. So even as Agésilas "questions" his return to Aglatide by speaking of the unreliability of the eyes and the heart, we must remember that he does so by way of justifying his return to his *and her* first love.

Everyone is happily and appropriately mated. "And," not "because," is the proper conjunction: *both* love and honor are satisfied. In the secondary characters honor is accommodated with love; in the principal characters, love is accommodated with honor. The play represents a curious blend of forms: of comedy, of romance ("if only the king would return to his first love!"—and he does), and of drama.

It would be difficult to say which form predominates, but the purely mechanical use of the concepts of *générosité* as a sort of lever to resolve the love dilemmas suggests that the prevailing mood is romantic. This impression is further enhanced by the experimental character of the verse: its varied lengths, its frequent oxymorons, its concentration on affective rather than hortatory *mots-clés*. Like the long interview in *Sertorius* between Pompée and the hero, the interview between Lysandre and Agésilas here seems out of place. And it is revealing that in this play it is Pompée's political counterpart who defends a pure sense of honor, the politically inferior Lysandre, while it is the king figure who speaks from Pompée's "impure" (or at least unconfident) position as *généreux*. This suggests that Lysandre, like Sertorius earlier, is "out of place" in this world, but actually he is out of place only in his confrontations with Agésilas-as-king. In the crucial love intrigues of the play, he is as indulgent as any of the lovers, as we have seen, and in fact is a worthy successor to the indulgent parents of the early comedies. Indeed, he seems less angry than perplexed when confronted with his king's behavior and, far from being a rival, he seems only a victim of that king. Similarly, Cotys seems overwhelmed by his mistress' behavior in their long *combat amoureux,* but both the prudent king and the haughty mistress are really functioning in only one mode of their being in both these instances: they are equally as strong *amoureux* as they are *généreux*. And since these other modes of being are sacrificed with relative simplicity, they seem chiefly pretexts to resolve the love interest of the play, a kind of dramatic ballast. But the ballast keeps the ship on an even keel even in the strange waters of this "romantic drama" in which the fantasy of the early comedies is so largely restored.*

In the plays beyond *Agésilas,* Corneille repeats certain previous conceptions of the hero. *Attila* (1667) represents a negative proof of the values of the *généreux.* Attila is punished "selon les lois constitutives de l'univers de la pièce" even as previous heroes had been saved according to the laws of the universe of their plays. And they are the same laws: the injunctions, imperatives, and equations of *générosité.* Attila is not born to be a king; he is a usurper, as Honorie reminds him:

> Ah! si non plus que vous je n'ai point le coeur bas,
> Nos fiertés pour cela ne se ressemblent pas.
> La mienne est de princesse, et la vôtre est d'esclave: (III, 4)

Attila is not a *généreux,* he is an *ambitieux*—or as Octar puts it at one point, a *politique.* (The real "guarantor of value" for Octar is the king hero, alluded to in the person of Mérouée.) True, he follows as rigorously as any previous hero the injunctions always to let the outer man manifest the inner man but the soul that is manifested is vicious and unworthy. Where in Cleopatre there was a discrepancy between station and means, here in Attila there is a perfect correlation between station (that of usurper) and means. More importantly, Attila is not some Nietzschean superman proving the inadequacy of lesser, "bourgeois" values in the world. He challenges the supreme aristocratic ethos even as he denies one of the key notions of that ethos: the equation between birth and function. Nor is Attila a precursor of Camus' Caligula,

---

*Couton reminds us that "nulle part ne se montre mieux quel génie de renouvellement habitait encore un écrivain de soixante ans, barbon en un siècle pour qui la vieillesse commençait à quarante ans." *Corneille,* p. 166.

a despondent existentialist despairing of the lack of values.
There definitely are values in the play and it is in their
name that Attila perishes, in order that the disrupted
world of the play might be restored. There is, of course,
the prediction of the *devins* which Valamir utters; there
is the reminder of Attila's offense against his brother and
the implications that the nosebleeds he suffers are the
sign of some outer force of retribution; there is Ildione's
dependence upon an outer necessity:

> Le ciel n'est pas toujours aux méchants si propice:
> Après tant d'indulgence, il a de la justice. (IV, 6)

Finally, at the peak of Attila's cruelty, even as he accepts
her view of him as God's instrument, there is Honorie's
warning:

> Lorsque par les tyrans il punit les mortels,
> Il réserve sa foudre à ces grands criminels,
> Qu'il donne pour supplice à toute la nature,
> Jusqu'à ce que leur rage ait comblé la mesure.
> Peut-être qu'il prépare en ce même moment
> A de si noirs forfaits l'éclat du châtiment,
> Qu'alors que ta fureur à nous perdre s'apprête,
> Il tient le bras levé pour te briser la tête,
> Et veut qu'un grand exemple oblige de trembler
> Quiconque désormais t'osera ressembler. (V, 3)

And this indeed does happen to Attila. (The explanation
is, of course, the orthodox Catholic one: God puts evil
to his own good purposes.)

Attila is, then, not the fulfillment of the Cornelian
*généreux*. He is the very opposite: the antihero. He is not
a model, but a warning, the self-made man brought to

the fate he deserves when he attempts to function beyond
his innate station. He is a shooting star in the firmament
of Cornelian heroes, meant to burn brightly but briefly.
His light is but reflected from the fixed stars of that firmament. Attila's imperatives are not sufficient to raise him
to the status of *généreux*.*

In *Tite et Bérénice* (1670), as certain observers have
noted,[8] Corneille is more Racinian than the Racine with
whom he vied in writing a play on the famous story of
renunciation:

> TITE: Je sais qu'un empereur doit parler ce langage;
> Et quand il l'a fallu, j'en ai dit davantage;
> Mais de ces duretés que j'étale à regret,
> Chaque mot à mon coeur coûte un soupir secret;
> Et quand à la raison j'accorde un tel empire,
> Je le dis seulement parce qu'il le faut dire,
> Et qu'étant au-dessus de tous les potentats,
> Il me seroit honteux de ne le dire pas.
> De quoi s'enorgueillit un souverain de Rome,
> Si par respect pour elle il doit cesser d'être homme,
> Eteindre un feu qui plaît, ou ne le ressentir
> Que pour s'en faire honte et pour le démentir? (V, 1)

Love has seldom been more paramount, appearance (kingship) and reality (passion) seldom so discrepant.

---

*According to Dort, the tyrant's bizarre death is "...la seule fin digne
d'Attila, de ce héros parvenu au bout de lui-même, qui succombe à sa
proper force, à son propre afflux de sang, qui meurt engorgé, victime de
sa liberté, de son propre éblouissement." *Pierre Corneille: dramaturge*,
p. 107. Dort's terms, as well as the thesis of his book (the destiny of the
hero) suggest that the fulfillment is more than Attila's—that it is the
"Cornelian hero's." The world of the play considered within the canon
does not seem to me to permit such an interpretation.

Yet, appearance and reality finally coincide: the lovers are paired off according to the hierarchy of their birth and station. The very fact that Corneille invented a possible mistress for his "odd man" allowed for (and, very likely for the spectator familiar with the dramaturgy, predicted) the final equations. One need only contrast Racine's procedure in which the tragic discrepancy between ideal and realization is built into the very structure of the action: two lovers contend for but one mistress. Someone, we might say of Racine's play at the very outset, is bound to utter the actual last word of the play: "Hélas!" Love and duty conflict *tragically* in Racine's *Bérénice*. Love and duty are *equally* respected in Corneille's *Tite et Bérénice*: the characters are pure; behavior is not in doubt; the situation is in doubt and some external event must resolve it. The event is *unexpected* but *explicable* "selon les lois constitutives de l'univers de la pièce." So it is with the Senate's decision. For just as l'Infante's command in *Le Cid* simply confirms a *fait accompli,* so too does the Senate's decision. And the Senate stands politically in the same relation to Tite as the king to Rodrigue: it is a dependent entity. Furthermore, in this play the harmony of person and station, of love and duty is achieved at all levels as it was not in *Le Cid*. Structurally, the role occupied by L'Infante in the earlier play, that of the rejected mistress, is not allowed to function in a vacuum of love-as-honor. Domitie is rewarded with Domitian. This "reward" thus redresses the balance between love and duty, between person and station. It restores the play to a perfect equivalence of values, allowing it to conclude with an equilibrium based not on the tensions with which it began but with an equilibrium of rest. "If only Domitian were an emperor...," "if only

Bérénice were a Roman . . ." come true and the outcome suspends the "vulgar commitments," the rigorous injunctions of the paradox of love-as-honor. Once again Corneille paints men not as they ought to be, but as they *would* be, both *généreux* and *amoureux*.

*Psyché* (1671), too, repeats the romantic mood of most of the plays since *Pertharite*. Corneille wrote the major portion of it, but Molière provided the scheme, the prologue, Act I, the first scenes of II and III, while Quinault provided the verses for those portions that were sung to music of Lully. This collaborative character as well as the purely spectacular character of the work caution against stressing its ideational aspects in a study of this kind. However, one aspect of the play does have some bearing on my thesis: the denouement in which Psyché is ascended into the heavens at Jupiter's command.

> Venez, amants, venez aux cieux
> Achever un si grand et si digne hyménée.
> Viens-y, belle Psyché, changer de destinée;
> Viens prendre place au rang des Dieux. (V, 6)

We have, of course, seen this denouement before: in *Andromède*. And, as in that play, the theology is Catholic in all its ramifications. Like Phinée, other mortals are "damned" for the sin of presumption. And, as in Catholic theology, more than one spectator might be bothered by the matter of why the Phinée of *Andromède* and the suitors of this play are not given sufficient beauty or reason to achieve Psyché's salvation. But that is another matter. This is the way things are—or could be, if . . . . For like *Andromède, Psyché* is not a *tragédie,* although, when first printed and attributed to Molière, the play was called a "*tragédie-ballet.*" The compound itself suggests softening of the tragic, especially as it evokes the *comédies-ballets* of Molière. The ballets carry us beyond the reality in which true tragedy operates and, combined with other aspects of the play, even beyond the ideality of certain of Corneille's political plays. We are in an "as if" world almost as soon as we leave Molière's king at the end of Act II, scene 1: a world of fantasy not unlike that of the grotto of Alcandre in *L'Illusion*, a lyrical anteroom of heaven to which we are transported at the beginning rather than at the end of the action (as in *Andromède*), It is a splendid world of gods and godlike men (or women) in which mundane creatures like the suitors are only intruders. Indeed, more so than in any other play (including the very similar *Andromède*) the purely physical is posited as the principal sign of a character's worth, an emphasis which makes this play the closest in theme to the earliest comedies. But, as we might expect in this far more aristocratic world, the theme of honor does not go unhonored, though it does not supplant the theme of love. It is a world in which the two can coexist, a world before the Fall, Paradise Regained.*

---

* In his study of Dryden's heroic plays, Thomas H. Fujirama regards honor and love as coequal passions which are victorious in a conflict with reason. "Reason" means here that adjudicative faculty which inhibits the free expression of any passion. Fujirama notes that this view of the relations among the psychic faculties was held by Restoration audiences as it is even in our own day by "naturalistic" and "skeptical" philosophers and psychologists (among them Freud). However, the critic also notes that the attitude toward the relation differed for the earlier audience: they welcomed the triumph of the passions of honor and love over reason. If there is what might be called an adjudicative reason in Corneille, it is not a reproving faculty, it is an approving faculty. Given the *rationale* of *générosité*—in particular, the equation of station and merit—reason enjoins the *généreux* to realize his sense of self as a hero and to seek out an equal as his lover: the nobly born behave nobly, the nobly born are drawn to the nobly born. See Fujirama's "The Appeal of Dryden's Heroic Plays," *PMLA, LXXV*, 37-45.

## 5

# Pulchérie and Suréna

## le généreux once more

Paradise is indeed in another world when we turn to Corneille's last two plays. *Pulchérie* (1672), said Mme de Sévigné, ". . . fait souvenir des anciennes."[1] Yet *Pulchérie* does not take us back to the paradoxes of love-as-honor. In its *combats amoureux,* opposing viewpoints are not harmonized, lovers do not drive each other to higher and higher levels of being. There is a conflict within the individual soul, a split that cannot be resolved through a chance, which, however precariously, will finally reveal itself to be destiny. Love and duty, the private self and the public self, are in dire conflict and sacrifice is unavoidable: that it is the public self which triumphs is undoubtedly what prompted Mme de Sévigné's comparison, although we should not fail to observe once again that the concept of "self" in the theme is more important than that of "public."

Yes, there are differences. In the political tetralogy one loved only whom one was born to love and destiny rarely made a mistake in the case of the central characters of the piece. This very rule created great "tragic potential" in certain secondary characters, but even their promptings of the heart were often flaccid, guilt-ridden, and in-effectual. In *Pulchérie,* the *promptings* of the heart be-come the *demands* of the heart, and so the conflict with the demands of *gloire* is keener even than in *Le Cid* or *Polyeucte. Gloire* is the stronger element at the outset and it remains so at the end. In this play the decision of the Senate need not *accommodate* the lovers, as in *Tite et Bérénice.* (True, the Senate shows itself the dependent body it should be in a world organized around the majesty of the *généreux* or *généreuse*). Even Pulchérie's earlier tergiversations upon her being named to the throne instead of her lover were based not on a reasoned, pru-dential fear of being unable to retain power but upon a refusal to demean herself by *appearing* to compromise her power. Her cultivation of the hope that the Senate will name Léon her consort, thereby doing the next best thing to naming him Emperor, is the last vestige of love, one which must be overcome *independently* of the Senate's decision if the victory of the public self is to be completed in the play. As it is. Even before the Senate renders its decision (or its indecision) , Pulchérie tells Justine:

> Je ne sais si le rang m'auroit fait changer d'âme;
> Mais je tremble à penser que je serois sa [Léon] femme,
> Et qu'on n'épouse point l'amant le plus chéri,
> Qu'on ne se fasse un maître aussitôt qu'un mari.
> J'aimerois à régner avec l'indépendance
> Que des vrais souverains s'assure la prudence;
> Je voudrois que le ciel inspirât au sénat
> De me laisser moi seule à gouverner l'Etat,     (V, 1)

So Pulchérie renounces the beloved Léon in order to marry the aged Martian who is in love with her. It is not because of his love that she rewards him with her hand;

it is for his loyal service. Similarly with Justine: she is given Léon not because she loves him, but because, as the new consort's daughter, her marriage to the empress' true love will legitimize that true love's ultimate ascension to the throne.

Love and duty are, then, not united but paired at the end of *Pulchérie*. Martian seems to make up for Sertorius' destiny. Yet, he does not get his mistress on the terms he wished for. Had he not already given evidence of expecting no more than this, had he himself not already suppressed love in the name of honor? With far more conviction than Sertorius, this aging lover rejects Pertharite's "il est temps de tourner du coté du bonheur" to declare that it is time to follow his mistress who has found it possible to say: "Je sacrifierai tout au bonheur de l'Etat" (IV, 2).

Such readiness prevents us from considering *Pulchérie* as a tragedy: love, the demands of the person, is consistently cast as the lesser value in the play and, consistently enough, it is this value which is "sacrificed" in the play. The best happens to the best. True, Martian's failure to possess his mistress in "the flesh" or, for that matter, in the heart, might be construed as an instance of limitations upon the human. And there is the same great tragic potential in Martian as in Sertorius: he is born too low or too late for empire, which makes him "tragic" even prior to falling in love; destiny seems to have erred. Moreover, chance comes to complicate destiny: he falls irrationally in love beyond his station and beyond his age.* When Pulchérie confronts him with his failure to

---

* Being the portrait of the artist as an old man, according to some critics. The identification between Corneille and Martian goes back to Fontenelle (*Oeuvres, II*, Première Partie, 346), and is heard more recently in Herland's *Corneille par lui-même*, p. 155.

conceal his love, his reply suggests the attempt to justify his love as rational. He says that love is inevitably born of "zèle" and "estime"— and this might sharpen our sense of the tragedy that he is born "out of place." Still, were we to grant that this tragic potential is not removed by the "happy ending"—indeed, that it is emphatically actualized in the denouement—we would once again only have an instance of the tragic relegated to the "secondary hero."

In *Suréna* (1674) this potential has shifted to a primary character: Suréna himself. The world of Corneille's last play is apparently centered around love as a destructive passion. The *éclat* of *généreux* behavior, symbolized in the panoply and splendor of the city of Séleucie, belies the reality. This is apparently better symbolized by Héca-tompyle, the private city of the heart to which, like so many of Racine's heroes and heroines, the first speaker of the play would flee. On the lips of the heroes and heroines of this play, the term *soupir* finds as great if not greater welcome as *gloire* or *devoir* on those of earlier heroes and heroines. "Un accord imprévu confondoit nos soupirs" (I, 1), Eurydice says of Suréna's reaction to her in their first encounter. And Pacorus fears lest the heart of his beloved "... pour un autre objet [il] soupire en mes bras" (II, 1). "Mes pleurs et mes soupirs rappelleront les siens" (III, 3) conjectures the vindictive Palmis, spurned by Pacorus for Eurydice. Apparently in vain does the king, Orode, enjoin these lovers to reverse the descent into the lower region of the soul:

C'est bien traiter les rois en personnes communes
Qu'attacher à leur rang ces gênes importunes, (III, 3)

The descent continues. The dramatic trajectory of almost

all the principals, shows a harried, "Racinian" quality.

That this should be so in the case of Pacorus, say, is not surprising. The *généreux secondaire* has often behaved in this way. But with the memory of so many *généreuses* who "bounced back," Eurydice's role as *amoureuse* seems the most compromising to date. She presents herself from the very beginning as more of an *amoureuse* than a *généreuse*. As she evokes an earlier time, a predramatic time, in which she was an *amante généreuse* (I, 1), the accents are suspiciously sentimental, even if there is nothing in the formulation to suggest that the love was "blind." Again, when the demands of station threaten to prevent her from possessing Suréna, she tells him:

> Je veux qu'un noir chagrin à pas lents me consume,
> Qu'il me fasse à longs traits goûter son amertume;
> Je veux, sans que la mort ose me secourir,
> Toujours aimer, toujours souffrir, toujours mourir.
> Mais pardonneriez-vous l'aveu d'une foiblesse
> A cette douloureuse et fatale tendresse? (I, 3)

The injunctions in force here are not those of love-as-honor. As the prosody suggests, through its parallel constructions, they are sensual in basis, a "Freudian" linkage of love and death as we might nowadays put it. In vain does this heroine seek to rise above her love in her confrontation with her lover. As Eurydice reserves to herself the right to dispose of her lover's hand (I, 3), she sounds like earlier queens making similar demands. But where a Pulchérie, for example, wished to be obeyed, this queen cannot hold to her demands upon herself, much less to those upon her lover:

> Moi? que ne puis-je, hélas
> Vous ôter à Mandane, et ne vous donner pas!

> Et contre les soupçons de ce coeur qui vous aime
> Que ne m'est-il permis de m'assurer moi-même! (I, 3)

It is Eurydice herself who gives us the clearest explanation *à la* La Rochefoucauld of how the head follows the dictates of the heart, or, in Cornelian terms, of how *estime* depends on *amour*:

> Il est si naturel d'estimer ce qu'on aime,
> Qu'on voudroit que partout on l'estimât de même;
> Et la pente est si douce à vanter ce qu'il vaut,
> Que jamais on ne craint de l'élever trop haut. (II, 2)

Much of Eurydice's cultivation of *généreux* behavior must finally be read as a means whereby she seeks to maintain the *status quo* in the hope that somehow she and Suréna can be united in the flesh as well as in the spirit. Thus, her injunction to Pacorus to make himself equal in *mérite* to her lover (unnamed on the occasion) is only a stall. In the last act, natural love expresses itself negatively but fully in her jealousy of Mandane. Finally, when her lover is clearly threatened with death, Eurydice gives in (too late) to Palmis' and the king's demand that Suréna marry Mandane, since this means that at least her lover will have been saved, that he will still exist as a *promesse de jouissance*. Eurydice does not, of course, finally enjoy Suréna as a *promesse de jouissance*: her lover has been slain. Love has apparently proved to be a destructive force, for in refusing to accept the injunction to wed Mandane and thereby renounce Eurydice, Suréna has been obliged to die. The love affairs of this play do not work out with the mathematical nicety of *Agésilas,* for example. Not even those who are left, Pacorus and Palmis, can be expected to be joined now, since Palmis is unreconciled to the outcome of events.

Orode lays the responsibility where it truly lies: in the discrepancy between Suréna's station and virtue:

> Et dans tout ce qu'il a de nom et de fortune,
> Sa fortune me pèse, et son nom m'importune. (III, 1)

And Suréna is still more specific:

> Madame, ce refus n'est point vers lui mon crime;
> Vous m'aimez: ce n'est point non plus ce qui l'anime.
> Mon crime véritable est d'avoir aujourd'hui
> Plus de nom que mon roi, plus de vertu que lui; (V, 2)

Suréna's real enemy is not Eurydice, nor love, nor is it even Orode in himself:

> Eurydice: Que le ciel n'a-t-il mis en ma main et la vôtre,
> Ou de n'être à personne, ou d'être l'un à l'autre!
> Suréna: Falloit-il que l'amour vît l'inégalité
> Vous abandonner toute aux rigueurs d'un traité!
> Eur.: Cette inégalité me souffroit l'espérance.
> Votre nom, vos vertus valoient bien ma naissance, (V, 2)

and to his sister just before he goes to his death: "Mon vrai crime est ma gloire, et non pas mon amour" (V, 3). Suréna is the supreme hero and as such he deserves (*mérite*) the supreme partner, Eurydice, the daughter of a king. His being corresponded and so had the right to respond to hers according to all the laws of *générosité*; their love was only to be expected. Love does not come to him as some kind of *"aveugle sympathie"* threatening his status as a *généreux*. But fate having forced the conflict between his heart and his soul (the division as expressed by Eurydice), he finally shows himself more of a *généreux* than an *amoureux*—a *généreux* who is apparently defeated.

As with the mistress, so then with the hero of the play himself. Like Sertorius, Suréna is troubled in his heart and troubled in his station. He is happier than Sertorius, of course, in that the woman he loves does love him. Yet, no more than Sertorius is he politically in a position to unite with his beloved in flesh as well as in spirit. His accents are even more passional than those of Sertorius when we first meet him:

> Et souffrez qu'un soupir exhale à vos genoux,
> Pour ma dernière joie, une âme toute à vous. (I, 3)

He is a *"soupirant"* of a kind with the other lovers of the play. He even appears to go further than Pertharite in his rejection of *généreux* values. When his mistress insists that he live and wed someone else in order to ensure a progeny whose glory will reflect on the glory of her own capacity for sacrifice, he retorts:

> Que tout meure avec moi, Madame: que m'importe
> Qui foule après ma mort la terre qui me porte?
> Sentiront-ils percer par un éclat nouveau,
> Ces illustres aïeux, la nuit de leur tombeau?
> Respireront-ils l'air où les feront revivre
> Ces neveux qui peut-être auront peine à les suivre,
> Peut-être ne feront que les déshonorer,
> Et n'en auront le sang que pour dégénérer?
> Quand nous avons perdu le jour qui nous éclaire,
> Cette sorte de vie est bien imaginaire,
> Et le moindre moment d'un bonheur souhaité
> Vaut mieux qu'une si froide et vaine éternité. (I, 3)

The "froide" suggests that the "bonheur" with which it

contrasts is a warm and sensual one, being an echo of the frankly sexual concerns already noted in Eurydice. *Suréna* is thus one of those plays in which, as the critic George Steiner has said, "what [Corneille] can tell us of the power of death of the heart is worth hearing outside the confines of the Comédie Francaise." [2] Moreover Jean Starobinski has pointed to the hero of this play and in particular to the speech I have just quoted as evidence of a split in Corneille between the psychology of the dramatist's characters and the ideology of the dramatist's audience.[3] The latter believes in or behaves according to the code of *générosité* with its injunctions of duty to house, state, king, etc. The hero believes only in himself and he does so existentially: he recognizes or comes to recognize that there are no received values—there are only the values a man forges for himself. And these are especially precarious. Like many another Cornelian play, then, *Suréna* is one of the earliest "existentialist tragedies" or, if we follow Steiner's thesis of the "death of the heart," betokens at least a shift from heroic comedy to a more truly tragic outlook.

Yet, it would be a mistake, I believe, to look upon *Suréna* in such ways. True, the intimations of the tragic are greater in this play than in any other Corneille has written. Nevertheless, the dramatist seems recalcitrant to carry through on the commitment to the tragic. And this is so whether we think of the tragedy as lying in the death of the heart or in the discrepancy between Suréna's merit and station—or both. For example, there is no gainsaying that the import of the speech cited is all that Starobinski says it is and there is no denying the power of the heart in the hero and his mistress. Yet, it should be noted that this is where the hero begins, that this "unheroic" speech is not Suréna's last in the play. Again, if we are to think of the tragedy as lying in the "death of the heart," we should note that, within the universe of the play, the heart is not *in the end* recognized as the *supreme* value.

> La tendresse n'est point de l'amour d'un héros:
> Il est honteux pour lui d'écouter des sanglots;
> Et parmi la douceur des plus illustres flammes,
> Un peu de dureté sied bien aux grandes âmes. (V, 3)

are the last words we hear Suréna utter. Yet, this does not mean he has ceased to love. Rather, in this moment before death he has overcome the *amoureux* in his character in order to become the last *amant généreux*. He does not reject love, but returns to the injunctions and equations of love-as-honor. Were he to die less gloriously, he would belie Eurydice's natural penchant for him in the first place. Similarly, in the case of Eurydice, there is a kind of "taking back" of the tragic implications of her role as *amoureuse*. In death, she too sounds more like a *généreuse*:

> EURYDICE: Non, je ne pleure point, Madame, mais je meurs.
> Ormène, soutiens-moi.
>                   ORMÈNE: Que dites-vous, Madame?
> EUR.: Généreux Suréna, reçois toute mon âme. (V, 5)

Given the situation, death seems the "logical" reaction on the part of Eurydice: the news of her beloved's death literally kills her. Still, the texture belies, as it were, the structure. The language is fraught with *généreux* values: like many another Cornelian hero and heroine, Eurydice wishes to die upright, "vertical," to recall Merian-Genast's analysis of the dramatist's language. And, of course it is as a *généreuse* that she addresses her lover for the last time. Again, when we recall that she had made a distinction between her soul (*âme*) and her heart (*coeur*) in refuting Pacorus' claims on her (II, 2), her use of *âme* here suggests that she sees herself more in the volitional, intellectual cast of a *généreuse* than in the sentimental or passional cast of an *amoureuse* in this moment of death. Finally, the tone is so calm that her death seems more willed than suffered, a notion which seems underscored in the rhyming contrast between *pleure* and *meurs*. Crying would be the act of a weakling in this circumstance; dying is the act of a hero, an instrument, as we have so often noted in Corneille, of self-affirmation.*

If the heart dies in this "tragedy," then, it does so with the approval of those in whom it dies. They subscribe to other, higher values. But do not these values "die?" Does not the tragedy really lie in the very discrepancy between station and merit which complicated the lovers' relations? At crucial moments in the action, various key characters clearly recognize that it is not love as a destructive passion which is responsible for Suréna's death at all. Nor is it easy to say of Suréna as of Sertorius that he is not a good example of this tragic, since he is *not* the best which the world *could* actually have offered. Though the world in which Sertorius found himself may be said to have deteriorated, notably in the corruption of Pompée, the main tenet of *générosité*, the identity between station

---

* Voltaire maintains that Eurydice's "Non, je ne pleure point, madame, mais je meurs" is by itself "très tragique" but that it is alone of this kind in the play. As I have suggested, it is in fact not alone of its kind in the play precisely in that it is not tragic. See *Commentaires, Oeuvres complètes* (Garnier edition), *XXXII*, 303.

and merit, was still maintained in the queen figures of the play, especially in Viriate. She is the best which the world of the play has to offer both in merit *and* in station, but she knows no tragic destiny. But in Suréna's world, the deterioration is far more complete. Orode may be said to correspond in corruption to the Pompée of *Sertorius,* but there is no character to correspond to Viriate. Eurydice, as a Princess of Armenia, is equal to her in station, but not in character (except, paradoxically, at the end, as I have noted). Furthermore, Suréna's merit is underscored here to an extent that even Sertorius' was not: we are reminded that it is due to Suréna's prowess that Orode actually remains on the throne. As Eurydice says of her lover very early in the action, he is:

> Des Parthes le mieux fait d'esprit et de visage,
> Le plus puissant en biens, le plus grand en courage,
> Le plus noble: (I, 1)

The estimate echoes Corneille's in his "Au Lecteur": ". . . le plus noble, le plus riche, le mieux fait, et le plus vaillant des Parthes," [4] and Corneille, himself echoing Plutarch here, must surely have known that Plutarch also characterized the hero as "le second des Parthes après le Roy, tant en noblesse qu'en richesse et en reputation; mais en vaillance, suffisance et experience au fait des armes, le premier personnage qui fust de son temps entre les Parthes, et au demourant en grandeur et baulté de corps ne cedant à nul autre." [5] The best that the universe has to offer and, one suspects, *could ever have offered.* But not a king. Fate has done Suréna one of these injustices Pauline (of *Polyeucte*) claimed it had done to Sévère, but here it makes no correction of its own mistakes.

Or does the mistake really lie with Suréna? As with the problem of locating the tragedy in the death of the heart, so with locating it in the discrepancy between Suréna's station and his merit: Corneille seems reluctant to follow through on the implications of the situation he has created. Suréna, he seems to tell us, is not out of place: the others of the play are. The "flaw" in the world of the play is not Suréna's secondary station, rather

> Quoi? vous vous figurez que l'heureux nom de gendre,
> Si ma perte est jurée, a de quoi m'en défendre,
> Quand malgré la nature, en dépit de ses lois,
> Le parricide a fait la moitié de nos rois,
> Qu'un frère pour régner se baigne au sang d'un frère,
> Qu'un fils impatient prévient la mort d'un père? (V, 3)

"In spite of nature, in spite of her laws," says Suréna. Like Oedipe, Suréna is not a victim, he is a judge.

However, unlike Oedipe, he does not challenge destiny to do right by him, because he does not come to see that destiny has done wrong by him. He concludes the speech from which I have just quoted:

> Mais, Dieux! se pourroit-il qu'ayant si bien servi,
> Par l'ordre de mon roi le jour me fût ravi?
> Non, non: c'est d'un bon oeil qu'Orode me regarde;
> Vous le voyez, ma soeur, je n'ai pas même un garde:
> Je suis libre. (V, 3)

He goes off to his death, of course, as he perhaps knows he will, considering that he is well aware of Orode's capacity for treachery. Is this speech ironic, our clue to (and perhaps his rueful admission of) the futility of his belief in a rational order according to which king equates with virtue? Is death the seal on this loss of belief? Perhaps. But, here again, Corneille seems to have hesitated before the tragic potential; earlier in the scene he has placed on the lips of Suréna quite another view of the death to which he willingly goes:

> J'aime mieux qu'elle soit un crime qu'un hasard;
> Qu'aucun ne l'attribue à cette loi commune
> Qu'impose la nature et règle la fortune;
> Que son perfide auteur, bien qu'il cache sa main,
> Devienne abominable à tout le genre humain;
> Et qu'il en naisse enfin des haines immortelles
> Qui de tous ses sujets lui fassent des rebelles. (V, 3)

Suréna will snatch victory out of defeat—and not merely that "spiritual" victory which some writers on tragedy see as peculiar to the form.[6] Rather, this is a victory on the natural plane, quite literally a strategic victory in the concrete, military sense of the term. There is nothing paradoxical in this view of death, for we then admire Suréna not for a mysterious vindication of himself *in spite of* destiny but a quite understandable vindication of himself *according to* destiny. Nor should we find a contradiction in the two different invocations of nature's laws by Suréna in the same scene: nature has a set of laws for the common and a different set of laws for the noble. Indeed, this distinction becomes clear if we think of "natural death" being for the common precisely because it is something to which one *submits*. The death which Suréna knows is one which he *commits*.

In the end, *we* may judge Suréna's fate as tragic, seeing the world as essentially made up of Orodes and Pacoruses who always defeat the Surénas, the best the world has to offer. Corneille himself lays the basis for such an interpretation, albeit hesitantly. But, if a tragedy,

*Suréna* is one without a clear-cut tragic "illumination." Even if Suréna's final remarks are to be construed as ironic, as I have suggested they might be, is this not a begrudging acknowledgement of the tragic? Moreover, it is significant that the play does provide just as much evidence for the view that Suréna really uses his death to defeat Orode. This deprives him, like so many other Cornelian heroes, of tragic potential. He knows no defeat, then, either on the natural or spiritual plane, from which he must snatch victory. Suréna's values remain intact. His is the last trajectory of fulfillment or realization; his death is the last phase of the entelechy of a *généreux*. He dies for honor and glory. Nor is the triumph of honor found only in the beyond. Palmis remains, but not to wed Pacorus as she might have in one of the "comedylike" tragedies (the blame might have been put on the father figure, Orode, instead of upon the son). Rather:

> PALMIS: Suspendez ces douleurs qui pressent de mourir,
> Grands Dieux! et dans les maux où vous m'avez plongée,
> Ne souffrez point ma mort que je ne sois vengée! (V, 5)

The final expression of the desire to rise again, the final words of a Cornelian play. They are to be regretted perhaps for their negative spirit, but, for all that, they are not untypical of their author: emphatic, self-confident, imperative, undefeated—Cornelian.*

---

* After using up the "passions ordinaires," Saint-Evremond writes, "Corneille s'est fait un nouveau mérite à toucher des tendresses plus recherchées, de plus fines jalousies, et de plus secrètes douleurs," *Oeuvres, I,* 218. Indeed—and we can also note with Lancaster that "if the reference, as seems probable, is to *Suréna,* it means that, according to Saint-Evremond, Corneille's interest in experimentation remained with him to the end." *History,* Part Four, *I,* 145. But neither the sounding of new passions nor the experimentation lead him to a basic change of outlook.

# Conclusion

# The Cornelian Universe

In looking at each play of Corneille I have tried to respect the values of the world of the work, not to judge them according to another set of values. I do not mean to imply that the world of a given play bears no resemblance to the world from which and for which it draws its examples of character and action. As Bénichou has insisted, one must be aware of the aristocratic milieu for which Corneille wrote. But respect for the values of the world of a play has led me to look at those values, whatever their historical reference, from one end of the play to the other, from the beginning of a world to its end. In following a given plot, I have been concerned not to lift out examples of this or that value, but to consider these examples in the context of the developing *and concluding* action. I have been especially concerned to understand the world in which a certain conception of the self has been imperiled, to see whether the peril to this conception has been or even could be real in the world of the play.

The world of Corneille is ordinarily thought of as the world of the political tetralogy: *Le Cid, Horace, Cinna, Polyeucte*. This, it is assumed, is the way things are in Corneille: a world of nobles torn by conflict between love and duty set against the political realities of an ascendant or established monarchy. The heroes of this world are truly heroes: exceptional protectors of values, defenders of the state, although the state is identified with themselves. Not unexpectedly, the historical echoes here of the heroes Corneille knew and of the world in which

Corneille lived suggest to many that this is the way things must be in Corneille. When it has not led to neglect of the rest of the canon, this realistic assumption has foreshortened critical perspectives of the canon on either side of the tetralogy. The near side of the tetralogy has been viewed in such terms as apprenticeship and anticipation, the far side in such terms as decline and repetition. Such evolutionary concepts have the virtue of treating the canon as a unit, correcting the misleading impressions which an exclusive concentration on the tetralogy has ensconced in non-French criticism in particular. However, if centered on the tetralogy, the evolutionary approach in its own way falsifies the genius of Corneille. Of no other French dramatist has so little been said about so much. It is ironic that, in attempting to give some account of the length, if not breadth, of Corneille's output, much historical criticism has failed to take into account Corneille's oft-expressed desire to renew himself, his prideful deference to *"invention"* and *"nouveauté."*

I have tried to show that this desired variety is reflected in the canon even in the purely ideological questions thought of as "Cornelian." Yet, I would not suggest that each play represents a radical departure from its predecessor. The relationship of love to duty is indeed a theme of the entire canon; there are definite characterological and ethical resemblances among the heroes whose separate destinies I have traced. But the relationship between love and duty is not always one of conflict, nor, when it is conflict, always one in which this value triumphs over that. The relationship is also one of suspension, assimilation, and adjustment. The hero is not always at odds with his beloved, nor, when he is, is he reconciled to her only in a paradoxical possession-in-renunciation. Hero and heroine are often—indeed, most often—united in both flesh and spirit.

Or, since the plural is more accurate, heroes and heroines. And they inhabit not a world but a universe of worlds. Reminding the reader that I have traced tendencies rather than described systems, I would summarize the five types of heroes and their worlds as follows:

1. The *damoiseau* in an idyllic world, or, as Nadal describes the world of the plays I have in mind, a pastoral-bourgeois worlds: *Melite* to *L'Illusion comique.* In these plays there is really no conflict between love and duty. Rather, the value of duty is either presupposed or ignored, in the etymological sense of the latter term. Love is the dominant value, but it in no way compromises duty. In the idyllic or mythological setting of the play, love is apparently all, but the appearance is all that really counts. There is no underlying reality, no implied set of values, in conflict with what we see and hear. In this world the concrete and the perceived, dramatically centered around the sensual, immediately convey the values of the world. The heroes and heroines of this world are more amiable than heroic, *gentilshommes* more than *généreux*. In literary terms we might call these plays fantasies (Greek: φαντασία, appearance), thereby indicating the generic resemblance between the so-called early comedies, one tragicomedy, *Clitandre,* and the one *"tragédie,"* as Corneille called *Médée.* As my individual analyses show, these last two plays show many characteristics of the comedies designated as such—particularly in the secondary characters. In them as in the comedies, value conflicts are not so much denied as suspended. *L'Illusion comique* obviously serves as a kind of résumé of this form, the most fantastical of the fantasies.

2. The *généreux* in a world presumed by many scholars to reflect the values of the world in which and for which Corneille wrote: *Le Cid* to *La Mort de Pompée*. I do not believe that Corneille writes a series of *pièces à clef* in the "political" plays of this and the following groups. However, on the other hand, I do not believe that this means there are no connections between Corneille and the France of Richelieu-Louis XIII or of Mazarin-Louis XIV. "L'enthousiasme cornélien baigne," writes Paul Bénichou, "tout entier dans l'atmosphère de l'orgueil, de la gloire, de la générosité et du romanesque aristocratiques, telle qu'on la respirait en France pendant le règne de Louis XIII, telle qu'elle remplit toute la littérature de l'époque."* And Bénichou also notes that though Cor-

---

* *Morales du grand siècle,* p. 14. I follow Bénichou more than Couton in this matter precisely because Couton's sense of realism in Corneille tends to make the dramatist more of a historiographer than an artist. Of course, like Couton, Bénichou finds a close correlation between the Cornelian hero and the rebellious aristocrats who wage the wars of La Fronde. However, Bénichou is less concerned to work out this part of the Cornelian canon as a series of *pièces à clef* than to see in it a spiritual record of the conflict. He points out that the dynamics of the rebellious aristocrat were very like those of the ascendant monarch: "L'idée d'une volonté suprême, s'exerçant librement et gratuitement, d'une majesté que rien ne limite, hante les esprits libres: leur propre rêve de puissance et de gloire se réalise de tout temps dans la royauté, où ils ont toujours aimé voir quelque chose d'irréductible" (p. 61). Finally, Bénichou notes that the Cornelian canon aims at a reconciliation of the conflict according to the tenets of the ancient feudal pact. I differ with Bénichou on only two points: (1) I would stress perhaps even more than he that there is a certain limit placed on the kings and heroes: the imperatives to a code of self-sufficiency which derives from their sense of self given with their noble birth. The critic himself points out that, with the rare examples of Cleopatre (*Rodogune*) and Attila, "l'orgueil véritablement héroïque répugne à détruire la loi morale" (p. 28). (2) It seems to me that the reconciliation gives the upper hand more to the king than to the rebellious aristocrat. For one thing, as Bénichou himself points out, the aristocrat is willing to accept the thesis that the king becomes abusive only because of evil counselors (Garibalde in *Pertharite*). For another, *l'ambitieux* turns out to be *le vrai roi* (for

neille is not a political theorist, "ses personnages argumentent souvent, intercalent dans le drame de l'écho des discussions politiques de son temps."[1] Yet, practical wisdom suggests that we have in these plays more the way things ought to be than the way they are with respect to the relationship between hero and society, between *généreux* and *généreuse*. I do not simply mean that the political resolutions differ from those which history provided, although we could note that Corneille is much less of a *frondeur* than some would have him. Rather, we get a heightening of the ideal.

There is no loss of value in these plays, no sacrifice of either love or duty, but a paradoxical preservation of these values presumably in conflict. As I have tried to show, this preservation is only implicit in *Le Cid,* whose actual resolution resembles more that of plays projecting a different world. But in *Horace, Cinna, Polyeucte,* and *Pompée,* the hero is a full-fledged *généreux,* realizing himself both in his political and amorous conflicts in a unitary way. As Péguy puts it:

C'est un balancement secret, douloureux, béni, malheureux, heureux, un retour et un retour, un balancement silencieux du même au même, de cet honneur et amour nommé honneur, à cet amour et honneur nommé amour.

Nous n'avons qu'un honneur. Il est tant de maîtresses, dit le vieux don Diègue. Mais l'idée de Rodrigue, et l'idée cornélienne, leur système d'être et leur système de pensée,

example, Don Sanche and Nicomède). Bénichou acknowledges this last fact and says that the very confusion of identity between aristocrat and future king is significant, but he fails to explain in what way (p. 69).

Fidao-Justiniani (*Qu'est-ce qu'un classique? 1: Le Héros ou du génie*) also shows the survival of heroic ideals in the century. Concerned primarily with critical concepts and with the latter half of the century, he does not cite Corneille too frequently in his illustrations.

c'est premièrement que nous n'avons qu'un honneur, deuxiè-
mement que nous n'avons qu'une maîtresse, troisièmement
que c'est la même unicité.[2]

As my analysis of this conception in the five plays shows,
I do not believe with Péguy that the paradox is tragic in
nature or that it issues in tragedy. Because it does not,
I would suggest a different designation of these plays from
that of *"tragédie"* which Péguy accepts: heroic comedy.
Corneille himself called some of his plays by this name
and Jean Rousset has suggested that it be extended to all
of the obviously noncomic plays of the canon.[3] The suggestion that Corneille's later plays as well as his "early"
ones are a variety of *comedy* is well taken. However, I
believe one can suggest still further generic distinctions
among the serious plays, so I would reserve the term
"heroic comedy" and all that it implies of grandeur for
precisely these five plays. In them, involved in a serious
conflict of values, the hero lives up to the great expectations based on the fact that he is clearly identified as
a *généreux* in station from the outset and is not obliged
to make sacrifices in order to realize his entelechy. He
knows no "tragic illumination" in the end, for he has
been "illuminated" from the beginning about those
values which he realizes or demonstrates in the action
of the play.

3. The *ambitieux* or unindentified *généreux* in an ultimately ideal world, one also reflecting the values of the
world in which and for which Corneille wrote, but only
in a final moment: *Le Menteur* to *Nicomède*. In the plays
I have called "heroic comedies," the *généreux* is clearly
identified as such from the outset. In particular, he
occupies his station without question and this unques-

tioned occupancy at once gives heightened interest to the love-duty conflict and provides the bases for its paradoxical resolution. In the plays from *Le Menteur* to *Nicomède,* Corneille still works on the preconceptions of the heroic comedies, but he deliberately disappoints the "great expectations" based on his audience's political assumptions (or, as for readers and spectators without those assumptions, to which he has conditioned his audience). The *généreux* is imperfect, defective in such a way that there is a discrepancy between station and behavior; usually, the defect is in station (*Rodogune* is a significant exception). The hero behaves heroically, but he is not born to the station (or woman) he would possess; the world of the plays is still political and, though not so frequently or so forcefully, the paradox of love-as-honor is still in force. Yet the prowess of the heroes casts them as self-made men and their aspirations as *ambitieux.* They also work out their ambition in a world charged with doubt and intrigue. However, their behavior is retroactively justified by a sudden revelation that they do indeed belong to a station dictating their kind of behavior; they are *finally* construed not as *ambitieux,* but as *généreux.*

This summary as well as my individual analyses suggest that many of these plays resemble detective stories, although they are "who-is-its" more than "who-dun-its." Furthermore, in view of the charged atmosphere of the plays and of the sensational, extravagant response to challenge by many of the characters, Georges May has appropriately included many of them (as well as others which I place elsewhere) in "l'ecole du mélodrame." [4] This designation is apt, except that I would note that I include the comedy *Le Menteur* under it only insofar as it projects the particular kind of dramaturgy Corneille will use in the plays which more obviously are melodramas: the patterns of the scene casting doubt followed by the scene providing guarantees of various kinds. Otherwise, *Le Menteur* quite obviously is a comedy. Finally, I trust that the analysis of *Rodogune* and *Nicomède* shows that I intend no pejorative judgment by the term "melodrama." In these two melodramas Corneille raises the genre to a level providing as much perspective on the values of the heroic comedies as any one of those plays.

4. The *amoureux* in a utopian world: *Pertharite* to *Psyché*. In these plays the relationship between love and duty veers toward a true division of the self. As in the fantasies, love is a private emotion, though one more sentimental than sensual in expression. We have, of course, noted this conception in certain of the melodramas, but now the expression is more insistent. At the same time, duty is also insistent, as it was in the heroic comedies. Political realities would seem to dictate certain lines of behavior to the *généreux* and *généreuse* if they are to be worthy of their predecessors in the heroic comedies or of their ideal counterparts in the mind of the spectator. Here, however, the discrepancy between the expectable and the actual is even sharper than it was in the melodramas. There is no doubt, as in the melodramas, about the station of the *généreux*, but love apparently reigns supreme. It does not so much triumph over duty as simply subordinate duty to its own demands. However, in the end, the hero is made happy as both *généreux* and *amoureux*. This solution is made possible neither by a retraction on the part of the "compromised" *généreux* (Rodogune) nor by a magnanimous gesture which similarly comes from within the *généreux* (Nico-

mède's clemency), but by an external development or one which was inherent only as an "outside possibility" in the political as distinguished from the characterological *données* of the play.

I would call these plays "romances," according to Henry James' use of the term:

> The only *general* attribute of projected romance that I can see, the only one that fits all its cases, is the fact of the kind of experience with which it deals—experience liberated, so to speak; experience disengaged, disembroiled, disencumbered, exempt from the conditions that we usually know to attach to it and, if we wish so to put the matter, drag upon it, and operating in a medium which relieves it, in a particular interest, of the inconvenience of a *related,* a measurable state, a state subject to our vulgar communities.*

Obviously, these plays have much in common with the plays I have designated melodramas: charged atmosphere, questions of identity, extravagant responses, denouements with *coups de théâtre,* etc. Georges May has thus included *Oedipe* in the plays he designated melodramas.[5] Yet, the denouements of these plays seem to me to set them apart from the melodramas, especially with respect to the love-duty relationship. The melodramas finally return us to the values of the heroic comedies, the concepts of love-as-

---

* "Preface to *The American*" in *The Art of the Novel,* p. 33. These plays also answer to Northrop Frye's concept of romance: "The romance is the nearest of all literary forms to the wish-fulfillment dream, and for that reason it has sociologically a curiously paradoxical role. In every age the ruling social or intellectual class tends to project its ideals in some form of romance, where the virtuous heroes and beautiful heroines represent the ideals and the villains the threats to their ascendancy. This is the general character of chivalric romance in the Middle Ages, aristocratic romance in the Renaissance, bourgeois romance since the eighteenth century, and revolutionary romance in contemporary Russia" (*Anatomy of Criticism,* p. 186).

honor. If the commitments of the world of the heroic comedies were suspended during the greater part of the action in the melodramas, they were restored in the end. But in the plays from *Pertharite* to *Psyché,* love and honor are upheld only partially or not at all throughout the action and in the denouement are upheld independently, "utopianly." We are thus closer to the world of the early comedies than we are to that of the tetralogy.

5. The *généreux* once more or the *amoureux* turned *généreux* in a real world: *Pulchérie* and *Suréna.* Here the political realities are closer to those which we might expect in a political play: intrigue and ambition, the hero without station, irrational love complicating duty. Nevertheless, just as practical wisdom suggests that the heroic comedies idealize the world of seventeenth-century France which they reflect, so such wisdom might suggest, at least in the case of *Suréna,* that this world is painted in perhaps too dark colors, that it is a kind of underworld in a modern rather than classical sense. Be that as it may, in these plays the relationship between love and duty is one of painful conflict. Passion is a law of the human heart, but self-realization is an equally imperious law in the political setting where this love figures. However, there are no *"fausses pistes"* as in the melodramas and no "saving conditions" as in the romances. Nor, this time, is the private self so easily assimilated into the public self. A choice must be made: orders to oneself and to others are the order of the day. The tone is imperative, the tone of a *généreux* returned thanks to a renunciation. If the hero is more of a true *généreux* than an *ambitieux* in the purely political sphere, he is *at first* more of an *amoureux* in the amorous sphere. He is utimately obliged to place duty before love in one case (*Pulchérie*) and to reassert the

paradox of love-as-honor in the other case (*Suréna*) in a world vastly different from that of the heroic comedies, where the paradox was maintained by the principals from beginning to end.

It is difficult to find a satisfactory subgenre for these plays. In terms of Goldmann's distinction between tragedy and drama cited in my Introduction, these plays could be called dramas, for the conflicts are resolved "selon les lois constitutives de l'univers de la pièce." True, we should, in particular, note the strong tragic intimations of *Suréna*. However, as I stated in my discussion of the play, I do not believe that Corneille fully commits himself to a tragic outlook: the hero is not crushed and, appearances not-withstanding, he triumphs according to the values he earlier upheld rather than through the paradoxical acqui-sition of a new insight putting him beyond the necessity which has presumably defeated him. As in *Pulchérie*—in fact, to an even greater extent because of the clear return to love-as-honor—we are back to the conceptions of the plays from *Le Cid* to *Pompée*. We might thus extend to both plays the rubric "heroic comedy," which Corneille applied to *Pulchérie,* although we would have to note that we return to the conceptions of that genre by force, as it were.

As my individual analyses have shown, these divisions express tendencies in the Cornelian canon. The worlds of the Cornelian universe are not shut off from one another like airtight compartments. There are proud *généreux* in the idyll of the fantasies, idyllic "authority figures" in the stern world of the first five heroic comedies, dynamic *ambitieux* in the detached world of the romances, perfect lovers in the charged atmosphere of the last two heroic comedies. Furthermore, the generic designations are only suggestive in many cases. Like *L'Illusion,* in the words of its creator, many a play is *"un étrange monstre."* Thus, even in projecting in their secondary characters many of the values of romance, *Oedipe* and *Sophonisbe* represent significant deviations from the form: in Oedipe himself, the play harks back to the world of the heroic comedies, while, in the person of Sophonisbe, one finds the basis for describing her play as a kind of antiromance. This relationship of a play to its "kind" also characterizes *La Suivante,* although to a lesser degree. Even within given "kinds," the dramaturgy is not always purely representative: *Cinna* shows much of the conjectural character of the melodramas in the behavior of Cinna and Emilie; their derogation from *générosité* is taken back, as it were, in the denouement. Finally, the most interesting plays of a given kind are not always those which bring the tendency to fullest definition: *La Mort de Pompée* is a too perfect example of a heroic comedy, a play based on the demonstration of the inherent excellence of the *généreux* and *généreuse; Héraclius* is an astonishing example of the melodrama, but its very feat of "pulling out all the stops," of ringing all the changes on the question of identity, makes it somewhat mechanical, a too elaborate exploitation of a tendency.

There are, then, important modifications of the categories of hero and play which I suggest; each play is its own thing, in the final analysis. Yet each of these categories, however tentative, implies that the universe or canon to which they belong presents a consistent view of the human condition. Critics propose varying terms to synthesize this view. I have already cited Rousset's suggestion to generalize the term "heroic comedy" for the entire canon. Corneille himself has used it for plays other than those to which I have restricted its use. Yet, of those to which he gave the name (*Don Sanche, Tite et Bérénice, Pulchérie*) only the last returns us to the tone and themes of the five plays I have included under the rubric. Even there, it is largely by force, as it were, that the *généreux* ceases to be *amoureux,* while, in fact, the stringent paradoxes of love-as-honor are never really restored. So it seems to me that to extend to the whole canon the term "heroic comedy" with all that it comports of fierce sense of self and paradoxical possession-in-renunciation—this would be to falsify the tone and themes of too many other plays. True, these concepts and this tone do form the "sounding board" against which Corneille played his more frequent themes and tones; I am not suggesting that Corneille did not really "believe" in them. But it is as if only critical pressure after the "Quarrel of *Le Cid*" led him to the explicit statement of these themes; as if against his natural bent, at least technically, he would show his critics that he was up to their demands—and then some!

Jean Schlumberger sees Corneille as essentially a writer of tragicomedy.[6] One would be tempted to generalize Schlumberger's term were it not for its pejorative connotations as applied to the serious plays and for its possible exclusion of the obvious comedies which make up one-fourth of the canon. Certain American critics have approached the problem of an over-all rubric in a different way: Borgerhoff, Edelman, and Wang[7] are all agreed that, whatever we call Corneille's plays, we cannot call them tragedies. I trust that my study has shown that this opinion is more than a mere assertion: Corneille does not write tragedies, in spite of three centuries of critical use of "tragedy" as an operating concept in discussing his work. I am not speaking only of those plays which Corneille called *"tragicomédies"* (the first designation of *Le Cid,* in fact) or of those he called *"comédies-héroiques."* I am speaking as well of those he designated *"tragédies"* according to the understanding of the term in his own day, resumed by Lanson as: "La tragédie est dans les âmes." That understanding was more comprehensive than this, to be sure. It ranged from the rather shallow acceptance of Aristotle's "flaw theory" by the *doctes* to the truly perceptive commentary on Aristotle by Racine. It also included certain more unusual commentaries on Aristotle and tragedy by Corneille himself, and I shall want to cite some of these in a moment. But here I would stress that the hesitancy expressed by Corneille in his successive designations of *Le Cid,* for example, reflects the peculiar state of tragic theory in the period. Indeed, Eugène Vinaver has claimed that "dans un siècle insensible à la beauté tragique," only Racine "eut la gloire d'en retrouver le secret."[8]

To assent to Vinaver's assessment of the seventeenth-century situation—at least in its implicit understanding of Corneille—is not to demean Corneille. With Vinaver, but in a critically more objective spirit, we can look on Corneille's dramatic practice as something other than tragedy. To see what this might be, it will be useful to recall in a fuller context Lanson's definition of *"le tragique"* which I cited earlier:

. . . le *pathétique* naît de la souffrance et de la plainte; le *dramatique* résulte du conflit, de l'incertitude, de l'attente anxieuse. le *tragique* est la manifestation, dans un cas doulou-reux, des limites de la condition humaine et de la force invisible qui l'étreint.

Il y a du pathétique sans tragique, du dramatique sans

tragique. Le tragique, toujours pathétique, n'est pas nécessairement dramatique, il l'est en proportion de l'incertitude
et de la lutte qu'il contient.

In this context, it is clear that the italicized terms are
metaphysical and moral in connotation. Then Lanson
goes on to observe:

> Par cette notion du *tragique* nous pourrons
> (a) discerner dans quelle mesure la tragédie française
> est tragique, et comment elle a suppléé au tragique.
> (b) découvrir du tragique avant et après la tragédie dans
> les oeuvres dramatiques du moyen âge ou du xixᵉ
> siècle.⁹

The introduction of a quantitative notion in this discussion of what Lanson clearly recognizes as an absolute
is perhaps puzzling, but undoubtedly Lanson's "discerner
dans quelle mesure" should be translated "see that" rather
than "see in what degree." For, from Lanson's second possibility (b), it is clear that for him the term *"tragédie"*
applies to the seventeenth century with its discovery that
"la tragédie est dans les âmes." That is, for Lanson, there
exists in the century a perfect consonance between the
moral category of the "tragic" and the esthetic category
of "tragedy"—at least, in those plays which internalize or
psychologize the concept of inimical fate. And by extension one can find on either side of this century other
dramatic examples which, whatever their rubric, do contain examples of the tragic understood as internalized
hostile fate. But, by this logic one can find examples
of works which have been called "tragedies" but which
do not contain examples of the "tragic" so defined. This
is to say that, historically if not logically, "tragedy" as an

esthetic category does not imply the moral category of the "tragic." In Lanson's view this discrepancy exists on either side of the seventeenth century. Lanson notwith-standing, it also exists within the century—most notably in the case of the "Father of French tragedy," Pierre Cor-neille.

That this is so is not surprising in light of French dramatic and critical conventions since the seventeenth century. In spite of his frequent derelictions and indeed, I am tempted to say, almost in spite of himself, Corneille may, in fact, be considered the "Father of French Classical Tragedy" defined as a "play in verse composed of five acts, in which the entire action develops in a single setting, in which the fictional duration is never longer than twenty-four hours and in which the heroes are great historical or mythical figures presented to the spectator in the last moments of their adventure—that is to say, at the time of the inevitable climax, a climax which ends in a catastrophe, generally the death of one or many of the characters." [10] Except for the very special character of the "catastrophe" in Corneille—to which I have already alluded in certain plays and to which I shall return more generally in a moment—Corneille's plays are "tragedies" according to this definition. Furthermore, they are "tragedies" in the psychological implications of Lanson's formulation: "la tragédie est dans les âmes." Moreover, the Cornelian hero's obvious concern for self, especially in the much-studied political tetralogy, neatly fits into the habit of French criticism which sees Corneille in that teleology of French dramatic literature which terminates in the writer in whom the concern for self is indeed tragic: Jean Racine. Therefore, as a psychological inquiry contained, however imperfectly, in a certain form consecrated as French

Classical Tragedy, the plays of Corneille are indeed "tragedies."

Yet, as an increasing number of responsible critics has
come to realize, surely the assumption that these "tragedies" contain the "tragic" must yield to one more accurate-
ly describing the trajectory of the hero. To use terms
familiar in such discourse: the tragic view of life, the
tragic vision is something which all men may know, peasant as well as king, politician as well as artist. Critics
have disagreed as to whether this knowledge must be the
final lesson of a *virtuous* man, with some arguing that, for
the wicked as for the virtuous, the tragic lies in man's
submission to necessity. Again, Oscar Mandel maintains
that tragedy is compatible with both spontaneity and
necessity, but that *inevitability* of suffering must be placed
at the kernel of a stable definition of tragedy, for "the
human situation which lies at the root of tragic art is
[thus] simple, perpetual, and (when it makes itself felt)
awesome. The situation is not simply that human effort
fails, but that failure lies implicit in the effort."[11] Many
a theory poses a paradoxical victory over this "implicit
failure," this defeat of man on the natural plane, while
other theories would describe as only pathetic those instances of defeat in which the defeat was avoidable or
short of the "limit case" use of the possibilities within
the universe of action— whether possibility be defined
here as virtue or sheer human energy. I have argued
primarily according to a "value theory of tragedy"
(Sewall's "the worst happens to the best"), but it seems to
me that by no theory of tragedy can Corneille be considered a tragic writer, for he does not allow for that
which one finds common in all tragic theory: initial defeat
of the human, a limitation on human possibility. In

Lanson's terms, he does allow for "conflit . . . incertitude
. . . attente anxieuse"—but there is no "force invisible qui
[l'] étreint." In Mandel's terms, "failure" is not "implicit."* This does not mean that the canon is a mono-
tonous series of heroic comedies. It does mean that,
though there are many heroes, they all have one essential
trait in common: an unlimited and, as the pattern of
action demonstrates, an illimitable confidence in man's
possibilities.

The pattern of action in Corneille engenders in the
spectator a different emotional climate from that of

---

* Mandel finds tragic situations in *Le Cid, Horace, Cinna, Polyeucte,*
and *Rodogune,* but it is worth noting that, except in the case of Polyeucte,
he takes some pains to show that the tragedy is somehow impure. Thus,
*Le Cid* offers a "posttragic redemption" which is "fairly shallow and perhaps regrettable" (p. 160); *Horace* is one of those cases "where we take
a step away from pure tragedy when we are no longer quite sure that
the original configuration involves the ruin that is to follow" (p. 37)
and the play can at best be described by Mandel as "at the very edge
of tragedy" (p. 38); *Cinna* falls among those "examples of tragic purpose
intercepted before they are fulfilled," since Maxime's confession "breaks
Cinna's dilemma" (p. 43); in *Rodogune* the "tragic situation is not necessarily the whole work of art," for "Corneille . . . quickly sketches in a
tragic dilemma, when Rodogune requires of her lover that he kill his
mother, but this is only one episode in a long intrigue" (p. 99). Still
more importantly, Corneille "cheats us" in this play by having Seleucus
"withdraw" from the tragic dilemma of killing his mother or losing his
mistress: "It goes without saying that a work which presents a purpose
in the midst of a tragic configuration, and then cheats us by simply
cancelling the purpose, is not likely to be a masterpiece" (p. 145). As
for *Polyeucte,* Mandel does not discuss the tragic situation in the detail
that he goes into for the other plays, but it is another instance when
the tragedy is not "coterminous with the work of art" (p. 145). I shall
not restate here my own interpretation of the play, but it seems to me
that Mandel might easily adduce the martyr-hero, Polyeucte, to illustrate
that ". . . tragedy does not deal with unflinching heroes, Achilles without
heels. A man so tough, and, we might add, so monomaniacal that no
harm can touch him is not a tragic hero" (p. 157). (All quotations from
*A Definition of Tragedy.*)

tragedy. May has spoken of curiosity and surprise as the emotions appropriate to Corneille, seeing in them *"les avatars modernes"* of fear and pity.[12] Nathan Edelman has shrewdly objected that:

> Some links do exist between the sets of words; but essentially they stand for two different modes of reaction; pity and fear are twin emotions, or one ambivalent emotion betokening the complex identity between spectator and tragic hero, whereas curiosity and surprise are successive states of the mind seeking answers to riddles: what is the identity between a spectator and a riddle?[13]

However, we need not agree with Edelman that there are no "affects" in the reaction to Corneille. It is true that surprise and curiosity, and particularly the latter, are appeals to the head instead of the heart. But this does not mean that when the head is at work the heart is not involved; the psyche defies such neat discriminations. Emotions of various kinds, depending on numerous motives, come into play during the professional activity of a mathematician, a philosopher, a physicist—or the spectator of a play in which the primary effects are those of surprise and curiosity. There are, of course, the various rewards which attach to the *results* of the inquiry: fame, money, station (or in a comedy, a desired marriage). But more importantly, the very activity of trying to "figure something out" puts the spirit into a state which differs from anxiety only in that its outcome promises to be positive rather than negative, helpful rather than harmful, a reaffirmation of human power to cope with the data of a given situation rather than a proof of the limitations of human power.

Curiosity and surprise, then, are more appropriately described as "betokening a state of *being*" parallel with, rather than continuous with, the tragic. They betoken the emotional climate of the Cornelian universe, a climate of excitement, expectancy, and possibility, even as terror and anxiety may be said to betoken the universe of a tragic writer. The latter climate issues specifically in what may be normatively and descriptively called *negative* emotions. (The usage here is descriptive. I am well aware that tragedy is not defeatist, that the "ambivalent emotion" of tragedy is not demeaning). Similarly, the emotional climate of the Cornelian universe issues specifically in *positive* emotions (the usage is again descriptive). As for the specific emotions, they will be various according to the kind of world or, in the literary terms I have employed, the form:

1. Delight in the fantasies and in their analogues, the romances.

2. Hope and what I shall call, for want of a better term, admiration in the heroic comedies. May has properly objected to the imprecision of this term,[14] and I would caution the reader that I am not speaking of that admiration which is based on a spiritual victory paradoxically won even as the hero is defeated. Yet the term "admiration" is Corneille's own, and it is more appropriate than any other in that there is an intense, positive emotional reaction to great deeds. Webster's dictionary defines admiration as "marveling esteem accompanied by gratification and delight." One may question the aptness of "gratification" and, even more so, of "delight" in connection with the Cornelian universe. Except for the comedies, "delight" is too thin a term to convey that compound of pride, power, and self-possession coinciding with our "marveling esteem" of Corneille's heroes here. But

whatever the emotions be named, the *fusion* of idea and emotion is just as great here as in the case of our response to tragedy. Indeed, I would say it is as difficult to separate the *idea* of possibility from the *emotion* of pride here as is is to separate the *emotions* of tragedy—or, as Edelman says, that ambivalent single emotion: fear-pity, pity-fear—from the *idea* of limitation or defeat "accompanying" these emotions in our response to tragedy.

3. The case of the melodramas is more complex: we do appear to be in a tragic climate of anxiety, but we are relieved in the end; the validity of hope is reaffirmed, our capacity for admiration restored. Of course, these last reactions are also said to express the sense of "illumination" in tragedy. But there is an important difference: in Cornelian "tragedy" the situation or events producing fear and pity prove to have been so many "*fausses pistes*," to have been merely conjectural.

As the interpretation of *générosité* indicates, the hero feels hope and admiration as an integral part of his conception of himself. That the spectator feels them may seem at first difficult to accept. These heroes seem so much above him not only because of their station but because of this very degree of self-possession. Yet, Péguy has written: "Les blessures que nous recevons, nous les recevons dans Racine; les êtres que nous sommes, nous les sommes dans Corneille." [15] Corneille himself comes close to meeting these specific objections in his own critical writings. As to the station of the hero, he writes:

Il est vrai qu'on n'introduit d'ordinaire que des rois pour premiers acteurs dans la tragédie, et que les auditeurs n'ont point de sceptres par où leur ressembler, afin d'avoir lieu de craindre les malheurs qui leur arrivent; mais ces rois sont hommes comme les auditeurs, et tombent dans ces malheurs par l'emportement des passions dont les auditeurs sont capables.[16]

As to the degree of self-possession of these heroes, their unfailing capacity to overcome the very "malheurs" Corneille cites, his remarks on *Nicomède* bear directly on this capacity in relation to the spectator:

> Ce héros de ma façon sort un peu des règles de la tragédie en ce qu'il ne cherche point à faire pitié par l'excès de ses infortunes; mais le succès a montré que la fermeté des grands coeurs, qui n'excite que de l'admiration dans l'âme du spectateur, est quelquefois aussi agréable que la compassion que notre art nous ordonne d'y produire par la représentation de leurs malheurs. Il en fait naître toutefois quelqu'une, mais elle ne va pas jusques à tirer des larmes. Son effet se borne à mettre les auditeurs dans les intérêts de ce prince, et à leur faire former des souhaits pour ses prospérités.
>
> Dans l'admiration qu'on a pour sa vertu, je trouve une manière de purger les passions dont n'a point parlé Aristote, et qui est peut-être plus sûre que celle qu'il prescrit à la tragédie par le moyen de la pitié et de la crainte. L'amour qu'elle nous donne pour cette vertu que nous admirons, nous imprime la haine pour le vice contraire. La grandeur de courage de Nicomède nous laisse une aversion de la pussillanimité; et la généreuse reconnaissance d'Héraclius, qui expose sa vie pour Martian, à qui il est redevable de la sienne, nous jette dans l'horreur de l'ingratitude.[17]

Citing the first paragraph of this passage in support, Herland speaks of admiration as "un nouveau sentiment tragique."* But this is misleading. The emotion may be

---

* "La notion de tragique chez Corneille" in *Mélanges de la Société toulousaine d'études classiques,* p. 278. In *Les Héroines de Corneille* Maria Tastevin notes that "l'admiration joue un grand rôle dans la genèse de l'amour cornélien" (p. 233).

new as applied to the plays denominated "tragedy" but this should only lead us to consider the aptness of the denomination for such plays. There is no need to go through a series of Cornelian *jeux d'esprit* in order to make Corneille ultimately tragic. He is not tragic either ultimately or fundamentally. Hope and admiration, the emotions appropriate to his system of "tragedy," put and maintain the spectator in an upward frame of mind; they are the emotional response to an affirmative, confident, and optimistic view of the human condition. Both pity and terror, as Corneille explicitly says in the "Examen" of *Nicomède,* are irrelevant in such a context. The terror points at most to the challenge which circumstances place before the hero, the pity is not pity at all. There is no need for man to feel pity or terror, for there is nothing to be afraid of, nothing to lament.*

We lack a term to express this view of the human condition. Aware of its basically untragic character, Prosser Hall Frye, a hostile critic of this point of view, has char-

---

* Racine translates and elaborates the relevant passage from Aristotle: "[Elle ne se fait] point par un récit, mais par une représentation vive qui, excitant la pitié et la terreur, purge *et tempère* ces sortes de passions. C'est-à-dire qu'en esmouvant ces passions, elle leur oste ce qu'elles ont d'excessif et de vitieux, et les rameine à un estat modéré et conforme à la raison." *Principes de la tragédie en marge de la Poétique d'Aristote,* texte établi et commenté par Eugène Vinaver, pp. 11-12. (Italics, in text, indicate Racine's elaboration.) Unlike his younger contemporary, Corneille does not seek a paradoxical coexistence of pity and terror in a modified form, but rather sees the emotions as sequential—terror, then pity: "La pitié d'un malheur où nous voyons tomber nos semblables nous porte à la crainte d'un pareil pour nous; cette crainte, au désir de l'éviter; et ce désir, à purger, modérer, rectifier, et *même déraciner en nous la passion* qui plonge à nos yeux dans ce malheur les personnes que nous plaignons, par cette raison commune, mais naturelle et indubitable, que pour éviter l'effet il faut retrancher la cause." *Discours de la tragédie,* M-L, *I,* 53 (my italics). He even goes on to doubt that catharsis ever takes place in tragedy and concludes "j'ai bien peur que le raisonnement d'Aristote sur ce point ne soit qu'une belle idée, qui n'ait jamais son effet dans la vérité." *Discours de la tragédie,* M-L, *I,* 57.

acterized it as "romantic" (in contrast with the laudable "classic") and has said of its dramatic expression: ". . . it is not tragedy at all, but a nondescript; for tragedy is impossible without an unflinching moral vision. The sole relief is to save our sympathy for the virtuous but unhandy hero and his cause and to cover his adversary with contumely. The resolution is purely human, it is a kind of *argumentum ad hominem*; there is no vestige of destiny about it." [18] And Frye goes on specifically to say of Corneille: "Classic by method and finally, perhaps by conviction, he was incurably romantic and was never wholly successful in conceiving an action thoroughly agreeable with his own formulae." [19] In terms of the antinomies which give Frye the title of his book, *Romance and Tragedy,* Corneille's theater, says the critic, belongs in essence if not in outer form to romance. These neo-humanistic strictures cast Corneille as a spiritual brother of those nineteenth-century "romantic" dramatists whom Frye berates later in his study. Yet, the critic's moral bias apart, the term "romantic" applied in this historical sense to Corneille is inept. The generic use of the term is appropriate for certain plays, as I have maintained, but in its usage by Henry James and Northrop Frye rather than Prosser Hall Frye. As these very romances show, for all his emphasis on an "open" dramaturgy and in spite of his metaphysic of "becoming," Corneille is not a precursor of Hugo or Musset or Vigny. His "open" dramaturgy is not the episodic dramaturgy of the "romantics"; Corneille's heroes do not just "become" *ad infinitum*—they become *something*. The "classic" Aristotelian concept of entelechy is more appropriate to Corneille than the "romantic" Hegelian dialectic.*

---

* Morse Peckham has provided the basis for an understanding of the familiar classic-romantic anthithesis according to which Corneille may

Still other critics speak of "le refus du tragique chez Corneille."[20] One appreciates the intent of such a formulation, but to speak of the "refusal of the tragic" is perhaps to do Corneille an injustice. To *refuse* is to acknowledge the existence of that which one refuses; the "refusal of the tragic" by Corneille would thus mean that he would be at best trying to deny existence to the tragic. Corneille has faults, but they are not those of the ostrich. We might call Corneille's view "untragic" or "antitragic," but the former term is at best a grab bag, while the latter too readily connotes the virtues of the ostrich associated with the concept of the "refusal of tragedy."

However, we do have a term at hand for the view of life which shows forth in Corneille's plays: comic. I realize that it is difficult for us to apply this term to Corneille because of the different practice we usually associate with it: the satirical depiction of human foibles, as in Molière. Yet, the critical fate of Molière's total practice is perhaps as instructive as the critical fate of Corneille's total

---

still be thought of as classic, Prosser Hall Frye's strictures notwithstanding. In his effort to define romanticism, Peckham does not speak of classicism, but, recalling Lovejoy, he does use as his starting point the thesis of the eighteenth-century "shift in European thought . . . from conceiving the cosmos as a static mechanism to conceiving it as a dynamic organism: static—in that all the possibilities of reality were realized from the beginning of things or were implicit from the beginning, and that these possibilities were arranged in a complete series, a hierarchy from God down to nothingness—including the literary possibilities from epic to Horatian ode; a mechanism—in that the universe is a perfectly running machine, a watch usually." "Toward a Theory of Romanticism," *PMLA, LXVI*, 9. Now Corneille is anything but static in his dramaturgy; one could claim that in Frye's terms he is not even technically classic. He is "dynamic" and "diverse"—two of the hallmarks of romanticism, according to Peckham. But he is not "organic" (the analogy with growing things, the key aspect of romanticism according to Peckham). Corneille remains "classic" in that he manipulates the given, the—or a—static view of the universe only to return to it. As we have seen, so many heroes *return to* the code of *générosité, turn out to be* the true king: "the possibilities were implicit from the beginning."

practice. The widespread view of Molière as a social satirist with a bourgeois outlook has tended to treat as "minor" those plays in which a very different outlook obtains: the *comédies-ballets* which make up nearly half of his work. These plays, often described significantly enough as "court plays," do not fit too easily into the liberal bourgeois ethos which sees Molière as a scourge of the *ancien régime* who, like many pessimistic contemporaries (Pascal, Bossuet, La Rochefoucauld), "exposes" *l'orgueil des grands* in the very heyday of *la grandeur.* Yet, heeding the "lessons" of the numerous court plays, certain critics have discovered in the great comedian not a bourgeois but an aristocratic poet in whom cruelty toward the Prud'homme is a marked trait. Nor does this "aristocratic ethos" express itself only in this negative way, as a play like *Amphitryon* shows, and as an attention to the balletic atmosphere of such "satires" as *Le Bourgeois gentilhomme* and *Le Malade imaginaire* also shows. In the *comédies-ballets* which make up the bulk of his work after *Le Tartuffe* (the original version of 1664), Molière is not reversing himself; he is only printing the "positive" from the "negatives" he took earlier in his career.

As for Molière and Corneille, we should remember that if the great comedian parodied his illustrious elder in *L'Impromptu de Versailles,* it was only after imitating him in *Dom Garcie de Navarre.* Of course, given Dom Garcie's extravagant character, we might see in the latter more proof of Molière's "intentional" criticism of Corneille in *L'Impromptu.* Yet, this would be to forget the presence of a truly Cornelian character in the play: the heroine. "Elvire," writes Fernandez, "est une héroïne de Corneille, une cousine de Pauline, un peu à la mode de Bretagne. Toujours, dit-elle, notre coeur est en notre pouvoir, et s'il montre parfois quelque faiblesse, la raison doit être maîtresse de tous nos sens."* It is true that even Elvire's *générosité* is inevitably compromised in the love she bears Dom Garcie, for, unlike her Cornelian counterparts, she cannot really be said to find in her lover a perfect reflection of herself. Nevertheless, her pity is dictated to her by her reason—she recognizes that Dom Garcie's vice is "incurable et fatal"—and her reason thereby teaches her that she cannot deny her lover the *estime* she otherwise owes him. Her love as seen in this gesture is not of the heedless, self-destructive kind in Racine's *Andromaque*, for example, but recalls rather Auguste's patronizing and self-congratulatory clemency in Corneille's *Cinna*. Though she is indeed touched by her lover's incurable malady, Elvire accepts him because "on doit quelque indulgence / Aux défauts où le Ciel fait pencher l'influence" (V, 6). One owes such indulgence to the victim himself, of course, but more fundamentally, one owes it to oneself. Elvire's love is narcissistic.

Molière's serious imitation of Corneille in the character of Elvire should make us wary of that tradition which pits Corneille against Molière almost as automatically as it does against Racine. To link Molière and Racine in this way against Corneille is to misconstrue both Molière comedy and Corneille "tragedy." Actually, with his un-limited confidence in man Corneille is the least tragic of writers. As for Molière, once we begin to see that not the limiting notions of satire but the expansive notions of what we can only call the "pure comic" are the real

---

* *La Vie de Molière,* p. 88. As for the Corneille-Molière affiliation, I do not mean to subscribe to the preposterous theses of G. Poulaille which are summarized in the title of his book: *Corneille sous le masque de Molière.* See Bibliography.

essence of his work, then we can begin to see his true relation to Corneille. Both the comedian and the so-called tragedian have an optimistic view of "man's fate." There is, to be sure, a crucial difference betwen the two: Corneille's optimism is more cerebral; Molière's is visceral and is grounded in a confident naturalism. In Cartesian terms, if the will follows the intelligence (*entendement*) so closely as to be identified with it in Corneille, in Molière the will follows the appetitive so closely as to be identified with it. (I am speaking of the relationship in those who defeat the comic butt.) Also, just as the will is passional in Corneille, so the appetitive is intelligent in Molière—witness the naturally wily Agnès and the numerous shrewd peasant types. There is, in sum, in the two writers a difference in both the psychical functions and in the ends to which man should direct those functions, but in each there is no doubt that man has it within his power to direct those functions to attainable ends. The difference from the truly tragic sense of human limitation in Racine could not be greater.

We might grasp the essential difference between Corneille and Racine by substituting "Corneille" for "comedy" and "Racine" for "tragedy" in Jacques Guicharnaud's apt contrast: "Comedy springs from the triumph of human definitions . . . ; tragedy, from the triumph of forces which refuse man peace." [21] Applied in this sense to Corneille, "comedy" does not deny the premises of Bergson's theory. To be sure, Bergson is hardly talking about "the triumph of human definitions"; one may even say that he is talking about the *defeat* of human definitions. However, he is talking about the defeat of *some* human being's definitions at the hands of a "life force" which, to extend Guicharnaud's language, grants the *rest* of humanity peace.

I thus apply the concept "comic" to Corneille in order to dramatize what I find in him: a very different sense from that of the "tragic" usually applied to his theater. Needless to say, I do not mean to extend this unique use of "comic" to those works to which another use is traditionally applied. I would simply note that there is a consonance between the more traditional use of the term and the special use I adopt here, especially if one pays less critical attention to the *butt* of comedy and more to those who make him their butt. Finally, on this matter of rubrics for a fundamentally similar outlook manifested in a variety of forms, I would call attention to Northrop Frye's distinction between two ways of developing the form of comedy: ". . . one is to throw the main emphasis on the blocking characters; the other is to throw it forward on the scenes of discovery and reconciliation. One is the general tendency of comic irony, satire, realism and studies of manners; the other is the tendency of Shakespearean and other types of romantic comedy." [22] The latter development obviously moves toward what Northrop Frye calls romance, the designation which, following James and Frye himself, I have applied to many of Corneille's plays. Using Frye's archetypes, one might place all of Corneille's serious plays under "romance," especially in what Frye calls its "sixth or *pensero* phase . . . the last phase of romance as of comedy. In comedy it shows the comic society breaking up into small units or individuals; in romance it marks the end of a movement from active to contemplative adventure." [23] The coincidence of the phases underscores the basically comic outlook I attribute to Corneille. I would, however, reserve the term "romance" to the more limited sense I have used in order to make distinctions within the Cornelian canon.

"There is no definition of tragedy," Leonard Wang has

maintained, "however broad and comprehensive, that will fit his [Corneille's] work."* And as Rousset has forcefully said:

> Tragédie? Il faudrait plutôt dire, comme Corneille le fait quelque fois, tragi-comédie ou comédie héroïque; ni le héros ni le climat de ces pièces ne sont vraiment tragiques: le tragique impose à l'homme une limite et le broie sous une force inéluctable; le héros cornélien ne connaît aucune limite, il peut tout, non seulement sur lui-même et sur les autres, mais sur l'événement, sur le destin; la mort elle-même est au pouvoir du héros, comme un instrument de sa liberté.†

---

* Except the psychological and technical definitions deriving from seventeenth-century tragic theory and practice (above pp. 272-275). See Wang's "The 'Tragic' Theatre of Corneille," *French Review, XXV*, 191. In "The Tragic Genius of Corneille" *Modern Language Review, XLV*, 164-176, Harold C. Ault maintains that it is precisely because the modern audience cannot recreate Corneille's period for itself that we must find the explanation for the dramatist's enduring "tragic" appeal elsewhere —in the "tragedy of the will of man in action." As Ault sees it (basing his thesis exclusively on the tetralogy), Corneille's heroes go "beyond humanity" (Rodrigue), are "barbarous" (Horace) and "fanatic" (Polyeucte); they thus "harden [their] hearts." Ault also darkly conjectures on the relations among principals beyond the "Fin du cinquième et dernier acte"—for example, echoing Nadal, on the inability of Chimene and Rodrigue to forget the bloody sword which lies between them; Auguste's possible suspicions and Maxime's possible jealousy; etc. More historical re-creation than the critic is willing to allow seems to me to serve as a corrective to Ault's interpretation. Furthermore, one may question his reading of various denouements—for example, that Chimene accepts Rodrigue only because of the king's command. (See my discussion of this aspect of *Le Cid*, above, pp. 77-79). Ault's categories of character description and his conjectures suggest that he is less interested in explaining the characters in their own world than in passing judgment on them.

† *La Littérature de l'âge baroque en France*, p. 213. Another perceptive critic, Valdemar Vedel, cannot bring himself to renounce the epithet "tragic" in discussing Corneille, in spite of his own awareness of the very special sense the epithet must take in Corneille: ". . . il ne s'agit pas dans les tragédies de Corneille d'un tragique inhérent aux conditions même de l'existence, d'une nécessité tragique, mais que tout peut tourner par suite d'un événement favorable: un saignement de nez dans Attila,

"Il peut tout"—although it should be stated immediately that the Cornelian hero *does not* do everything. Corneille's "comic base" is narrow, if, paradoxically enough, lofty. Brasillach notwithstanding, the comparison with Shakespeare falls short.[24] The number of types, the range of emotions is limited. But there are a number of types, not *a* Cornelian hero, but Cornelian heroes. Between them the plays in which the *damoiseau* and the *amoureux* are the types of hero make up more than half the Cornelian canon. This simple statistic is not sufficient in itself, but it does serve as a caution that we cannot confine Corneille within the political tetralogy which has confined Cornelian criticism for three centuries.

Corneille's confidence in the human condition is not arrived at through appeal to a higher power in which man finds the basis for a renewed confidence in a set of values whose source is superhuman. Corneille does not move *through* the tragic, through the awareness of man's limitations as he is constituted, to some "doctrine" of "saving grace" assuring man that he is, in Niebuhr's trenchant phrase, "beyond tragedy."* In Corneille this "grace" is already given. The religious expression of this relationship between man and his destiny is appropriate. In noting in the pupils and his teachers a consonance of outlook, we need not argue for or against Brasillach that Corneille's Jesuit education is responsible for his outlook.[25] In the

---

le meurtre opportun du tyran dans *Héraclius*, une émeute militaire dans *Othon* et *Nicomède*; ou bien c'est grâce à un sentiment de justice ou de générosité éveillé dans l'âme du souverain (*Pertharite, Cinna*). Cela veut dire encore qu'en dépit de tout son esprit tragico-héroïque le drame de Corneille n'a pas de la vie la conception tragique proprement dite." *Deux Classiques français,* p. 234.

---

* The title of one of Niebuhr's books. Its subtitle is: *Essays on the Christian Interpretation of History.*

same years that the Jansenists were forging their dark
view of the human condition, with the concomitant need
to get "beyond tragedy" through the *"mystère de Jésus
Christ,"* Corneille was depicting an opposite view of man
as already saved. Whether the "salvation" is fundamentally
as Christian as Pascal's is a matter of argument, but we
can at least note once again that there is as respectable a
body of theology for Corneille as against him. As I have
said in connection with Corneille's "religious tragedy,"
his view is Pelagian rather than Augustinian. With
Descartes, that other controversial *"bien pensant"* of the
seventeenth century, Corneille may be said to depict man
before the Fall, even as Pascal and Racine may be said
to depict him after the Fall.

To describe Corneille's awareness in these terms is not
to explain him away. It is rather to point in another
domain to the split (some would call it a tension) which
characterizes Western man's traditional attempts to eva-
luate the human condition. Nor does pointing up Corneille's relationship to the Jesuits mean that both he
and they, being essentially elements of the Counter Refor-
mation,[26] are no longer relevant. It is true that the
aristocratic view of character and society on which I have
claimed Corneille bases his esthetic effects might be invoked by critics of a certain ideological bent to "prove"
the inadequacy of Corneille for the "Age of the Common Man" (or, in the case of some critics, to try to
replace the Common Man with the Hero). Again, such
critics might try to find in Corneille a "precursor" of the
ideological concerns of their own times. Bénichou has
observed that the dominant current of Corneille criticism,
that best represented by Lanson, tended to reconstruct
the ethos of the plays according to its own ethos, "les

idées morales de la bourgeoisie conservatrice," [27] and we had the Corneille of duty over love. Recent reconstructions have given us the Cornelian hero in existentialist and Marxist terms. Thus, to recall Starobinski's thesis: profoundly at variance with *idées reçues* of Corneille's audience and perhaps, in fact, with the other inhabitants of his world, the hero is a precursor of *"l'homme absurde."* Or, with Bernard Dort, proceeding chronologically through the canon we would trace the necessary alienation of the hero, whose oppression at the hands of absolute monarchy is another instance of the historical dialectic, a lesson for our own time with its oppressors of the un- (or under-) privileged. One can sympathize with such attempts to relate the past to the present, but one can also question the accuracy of such formulations applied to the Cornelian universe. Far from the "alienation" —either existential or historical—of the hero in his world, Bénichou concludes that "le but vers lequel tend Corneille, c'est de concilier finalement la royauté et les 'gens de coeur.' "* And even the most reflective of

---

* *Morales,* p. 68. In his *Etudes sur le temps humain* (pp. 89-102), Georges Poulet contends that the primacy of the present in Corneille's plays tends to portray a hero divested of both past and future; the hero's essence is self-derived rather than inherited. This is obviously counter to the sense of the political past which I find so significant in the plays. I would note that, in studying the texture of Corneille's language, Poulet has given insufficient account of the dramatic context of the hero's concern with self. The dramatic basis of so many of the plays of the middle and late periods is the legitimacy of a given hero's claim to the throne—for example, the melodramas revolving around the question of identity. Thus, Poulet contends that Corneille "nous donne dans *Don Sanche* un personnage sans passé, sans aïeux et sans race, dont la grandeur d'âme est une fidélité au seul mot présent et agissant:

Se pare qui voudra du nom de ses aïeux,

Moi, je ne veux porter que moi-même en tous lieux. (I, 3)"

(*Etudes sur le temps humain,* p. 96) But this is Carlos who speaks—who turns out to be the heir to the throne, Don Sanche!

Corneille's heroes can hardly be described as introspective or soul-searching. Indeed, Borgerhoff complains of the "outwardness" of Corneille's heroes: "Their consciousness is all directed toward combating the disintegrating forces which are attacking them from outside." [28] Precisely, because these forces "threaten" a fixed sense of self; they do not lead the hero to cast a new sense of self. The resolutions of even the most seemingly "existentialist" plays—those based on the theme of identity—center around the sense of self the hero receives as a *généreux,* as a noble-born—and as a *king,* the most noble-born at that!

The nobly born behave nobly. The *généreux* (and, so often, *généreuse*) inherently possesses the qualities which an existentialist or pragmatic orientation views as acquired. Not for Corneille's heroes such notions as *"l'homme se fait,"* "existence precedes essence," "handsome is as handsome does." The hero *real-izes* his heroism; in Aristotelian terms once again, the hero actualizes his potential, he realizes his entelechy, his innate excellence. As Dort recognizes in his provocative book, for the dramatist who chooses politics as his setting for such ideas, the supreme realization is the throne, and when the hero is not a king, certain tensions arise. In a world of ready-made men, the self-made man can be a problem. But, as I have tried to show, the heroes who are at first presented as self-made men are really not self-made in the long run. Dort misconstrues Corneille's relation to his time in viewing the dramatist as a judge of that time, a teacher of a political lesson. That the lesson has strong Marxist overtones in Dort is not objectionable because it is Marxist, but that it is so limiting in the case of this artist so desirous of pleasing his public. Whatever Corneille's political views, it is clear that in depending on the political currents of his time, he can achieve those effects of *"nouveauté"* and *"invention"* so dear to him in his own reviews of his plays. For an audience expecting from the hero behavior consonant with its own conception of *générosité*, the conspiracy of Cinna can be a surprising thing; for an audience accustomed (by Corneille as well as by its own political assumptions) to ideally royal behavior from a queen, Cleopatre's treachery and Rodogune's flirtation with treachery can be dramatically exciting; for an audience accustomed to the stern postulates of love-as-honor, Pertharite's or Thésée's readiness to sacrifice a kingdom to *l'amour tendre* can be a puzzling and perhaps a tempting possibility. Corneille does not *preach* honor and glory and the sacrifice of love to duty. He *uses* these themes (and the last one far less often than has been believed).

What counts, then, for those seeking instruction or enlightenment from the literary works of the past is not the possible parallels with one's own time, but the view of the human condition which the works imply; what remains beyond the historical context is the outlook in the given writer's use of the context. Corneille's use is comic in the large sense of that term which I have posited. As I have noted, even in such plays as *Rodogune, Sertorius,* and *Suréna*—the "problem plays" of the canon—the underlying view is comic: a confidence in human possibilities. Only with reservations can one speak of a value tragedy as present even in two of these plays: the worst happens only to the second-best (Seleucus and Sertorius) and, at that, in the case of Sertorius, in only one dimension of his being. The values of the world of the play do not allow us to generalize their fate as "man's fate." We cannot, that is, apply the absolute of the tragic to the world in which they work out their unhappy fates. The Seleucuses and the Sertoriuses (as well as the inverted example of the tragic, Cleopatre) do not finally set the norms of the worlds in which they figure.

Corneille's worlds form an Olympus peopled by such *généreux* men and women as Polyeucte, Pauline, Rodogune, Nicomède, and Oedipe; an Arcadia peopled by such sweet and subtle young *damoiseaux* as Melite, Tirsis, Doris, Rosidor, and Clindor; a utopia peopled by such perfect lovers and virtuous nobles as Pertharite, Andromède, and Psyché; a perfect kingdom ruled by such kingly souls as Pulchérie and Suréna. All are triumphant and fulfilled for reasons clear to their ethical understanding and to ours. "Au fond," writes Péguy, "il n'y a pas une femme de Corneille dont on puisse dire: *C'est une malheureuse*; et il n'y a tout de même pas un homme de Corneille dont on puisse dire: *C'est un malheureux*." [29] Value in Corneille's men and women is something to be realized, not denied. They are on their best behavior, for this is the only kind of behavior of which they are capable. And of which we are capable, if, being men and women even as they, we wish to follow their example. That example is no more limited to a particular time and place—Corneille's say—than is the example of the original Cids and Caesars on whom Corneille so often models his heroes. Corneille's heroes are heroes for all times, the "Cornelian face" of that figure Joseph Campbell has studied in *The Hero with a Thousand Faces*:

The godly powers sought and dangerously won are revealed to have been within the heart of the hero all the time. He is the "king's son" who has come to know who he is and therewith has entered into the exercise of his proper power —"God's son," who has learned to know how much that title means. From this point of view the hero is symbolical of that divine creative and redemptive image which is hidden within us all, only waiting to be known and rendered into life.[30]

Our world may not be hierarchically structured like the Cornelian heroes', but the "moral" of their example is nonetheless ours: there is nothing inherent in ourselves or in our world which prevents us from realizing our entelechy.

Tragic viewers will not be drawn to Corneille—they will note with varying degrees of irony that men and women do not live on Olympus, in Arcadia, or in Paradise and that man's government is not a perfect kingdom. They can remind "Cornelians" of La Bruyère's famous formulation that Corneille showed men as they ought to be, while Racine showed them as they are.* The formulation is usually made to apply to the political tetralogy in particular. Yet, having reviewed the entire canon we might revise La Bruyère by saying that Corneille shows men not only as they ought to be, but also as they might be, as they would be, as they could be, and as they have to be. Corneille's vision is more varied. As Sartre has said:

We believe the statement should be reversed. Racine paints psychologic man, he studies the mechanics of love, of jealousy in an abstract, pure way; that is, without ever allowing moral considerations or human will to deflect the inevitability of their evolution. His *dramatis personae* are only creatures of his mind, the end results of an intellectual analysis. Corneille, on the other hand, showing will at the very core of passion,

---

* *Caractères* in *Oeuvres complètes* (Pléiade edition), p. 84. The opposition also informs Turnell's *The Classical Moment,* with Corneille representing, in terms I do not think unfaithful to Turnell's thesis, the "ascendant" monarchy and Racine the "descendant" monarchy.

gives us back man in all his complexity, in his complete reality.*

One may question the logic of "deflecting an inevitability," and my own reading of Corneille has led me to beleive that if Corneille's heroes are deflecting anything, it is the threat to the evolution of their own ascendancy, to the realization of their entelechy. Nevertheless, accepting the spirit of Sartre's appraisal, it is clear that he takes his stand with Corneille. Sartre thus clearly reformulates the Corneille-Racine contrast which has been diluted to a comparison in over two centuries of academic criticism with its teleology culminating in Racine. For, Corneille is not a precursor of Racine or a "Racine malgré lui." He has a vastly different vision, one which no more need be regarded "escapist" than Racine's "defeatist."†

In an age in which the tragic view enjoys great prestige,

---

* Jean-Paul Sartre, "Forgers of Myths. The Young Playwright of France," *Theatre Arts*, XXX, 329. Quoted in English, since I have been unable to locate the French expression of the passage. Merian-Genast maintains that a study of Corneille's language shows "dass Corneille nicht so sehr der Dichter des Willens als der des Stolzes ist" ("Corneilles Wertgefühl im Spiegel Seiner Bildersprache," in *Festschrift für Ernst Tappolet*, p. 228). Finally, it should be noted that others have reversed La Bruyère's formulation. Thus, André Rousseaux cites with approval the reversal I have already quoted from Péguy: "Les blessures que nous recevons, nous les recevons dans Racine. Les êtres que nous sommes, nous les trouvons dans Corneille." "Corneille ou le mensonge héroïque," *Revue de Paris*, XLIV, 51. The "mensonge" in Corneille, as the critic sees it, has nothing Racinian or Pirandellian about it: neither the lies with which one cultivates the illicit nor those which make life bearable, it is "le jeu que l'homme joue par vertu, par noblesse et générosite" (64).

† André Malraux has situated himself along with Bernanos, Giono, and Montherlant in what he calls "la tradition héroïque de la France, sa tradition cornélienne" which he cites as running counter to another tradition, "celle des gens à qui on ne la fait pas, qui veulent savoir ce dont ils parlent. Les rectificateurs des rêves. Les moralistes, après tout." "Lignes de force," *Preuves*, No. 49 (March 1955), 8—republication of an interview which first appeared in *Labyrinthe* [Genève], February 15, 1945. Malraux also finds that the "tradition cornélienne" has a strong link in Pascal. Malraux thus echoes Vedel's interpretation of Corneille as "tragico-héroïque." I would record that Pascal joins his Jansenist *confrères* in an attack upon just that special kind of confidence in human

especially among American literary intellectuals, Corneille will perhaps seem irrelevant. The "realism" of much contemporary criticism—often expressing a bias founded on a pessimistic interpretation of Freud, the modern thinker who has most influenced prevalent notions of the self, or a bias grounded in a pessimistic "phenomenology" stressing the "naiveté" of essentialistic thinking—such "realism" more readily finds in Racine its notion of the self as an "exile" in its own "kingdom." Do we then damn with faint praise to see in Corneille a magnificent example of a "comic" vision in which honor and instinct are reconciled without compromise? Perhaps. But praise and damnation are themselves irrelevant here; they have more to do with the spectator's "dynamics" than with the "dynamics" of the Cornelian heroes. I have been primarily concerned in these pages to describe the Cornelian universe. The reader may draw whatever lessons *his* vision of life dictates as I return him to Corneille, his heroes, and their worlds.

---

nature which Corneille proclaims throughout his work: *"Comminitum cor*, saint Paul, voilà le caractère chrétien. *Albe vous a nommé, je ne vous connais plus* [*Horace*, II, 3], Corneille, voilà le caractère inhumain. Le caractère humain est le contraire." (*Pensées*, ed. Brunschvicg, No. 533, *II, 423*).

# Footnotes

### Introduction

[1] *A New Latin Dictionary* (commonly called "Harper's Latin Dictionary").

[2] *Dictionnaire général de la langue française* (1926).

[3] "Corneille: The Play as Magic" in *Play within a Play*, pp. 47-61, a modification of my "Pierre Corneille's *L'Illusion comique:* The Play as Magic," *PMLA, LXXI,* 1127-1140.

[4] "Intellectualism in Corneille: The Symbolism of Proper Names in *La Suivante,*" *Symposium, XIII,* 293.

### 1
### *Melite* to *L'Illusion comique: le damoiseau*

[1] For the dates of the plays through *La Place Royale* I have relied on L. Rivaille, *Les Débuts de P. Corneille,* p. 26.

[2] For a study of names in Corneille see L. Harvey, "Intellectualism in Corneille: The Symbolism of Proper Names in *La Suivante,*" *Symposium, XIII,* 290-293.

[3] *Morales du grand siècle,* passim.

[4] For a review of this question, see L. Rivaille, *Les Débuts,* pp. 58-63.

[5] "The Dénouement of *Mélite* and the Role of the Nourrice," *Modern Language Notes, LXXI,* 201.

[6] *History,* Part One, *II,* 520-521.

[7] *The French Tragi-Comedy,* p. xxiv.

[8] *Tragédie cornélienne,* p. 206.

[9] *History,* Part One, *II,* 594.

[10] M-L, *I,* 446, n. 2.

[11] *Ibid.,* 376-377.

[12] For further study of the theme of nobility in *La Veuve* see L. Harvey, "The Noble and the Comic in Corneille's *La Veuve,*" *Symposium, X,* 291-295.

[13] "Examen," M-L, *II,* 123.

[14] *History,* Part One, *II,* 609.

[15] *Le Sentiment,* p. 111.

[16] *The Vision of Tragedy,* p. 31.

[17] *Esquisse d'une histoire de la tragédie française,* p. 3.

[18] *Ibid.,* p. 4. Italics in text.

[19] *Ibid.,* pp. 7-8.

20 *Ibid.*, p. 47.

21 "Un Tricentenaire," *La Nouvelle Revue Française, XLV* (septembre 1935), 403.

22 *Le Sentiment,* especially "Deuxième Partie, Ch. 1."

23 "*L'Illusion comique* of Corneille: The Tragic Scenes of Act V," *Modern Language Notes, LXXIII,* 421-427. For a discussion of the theme of illusion touching other plays as well as *L'Illusion,* see Philip Koch, "Cornelian Illusion," *Symposium, XIV,* 85-99.

24 *Play within a Play,* p. 61.

## 2
### *Le Cid* to *Pompée: le généreux*

1 The final version is found in M-L, *III.* The original version from which I quote has been edited by Maurice Cauchie. See Bibliography.

2 *En Lisant Corneille,* p. 111.

3 *Tragédie cornélienne,* pp. 104-112 and passim.

4 "Observations sur *Le Cid,*" M-L, *XII,* 442-443.

5 *Le Sentiment,* p. 166.

6 "Les Sentiments de l'Académie Française sur la tragi-comédie du Cid," M-L, *XII,* 477.

7 *Ibid.*, p. 482.

8 "Avertissement" (accompanying editions from 1648 to 1656), M-L, *III,* 82-83.

9 In the "Introduction" to his translation of the play in his *The Chief Plays of Corneille,* p. 8, n. 6.

10 *Le Sentiment,* p. 179.

11 "Les Sentiments," M-L, *XII,* 482.

12 *Ariosto, Shakespeare and Corneille,* pp. 380-383.

13 *Ibid.*, p. 383.

14 "Remarques sur la technique dramatique de Corneille" in *Studies by Members of the French Department of Yale University,* p. 121.

15 *Le Sentiment,* p. 280.

16 "Preface to *The American*" in *The Art of the Novel,* p. 33. Italics in text.

17 "Examen," M-L, *III,* 275.

18 *Horace, ou la naissance de l'homme,* p. 65.

19 *Horace, ou la naissance de l'homme,* p. 32.

20 *Ariosto, Corneille and Shakespeare,* p. 383.

21 *Renunciation as a Tragic Focus,* pp. 70-71.

22 Reported by Voltaire as a "tradition." *Commentaires, Oeuvres complètes, XXXI,* 394.

23 E. Merian-Genast, "Corneilles Wertgefühl im Spiegel seiner Bildersprache." See Bibliography.

## 3
### *Le Menteur* to *Nicomède: l'ambitieux*

1 "Examen," M-L, *IV,* 285.

2 *Ibid.*, p. 422 and note 1.

3 "Avertissement," (1647, 1652, 1655), M-L, *IV*, 416.

4 *Ibid.*

5 M-L, *I*, 79.

6 M-L, *IV*, 283-284.

7 *Ibid.*, pp. 426.

8 *Ibid.*

9 From Sewall's discussion of tragedy, *op. cit.*, p. 31.

10 M-L, *V*, 505.

11 "Examen," M-L, *V*, 508-509.

12 "Au Sujet d'Adonis," in *Oeuvres* (Pléiade), *I*, 483.

13 "Examen," M-L, *V*, 505.

14 *La Vie de Molière*, p. 64.

### 4
### Pertharite to Psyché: l'amoureux

1 *Commentaires, Oeuvres, XXXII*, 142.

2 "William Dean Howells and the Roots of Modern Taste," in his *The Opposing Self*, p. 93.

3 See Couton, *Corneille*, pp. 138-141.

4 "Examen," M-L, *VI*, 130.

5 *Le Sentiment*, p. 236.

6 "Au Lecteur," M-L, *VI*, 357.

7 "The Philosophy of Sophocles" in *Greek Tragedy* (Anchor edition), pp. 150-155.

8 For example, Turnell in *The Classical Moment*, p. 189, and Dort, *Pierre Corneille: dramaturge*, p. 119.

### 5
### Pulchérie and Suréna: le généreux once more

1 Quoted in M-L, *VII*, 373.

2 *The Death of Tragedy*, p. 102.

3 "Sur Corneille," *Les Temps Modernes*, 10e année (novembre 1954), 729.

4 M-L, *VII*, 460.

5 *Ibid.*, n. 3 (Amyot's translation).

6 D. D. Raphael, *The Paradox of Tragedy*, p. 28.

### Conclusion

1 *Morales*, p. 72.

2 *Note conjointe sur M. Descartes* in *Oeuvres en prose* (Pléiade edition), p. 1384.

3 *La Littérature de l'âge baroque en France*, p. 213.

4 *Tragédie cornélienne*, pp. 202-207.

5 *Ibid.*

6 *Plaisir à Corneille*, p. 15.

7 Borgerhoff, *The Freedom of French Classicism*, p. 74; Edelman, review of May, *Tragédie cornélienne*, in *Romanic Review, XLI*, 135-141; Wang, "The 'Tragic' Theatre of Corneille," *French Review, XXV*, 182-191.

8 *Racine et la poésie tragique,* p. 47.

9 *Esquisse,* p. 3 for both passages. Italics in text.

10 Jacques Guicharnaud, "Tragedy," in *Dictionary of French Literature,* ed. Sidney D. Braun.

11 *A Definition of Tragedy,* p. 162.

12 *Tragédie cornélienne,* p. 114.

13 Review of May, *Tragédie cornélienne,* in *Romanic Review, XLI,* 140.

14 *Ibid.,* 113.

15 *Victor-Marie, Comte Hugo* in *Oeuvres en prose* (Pléiade edition), p. 770.

16 M-L, *I,* 54.

17 "Examen," M-L, *V,* 507-508.

18 *Romance and Tragedy,* p. 54.

19 *Ibid.,* p. 205.

20 For example, Nadal, *Le Sentiment,* p. 141.

21 *Modern French Theatre,* p. 44.

22 *Anatomy of Criticism,* p. 166.

23 *Ibid.,* p. 202.

24 *Corneille,* passim.

25 See especially in his *Corneille* the section entitled "Enfances" (pp. 15-46).

26 For this affiliation see Gonzague de Reynold, *Le Dix-septième Siècle; le classique et le baroque,* p. 146.

27 *Morales,* p. 25.

28 *The Freedom of French Classicism,* p. 63.

29 *Victor-Marie, Comte Hugo* in *Oeuvres en prose* (Pléiade edition), p. 785. Italics in text.

30 *The Hero With a Thousand Faces,* p. 39.

# Appendix

## Plot Résumés of Plays Discussed at Length

The order is chronological. The numbers in parentheses refer to pages on which the play is discussed. I have retained the French spelling of proper names of the play's characters.

### Melite
#### (pp. 26-37)

Eraste, in love with Melite, introduces her to his friend Tirsis, and, soon after, becoming jealous of their attentions to one another, arranges to send some love letters, supposedly from Melite, to Philandre, fiancé of Cloris, sister of Tirsis. Philandre, persuaded by the letters and Eraste's arguments, shows the letters to Tirsis. This poor lover falls into despair, and withdraws to the home of his friend Lisis, who then gives false alarms of Tirsis' death to Melite. She faints at the news, thus giving evidence of her true affections. Lisis disabuses her and has Tirsis return to marry her. However, Cliton, seeing Melite fainted, believes her dead and carries the news to Eraste, as well as the news of Tirsis' death. Seized with remorse, Eraste goes mad. However, brought back to his senses by La Nourrice, who tells him that the lovers are still alive, he goes to Melite to ask forgiveness for his ruse, and obtains from the two lovers the hand of Cloris, who will have no more to do with the fickle Philandre.

### La Veuve
#### (pp. 39-50)

In love with Clarice, widow of Alcandre and mistress

of Philiste, his best friend, Alcidon pretends, out of fear that Philiste sense his love for the widow, to be in love with Doris, Philiste's sister, who, undeceived by his attentions, consents to marry Florange, whom her mother proposes. The false friend, under a pretext of avenging the affront which the latter marriage means to him, gets Celidan to consent to kidnaping Clarice for him, and they take her to Celidan's castle. Philiste, misled by the false resentment of his friend, breaks up Doris' engagement to Florange: upon which Celidan entreats Alcidon to go back to Doris and to sur-render Clarice to her true lover. Being unable to persuade him to do so, Celidan suspects some treachery on his part, and puts on an act of his own so well that he fools Clarice's nurse, who has been in cahoots with Alcidon, and had even made her mistress' kidnapping easier for him. All of which leads Celidan to take sides against the perfidious Alcidon: so that in returning Clarice to Philiste, he obtains from him his sister Doris as a reward. (Somewhat free translation of Corneille's *Argument*.)

### La Suivante
(pp. 50-61)

Théante, tiring of his suit with the *suivante* Amarante and ambitious for social advancement, confides in his friend Damon that he has urged Florame to pay court to Amarante so that he have access to the latter's mistress, Daphnis. Damon, however, tells Théante that Florame, too, is using Amarante in order to be near Daphnis. Amarante, herself in love with Florame, but doubtful that her father, Géraste, will approve of his court because of his lowly station, is surprised to hear her father approves of her "lover." But under this anonymous designation the father means Clarimond, with whom Amarante has falsely claimed her mistress is in love. Damon schemes with Théante to engage Clarimond and Florame in a duel, so that these two suitors must face either compromise of honor or death (or both) and so leave the field open to him in his pursuit of Daphnis. But Damon is a double agent and reports Théante's plans to Florame. When Florame agrees to a duel with Clarimond, he asks Théante to serve as his second. Under these circumstances, Théante is less eager for bloodshed and gladly withdraws from the amorous lists. Later, bargaining with Florame for the hand of his sister Florise, Géraste changes his mind and orders his daughter to marry Florame, again not mentioning his choice by name. Desolate when he learns of this "change," Florame grimly determines to slay the "treacherous" father but his loyalty to the daughter holds him back. When Géraste and Daphnis finally do name names, the misunderstanding is cleared up and father and daughter, sister and brother go off to unite in a common family. Amarante concludes the play in a bitter complaint against the social circumstances and personal ambitions which have prevented her from having her heart's desire.

## Le Cid
### (pp. 68-87)

Chimene, daughter of Don Gomes (Comte de Gormas), is reassured by her governess, that, in spite of anxieties about the possibility of marrying Rodrigue, the man she loves, nothing stands in the way. However, Don Gomes and Don Diegue, Rodrigue's father, quarrel when the latter receives a royal honor. Insulted, Diegue demands that his son defend the family's honor. When the son does so at the price of Gomes' life, a price whose consequences please L'Infante, the king's daughter, who is in love with Rodrigue, Chimene demands in turn the life of her lover, slayer of her father. With the kingdom besieged from without, the king, having charged Rodrigue with its defense, teases Chimene into believing that Rodrigue has perished. Chimene's reaction proves that she loves Rodrigue, but she persists in seeking his head in payment for her father's life and even makes it clear to her lover in a series of confrontations that he must accept her enmity as the very sign of their mutual worthiness of each other. Combatting Sanche, Chimene's champion, Rodrigue, now a national hero, triumphs, encouraged by his mistress' evident hope that he not perish. He returns to submit himself for a final time to her wishes, but, in spite of her continuing estrangement, their mutual fate is presumably decided by the king's word to both that their enmity cease.

### *Horace*
### (pp. 87-96)

In order to decide the conflict between Alba and Rome, a personal combat between the Roman family of Horace and the Albine family of Curiace is arranged. Ironically, young Horace is married to Sabine, Curiace's sister, while Camille, young Horace's sister, is engaged to Curiace. Young Horace's two brothers are reported killed and young Horace fled in the combat between the camps. However, young Horace has really survived and when he returns, it is with the symbols not of defeat but of victory. Camille curses Rome before her brother and is killed by him. In a "trial" before the King, young Horace, "defended" by his father, is absolved and his wife enjoined to be loyal to him in spite of his "murder" of her brother.

### *Polyeucte*
### (pp. 99-128)

Polyeucte, an Armenian nobleman, is humanely reluctant to announce his conversion to Christianity to his recently taken wife, Pauline, daughter of the feeble governor of Armenia, Félix. Pauline had wed Polyeucte after an earlier interest in Sévère, a relatively low-born suitor, had come to naught because of her father's disapproval. Sévère now returns in triumph, exalted by his victories in the name of Rome, prepared to reclaim his mistress. But the latter now enjoins him to preserve her marriage by dissuading her husband from his "foolish" conversion. However, Polyeucte himself would consign Pauline to Sévère's hands while he himself persists in his Christian ways. He smashes the pagan idols and drives the vacillating Félix to martyr him. After Polyeucte's death, Pauline and her father are converted, while Sévère sympathetically promises to relieve the persecuted Christians through his good offices with the Emperor.

### Le Menteur
### (pp. 130-138)

Dorante, a young blade boasting a glorious past as a soldier and lover, falls in love with Clarice, whom he takes for Lucrèce. In spite of the misgivings of his *suivant,* Cliton, he pursues "Lucrèce" in a series of elaborate lies which compound the misunderstanding. The girls allow him to persist in the misunderstanding, actively abetting it in various ways —for example, allowing him to think he is addressing one while it is really the other during a rendezvous at which he cannot see them. Forced to wed the real Lucrèce, both as a result of his misunderstanding and circumstances, he does so without regret, having discovered that he is drawn to her.

### Rodogune
### (pp. 139-167)

Seleucus and Antiochus, twin sons of Cleopatre, queen of Syria, are both in love with the Parthian princess, Rodogune, who had also been their father Demetrius' fiancée while he was a prisoner of the Parthians. He had entered into this relationship in retaliation for Cleopatre's own politically inspired marriage to the now dead brother of Demetrius after Demetrius' reported death. In spite of this latter relationship, Cleopatre is apparently prepared to allow one of the twins to wed Rodogune, at the same time giving the throne to the winner. However, she promises instead to name as the first born, and thus as emperor, the one who will kill Rodogune. The latter, in turn, makes herself the prize for the twin who will kill his mother. Seleucus balks at both offers and is murdered by Cleopatre. Her further plan to poison Antiochus and Rodogune is discovered. Scornfully refusing reconciliation, Cleopatre dies by drinking the poison intended for the others.

## Nicomède
### (pp. 172-182)

Nicomède, son of Prusias, king of Bithynia, through a first marriage, is opposed for the succession by the king's second wife, Arsinoé, who wishes to place their son, Attale, first in line. Nicomède's position is further complicated in that Rome, through its emissary Flaminius, is suspicious of him as a follower of Annibal and because of his projected marriage to Laodice, queen of Armenia. In spite of the machinations of his enemies—father, stepmother, and Roman emmisary— Nicomède, saved from prison by his reconciled stepbrother, forgives those enemies, submitting to his father's rule until such time as it will be proper for him to assume it himself.

## Pertharite
### (pp. 183-202)

The usurper of the Lombard throne, Grimoald, inspired by an evil counselor, Garibalde, wishes to abandon his beloved Edüige, sister of the presumably dead king, Pertharite, in order to marry Rodelinde, widow of Pertharite, and thereby shore up his throne. The "widow" accepts his offer on the grounds that he slay her children, an offer made to save their honor rather than out of personal ambition. Before the threat is carried out, Pertharite returns—not to act as a king, but to concede his wife as well as his kingdom. Garibalde attempts to slay the returned king, but the latter slays his pursuer, thereby rehabilitating himself as a *généreux,* in the eyes of his own wife and Grimoald. The latter would even relinquish his ill-gotten throne, but Pertharite proposes instead that he and Grimoald share the kingdom with, of course, Edüige married to Grimoald.

### Oedipe
(pp. 202-217)

With Thebes plague-ridden, Dircé, daughter of the long-dead king Laius, urges her lover Thésée to leave. The latter will not, unless she accompany him. But the present king, Oedipe, wary of the political implications of such an alliance, refuses, claiming that he promised Dircé to his cousin. As the blood of Laius, she wishes to make the sacrifice demanded by the latter's ghost in expiation of the former king's death. The wish is refused since it has been learned that Laius' son lives. Now Thésée offers himself as the missing son and thus the demanded victim, for his own origins are somewhat obscure. But before this development can be brought to its fulfillment, he must show himself to be Laius' murderer. When the messenger who carried away the infant son of Laius appears, he is first identified by the grown Oedipe as one of the "brigands" Oedipe has combatted at a crossroads where he slew the oldest. He then recognizes himself as the murderer of Laius, but not yet as the latter's son. This final identification occurs when Oedipe learns from Iphicrates, his "father's" messenger, that his "father," Polybe, has died declaring that Oedipe is not his son but that he had received him through Iphicrates from a Theban. Iphicrates recognizes Phorbas as the Theban in question and Oedipe himself as Laius' son and slayer. Oedipe blinds himself, while Jocaste and Phorbas slay themselves and Thésée and Dircé wed.

### Sertorious
(pp. 220-229)

Sertorius, faithful general of Queen Viriate, with whom he is in love, is offered marriage by Aristie, first wife of Pompée, who wishes thereby to avenge herself on Pompée who divorced her at the Emperor Sylla's command. Sertorius is also trying to avoid disruption in his own country through Perpenna, rebellious general who wishes to accede to the throne by marying Viriate. Pompée arrives and beseeches Sertorius to

discontinue the enmity with Rome. He also attempts to dissuade Aristie from wedding Sertorius for both personal and
political reasons. When Sylla dies, Pompée can rejoin Aristie,
but in the political confusion which ensues, Perpenna slays
Sertorius. Pompée overcomes the usurper and turns him over
to the townspeople, who put Perpenna to death. Pompée and
Aristie rewed and enter into happy political alliance with
Viriate.

### Agésilas
### (pp. 230-238)

Contrary to his country's custom, Agésilas, king of Sparta,
wishes to marry the foreigner, Mandane, a Persian noble-
woman. His rival for Mandane is Cotys, king of Paphlagonia,
who is supposed to wed Elpinice, daughter of Agésilas' min-
ister, Lysandre, while Aglatide, Elpinice's sister is to wed
Spitridate, a Persian nobleman, who is actually in love with
Elpinice. Aglatide is herself eager to wed Agésilas, chiefly
because he is a king. He had, in fact, once encouraged her to
believe he might be interested in marrying her. Agésilas fears
the political power implicit in Lysandre's plans to marry his
daughters to foreigners, but he must also fear the threat to
his throne immanent in his own desire to join in an un-
popular union with Mandane. Elpinice also complicates things
by refusing to marry Spitridate unless he gives his sister to
Cotys, but Mandane wishes to protect Spitridate from Agésilas's vengeance by agreeing to marry Agésilas. In the face of
these intricate threats and counterthreats, Agésilas decides to
marry Aglatide, thereby leaving the remaining couples in a
position to follow their hearts.

### Suréna
### (pp. 247-258)

Eurydice, an Armenian princess, is betrothed to Pacorus,
son of Orode, king of the Parthians, although she loves and
is loved by Suréna, Parthian general who shores up Orode's

power and who is the brother of Palmis, Pacorus' former mistress. To bind him politically, Orode would wed Suréna to his daughter, Mandane; Suréna refuses the honor as "above" him. Eurydice also refuses to carry through with the wedding to Pacorus in spite of Palmis' entreaties to do so by way of saving Suréna's life. Eurydice finally yields, but only to discover that Suréna has been slain. Eurydice succumbs herself as Palmis swears to avenge her brother's death.

# Bibliography

*Editions of Corneille*

*Oeuvres de P. Corneille,* ed. Ch. Marty-Laveaux, 12 vols. Paris, Hachette, 1862-1868. (Les Grands Ecrivains).

*Clitandre,* ed R.-L. Wagner. Lille, Giard; Genève, Droz, 1949. (Textes Littéraires Français).

*La Veuve,* ed. Mario Roques and Marion Lièvre. Genève, Droz; Lille, Giard, 1954. (Textes Littéraires Français).

*Le Cid,* ed. Maurice Cauchie. Paris, Marcel Didier, 1946 (Textes Littéraires Français).

*L'Illusion comique,* ed. Robert Garapon. Paris, Marcel Didier, 1957. (Société des Textes Français Modernes).

*Mélite,* ed. Mario Roques and Marion Lièvre. Lille, Giard; Genève, Droz, 1950. (Textes Littéraires Français).

*Rodogune,* ed. Jacques Schérer. Paris, Droz, 1946. (Textes Littéraires Français).

*Sertorius,* ed. Jeanne Streicher, Genève, Droz; Paris, Minard, 1959.

*References*

Aristotle. *Aristotle's Theory of Poetry and Fine Art, with a Critical Text and Translation of the Poetics,* ed. and trans. S. H. Butcher. 4th ed. London, Macmillan and Co., Ltd.; New York, The Macmillan Company, 1907.

Ault, Harold C. "The Tragic Genius of Corneille," *Modern Language Review,* XLV (1950), 164-176.

Bailly, Auguste. *L'Ecole classique française: Les Doctrines et les hommes.* Paris, Colin, n.d.

Bénichou, Paul. *Morales du grand siècle*. Paris, Gallimard, 1948.

Boorsch, Jean. "Remarques sur la technique dramatique de Corneille," in *Studies by Members of the French Department of Yale University*, ed. Albert Feuillerat. New Haven, Yale University Press, 1941. Pp. 101-162.

Borgerhoff, E. B. O. *The Freedom of French Classicism* Princeton, Princeton University Press, 1950.

Brasillach, Robert. *Pierre Corneille*. Paris, Arthème Fayard, 1938.

Caillois, Roger. "Un Roman cornélien," *Nouvelle Revue française,* (mars 1938), 477-482. Review of André Rouveyre's *Silence* (Mercure de France, 1937).

Campbell, Joseph. *The Hero With a Thousand Faces*. The Bollingen Series XVII. New York, Pantheon Books, 1949.

Canfield [Fisher], Dorothea Frances. *Corneille and Racine in England*. New York, Columbia University Press, 1904.

Cayrou, Gaston. *Le Français classique: Lexique de la langue du dix-septième siècle*. Paris, Didier, 1948.

Cherpack, Clifton. *The Call of Blood in French Classical Tragedy*. Baltimore, The Johns Hopkins Press, 1958.

Cotgrave, Randle. *A Dictionarie of the French and English Tongues*. Reproduced from the first edition, London, 1611. Columbia, University of South Carolina Press, 1950.

Couton, Georges. "Comment dater les grandes pièces de Corneille," *Revue d'Histoire du Théâtre,* 8e année, 1 (1956), 15-23.

———. *Corneille*. Paris, Hatier, 1958.

———. *La Vieillesse de Corneille* (1658-1684). Paris, Maloine, 1949.

———. *Réalisme de Corneille: Deux Etudes--La Clef de "Mélite"; Réalités dans le Cid*. Paris, Société d'Edition "Les Belles Letres," 1953.

Crétin, Roger. (real name of Roger Vercel). *Les Images dans l'oeuvre de Corneille*. Paris, Champion, 1927.

Croce, Benedetto. *Ariosto, Shakespeare and Corneille,* trans.

Douglas Ainslie. New York, Henry Holt and Company, 1920.

Currie, Peter. *Corneille: Polyeucte.* Studies in French Literature, No. 3. London, Edward Arnold, Ltd., 1960.

Dort, Bernard. *Pierre Corneille: dramaturge.* Paris, L'Arche, 1957.

Edelman, Nathan. Review of G. May, *Tragédie cornélienne, tragédie racinienne. Romanic Reveiw, XLI* (1950), 135-141.

Faguet, Emile. *En Lisant Corneille.* Paris, Hachette, 1913.

Falk, Eugene H. *Renunciation as a Tragic Focus: A Study of Five Plays.* Minneapolis, University of Minnesota Press, 1954.

Fergusson, Francis. *The Idea of a Theater.* Princeton, Princeton University Press, 1949.

Fernandez, Ramon. *La Vie de Molière.* Paris, Gallimard, 1929.

Fidao-Justiniani, J. E. *Qu'est-ce qu'un classique? Essai d'histoire et de critique positive; le héros, ou du génie.* Paris, Firmin-Didot, 1930.

Fontenelle, Bernard Le Bouvier de. *Oeuvres de Fontenelle.* 3 vols. Paris, A. Belin, 1818.

Frye, Northrop. *Anatomy of Criticism: Four Essays.* Princeton, Princeton University Press, 1957.

Frye, Prosser Hall. *Romance and Tragedy.* Boston, Marshall Jones Company, 1922.

Fujirama, Thomas H. "The Appeal of Dryden's Heroic Plays," *PMLA,* LXXV (1960), 37-45.

Goldmann, Lucien. *Jean Racine: dramaturge.* Paris, L'Arche, 1956.

Guicharnaud, Jacques. *"Tragedy"* in *Dictionary of French Literature,* ed. Sidney D. Braun. New York, Philosophical Library, 1958.

———. (with June Beckelman). *Modern French Theatre: From Giraudoux to Beckett.* New Haven, Yale University Press, 1961.

Haley, Sister Marie Philip. *"Polyeucte* and the *De Imitatione Christi,"* *PMLA,* LXXV (1960), 174-183.

Harvey, Lawrence E. "Intellectualism in Corneille: The Symbolism of Proper Names in *La Suivante*," *Symposium*, XIII (1959), 290-293.

———. "The Dénouement of *Mélite* and the Role of La Nourrice," *Modern Language Notes*, LXXI (March 1956), 200-203.

———. "The Noble and the Comic in Corneille's *La Veuve*," *Symposium*, X (1956), 291-295.

Hatzfeld, Adolphe, and Arsène Darmesteter. *Dictionnaire général de la langue française*. 2 vols. Paris, Delagrave, 1926.

Herland, Louis. *Corneille par lui même*. Paris, Aux Editions du Seuil, 1954.

———. *Horace, ou la naissance de l'homme*. Paris, Les Editions du Minuit, 1952.

———. "La notion de tragique chez Corneille," in *Mélanges de la Société toulousaine d'études classiques*. Toulouse, Privat, 1946. I, 265-284.

Hubert, J. "The Conflict between Chance and Morality in *Rodogune*," *Modern Language Notes*, LXXIV (1959), 234-239.

James, Henry. *The Art of the Novel: Critical Prefaces*. New York, Charles Scribner's Sons; London, Charles Scribner's Sons, Ltd., 1950.

Jaspers, Karl. *Tragedy Is Not Enough*, trans. by Harold A. T. Reiche, Harry T. Moore, and Karl W. Deutsch. Boston, Beacon Press, 1952.

Kitto, H. D. F. *Greek Tragedy: A Literary Study*. Garden City, New York, Doubleday and Company, Inc., 1954. (Anchor Edition).

Koch, Philip. "Cornelian Illusion," *Symposium*, XIV (1960), 85-99.

La Bruyère, Jean de. *Oeuvres complètes,* ed. Julien Benda. Paris, Bibliothèque de la Plèiade, 1957.

Lancaster, H. C. *A History of French Dramatic Literature in the Seventeenth Century*. 9 vols. Baltimore, The Johns Hopkins Press; Paris, Les Presses Universitaires, 1929-1942.

——. *The French Tragi-Comedy: Its Origin and Development from 1552 to 1628.* Baltimore, J. H. Furst Company, 1907.

Lanson, Gustave. *Corneille.* Paris, Hachette, 1898.

——. *Esquisse d'une histoire de la tragédie française.* New York, Columbia University Press, 1920.

Lemonnier, Léon. *Corneille.* Paris, Tallandier, 1945.

Lewis, Charlton T., and Charles Short, eds. *A New Latin Dictionary* founded on the translation of Freund's "Latin-German Lexicon." New York, Harper and Brothers, 1922.

Lockert, Lacy, ed. *Moot Plays of Corneille.* Nashville, Vanderbilt University Press, 1959.

——. *Studies in French Classical Tragedy.* Nashville, Vanderbilt University Press, 1958.

——, ed. *The Chief Plays of Corneille.* Princeton, Princeton University Press, 1957.

Lodge, Lee Davis. *A Study in Corneille.* Baltimore, John Murphy and Co., 1891.

Malraux, André. "Lignes de force," *Preuves,* 5e année, No. 49 (mars. 1955), 5-15.

Mandel, Oscar. *A Definition of Tragedy.* New York University Press, 1961.

Martinenche, Ernest. *La Comedia espagnole en France de Hardy à Racine, 1600-1660.* Paris, Hachette, 1900.

May, Georges. *Tragédie cornélienne, tragédie racinienne: Etude sur les sources de l'intérêt dramatique.* Urbana, University of Illinois Press, 1948.

Merian-Genast, E. "Corneilles Wertgefühl im Spiegel Seiner Bildersprache," in *Festschrift für Ernst Tappolet.* Basel, Schwabe, 1935. Pp. 219-228.

Molière [Jean-Baptiste Poquelin]. *Oeuvres complètes,* ed. Maurice Rat, 2 vols. Paris, Bibliothèque de la Pléiade, 1956.

Montchrestien, Antoine de. *Les Tragédies de Montchrestien,* ed. L. Petit de Julleville. Paris, Plon, 1891.

Moore, W. G. *Molière: A New Criticism.* Oxford, Clarendon Press, 1949.

Nadal, Octave. *Le Sentiment de l'amour dans l'oeuvre de Pierre Corneille.* Paris, Gallimard, 1948.

Nelson, Robert J. "Pierre Corneille's *L'Illusion comique*: The Play as Magic," *PMLA*, LXXI (1956), 1127-1140.

————. *Play within a Play*: *The Dramatist's Conception of His Art—Shakespeare to Anouilh.* New Haven, Yale University Press, 1958.

————. "The Dénouement of *Le Cid*," *French Studies*, XIV (1960), 141-148.

————. "The Unreconstructed Heroes of Molière," *Tulane Drama Review, IV* (March 1960), 14-37.

Niebuhr, Reinhold. *Beyond Tragedy*: *Essays on the Christian Interpretation of History.* New York, Charles Schribner's Sons, 1937.

Pascal, Blaise. *Pensées.* ed. Léon Brunschvicg. 3 vols. Paris, Hachette, 1904. Les Grands Ecrivains.

Peckham, Morse. "Toward a Theory of Romanticism," *PMLA,* LXVI (1951), 5-23.

Péguy, Charles. *Oeuvres en prose*: *1909-1914,* ed. Marcel Péguy. Paris, Bibliothèque de la Pléiade, 1957.

Poulaille, Henri. *Corneille sous le masque de Molière.* Paris, Grasset, 1957.

Poulet, Georges. *Etudes sur le temps humain.* Paris, Plon, 1950.

Racine, Jean. *Oeuvres de J. Racine,* ed. Paul Mesnard. 8 vols. Paris, Hachette, (1865-1873). Les Grands Ecrivains.

————. *Principes de la tragédie en marge de la "Poétique" d'Aristote,* texte établi et commenté par Eugène Vinaver. Les Editions de l'Université de Manchester; Paris, Nizet, 1951.

Raphael, D. D. *The Paradox of Tragedy.* Bloomington, Indiana University Press, 1960.

Reynold, Gonzague de. *Le Dix-septième Siècle; le classique et le baroque: suivi de trois études sur Malherbe, Molière, Madame de Lambert.* Montréal, Editions de l'Arbre, 1944.

Riddle, Lawrence Melville. *The Genesis and Sources of*

*Pierre Corneille's Tragedies from "Médée" to "Pertharite."* Baltimore, The Johns Hopkins Press, 1926.

Rivaille, Louis. *Les Débuts de P. Corneille*. Paris, Boivin, 1936.

Rousseaux, André. "Corneille ou le mensonge héroïque," *Revue de Paris*, 44e année July 1 (1937), 50-73.

Rousset, Jean. *La Littérature de l'âge baroque en France: Circé et le paon*. Paris, José Corti, 1953.

Saint-Evremond [Charles de Marguetel de Saint Denis, Seigneur de]. *Oeuvres de Saint-Evremond*, ed. René de Plainhol. 2 vols. Paris, La Cité des Livres, 1927.

Sartre, Jean-Paul. "Forgers of Myths: The Young Playwrights of France," *Theatre Arts*, XXX (June 1946), 324-335.

Schérer, Jacques. *La Dramaturgie classique en France*. Paris, Nizet, 1950.

Schlumberger, Jean. *Plaisir à Corneille (Promenade anthologique)*, 12th ed. Paris, Gallimard, 1936.

Segall, J. B. *Corneille and the Spanish Drama*. New York, Columbia University Press, The Macmillan Company: Agents, 1902.

Sellstrom, A. Donald. *"L'Illusion comique* of Corneille: The Tragic Scenes of Act V," *Modern Language Notes*, LXXIII (1958), 421-427.

———. "The Structure of Corneille's Masterpieces," *Romanic Review*, XLIX (1958), 269-277.

Sewall, Richard. *The Vision of Tragedy*. New Haven, Yale University Press, 1959.

Starobinski, J. "Sur Corneille," *Les Temps Modernes*, 10e année (novembre 1954), 713-729.

Steiner, George. *The Death of Tragedy*. New York, Alfred A. Knopf, 1961.

Tastevin, Maria. *Les Héroïnes de Corneille*. Paris, Librairie Ancienne Edouard Champion, 1924.

Thibaudet, Albert. "Un tricentenaire," *La Nouvelle Revue Française*, XLV (septembre 1935), 401-412.

Trilling, Lionel. *The Liberal Imagination: Essays on Litera-*

*ture and Society*. New York, The Viking Press, 1950.

———. *The Opposing Self*. New York, The Viking Press, 1955.

Turnell, Martin. *The Classical Moment: Studies of Corneille, Molière and Racine*. Norfolk, Conn., New Directions, 1948.

Valéry, Paul. *Oeuvres*, ed. Jean Hytier. 2 vols. Paris, Bibliothèque de la Pléiade, 1957. Vol. 1.

Vedel, Valdemar. *Deux classiques français vus par un critique étranger: Corneille et son temps—Molière,* traduit du danois par Madame E. Cornet. Paris, Librairie Ancienne Honoré Champion, 1935.

Vinaver, Eugène. *Racine et la poésie tragique*. Paris, Nizet, 1951.

Vincent, Leon H. *Corneille*. Cambridge, Mass., Riverside Press, 1901.

Virtanen, Reino. "Nietzsche and Corneille," *Symposium,* XI (1957), 225-239.

Voltaire [François-Marie Arouet de]. *Commentaires sur Corneille* in *Oeuvres complètes de Voltaire,* ed. Louis Moland, 52 vols. Paris, Garnier, 1877-1885. Vols. 31-32.

Wang, Leonard. "The 'Tragic' Theatre of Corneille," *French Review,* XXV January (1952), 182-191.

# INDEX